Understanding Silicon Valley

Understanding Silicon Valley

THE ANATOMY OF AN
ENTREPRENEURIAL REGION

EDITED BY

Martin Kenney

STANFORD UNIVERSITY PRESS

STANFORD, CALIFORNIA

Stanford University Press
Stanford, California
©2000 by the Board of Trustees of the
Leland Stanford Junior University
Printed in the United States of America

Library of Congress Cataloging-in-Publication Data

Understanding Silicon Valley : the anatomy of an entrepreneurial region /
edited by Martin Kenney.
   p. cm.
   Includes bibliographical references and index.
   ISBN 0-8047-3733-9 (alk. paper) — ISBN 0-8047- 3734-7 (paper : alk. paper)
   1. Santa Clara County (Calif.)—Economic conditions.   2. Santa Clara
County (Calif.)—Social conditions.   3. High technology industries—
California—- Santa Clara County.   4. Business enterprises—California—
Santa Clara County.   I. Kenney, Martin

HC107.C22 S3975   2000
330.9794'4—dc21   00-034523

This book is printed on acid-free, archival-quality paper.

Original printing 2000
Last figure below indicates year of this printing:
09 08 07 06 05 04 03 02 01 00

Typeset in 10/13 Palatino

Acknowledgments

My thanks to two extremely able student assistants, Kimmy Pang and Kalela McConnell. Their cheerful assistance made the process of assembling and editing this book much easier. Laura Comay, the acquisitions editor at Stanford University Press, has been extremely helpful and supportive. Finally, I would like to thank my colleagues in the Department of Human and Community Development and at the Berkeley Roundtable on the International Economy for creating a congenial place to work.

Contents

Part III: General Explanations

Foreword

JOHN SEELY-BROWN

When I first came out to the West Coast, I never imagined I would find myself writing a foreword about Silicon Valley. I was deeply suspicious of the place. My intellectual roots were in Cambridge, Massachusetts, where I had come to believe that the whole Silicon Valley thing that people were starting to talk about (the term, we learn here, was coined in 1971) was wildly overhyped, the people subject to mind rot, and the West Coast culture just a bit crazy. So my move to Silicon Valley was made with great trepidation. Indeed, my second thoughts were so strong, that to diminish cognitive dissonance between East and West and to prevent immediate retreat, I sold my home next to Harvard Square before moving. I wanted to eliminate anything that would make the return to "civilization" too easy—or so I thought. That was all in the fall of 1978.

Two decades later, I realize that my career at the Xerox Palo Alto Research Center (better known as Xerox PARC) has afforded me a much wider view of civilization. In particular, it has provided me with endless opportunities to meet with visitors from all parts of the world and in turn to visit nearly all parts of the world. Everyone takes Silicon Valley seriously now. With these visits, hardly a day goes by that I don't get asked to explain the magical brew that makes up Silicon Valley. What is it? What makes it so special? Can it be copied? If not, why not? And if yes, how? And what about that famous culture? What does it feel like to work for a large East Coast company and yet be a part of the Valley? Does this give me a different perspective—having to bridge those two quite different cultures daily? And how are those cultures different?

These are complex questions that raise serious issues about development—at the regional, national, and even global level. I am not sure I've ever answered them to the complete satisfaction of the people who asked. I'm pretty sure I cannot do them justice in these few short pages. But I would like to try at least to raise some of the points that seem to me most significant in trying to answer these questions.

But let me first say that I have often had the good fortune to address these questions at academic workshops. How quickly I learned (albeit the hard way) that simplistic generalizations don't cut it in the academy. Analytic precision, grounded in deep empiricism with only a speck of speculation, is the coin of the day. So it should be. And this book is an example of excellent empirical research, deep scholarship, tested and testable hypotheses, all conducted with a substantial cross-disciplinary flavor. Its deep engagement with the subject has provided evidence to support some of my theories, challenged others, and directed me to new grounds for speculation. I think it will do this for anyone prepared to read it closely.

My little contribution, however, may deviate from the high standards set in the following pages, so I feel particularly privileged to be able to get my words in first. I want to start with some of my own personal beliefs about the Valley and follow these with some speculative remarks that emerge from my long-time collaboration with Paul Duguid about the dynamics of knowledge creation and flow, both within the firm and throughout a particular region. For yes, even in today's web-based world, geography matters—perhaps even as much as in the past, but now for different reasons. Then I'll end with a couple of words on why it is so difficult to replicate the ongoing experiment that is Silicon Valley.

At the center of all questions about the Valley lies the matter of innovation—for the Valley occasionally appears like a perpetual innovation machine. I say "innovation" rather than simply "invention," because innovation, to me, means invention implemented. And I have grudgingly come to realize that invention is often the easy part of innovation. The hard part is usually the implementation. Here I was particularly interested in Stuart Leslie's well-chosen quotation from a letter of Frederick Terman. Terman was the Stanford University dean who played godfather to Hewlett Packard and so many other early start-ups in the Valley. When he left the university to work on radar during World War II, he wrote back to a colleague at Stanford, "I had never before realized the amount of work required to make a device ready for manufacture after one had a good working model." It was a lesson he clearly learned well as he guided young Stanford graduates to innovative success.

Implementation, I would say, requires the three Fs—focus, focus, focus. First, one must focus on a single value proposition pertaining to the initial invention. Sounds easy, but this focus is hard because a single invention will often support many different value propositions. Deciding on the right one to pursue requires discipline, experience, and a touch of luck. After that, you must focus on assembling a dedicated team to design and develop the invention into a product, then to market that product qua its value proposition, then to create appropriate partnerships around delivering and amplifying its value, and finally, to get mindshare for it. And while doing all this—which is never as linear a process as the above makes it appear—you also need to focus on your competition. Indeed, you need to be permanently paranoid about the likelihood that someone else has the same idea and is moving faster than you are.

The risk of competition and the risk of failure more generally are central to this whole process. If you hit it just right, you can win big; but if you focus wrongly on any one of the above issues, especially if you misjudge the customer value proposition, it all may come crashing down around you. Fine, risk is the coin of the day for any type of innovation. But Silicon Valley puts its own spin on risk. Here taking risks around radical innovations is respected and encouraged. Be shrewd, you will be told, and don't be timid: go for it.

Silicon Valley has developed some powerful ways to deal with the risk it pushes you toward, however. You can see this if you take the advice to go for it and set out to get a new company off the ground. For this, you need money (today, that's often the easy part). You need legal help to start the company and protect your intellectual property, or "IP." You need design talent to help define and craft your product. You will need marketing talent to position and validate your product concept. You need help to manufacture, test, and service it, and so on.

As the authors in this book explain, a good deal of Silicon Valley's strength lies in the way it helps you deal with these matters, effectively helping you both take risk and share risk. Some of these tasks you will want to take on in your firm—so you need to hire the right risk-taking folks to join your firm. But many of these tasks you will want to out-source to experts or consultants well seasoned in the challenges you face and perhaps willing in one way or another to help you spread your risk.

Where do you turn for that? That is not one of the hard questions to answer about Silicon Valley. My fifteen-minute drive from home in Palo Alto to work in the foothills behind Stanford University takes me by one of the best design firms in the world. Next I pass one of the best legal firms for start-ups in the country. If I continue down the road, I encounter one of the best marketing firms in the region. (These are some of the nontechnological firms that make up what Martin Kenney and Urs von Burg insightfully describe as the Valley's second economy.) And all around lie not only the competitors of these firms but also countless other potential partners, such as the numerous specialty shops and foundries that provide fast turn-around on submodules for a product.

That there are so many kinds of help and so many suppliers for each kind is not surprising. But what may be surprising is just how good these resources are and how well the strengths of each are recognized. As I like to think of it, the knowledge *in* these firms is extraordinary, and so is the knowledge *about* them. These two are closely connected. The knowledge in any one of these grows daily because of the intensity of the competition. And that competition is intense because in Silicon Valley, people know so much about their competitors. The amount of knowledge available about the players in the valley is incredible. As Martin Kenney and Richard Florida show clearly in their chapter, venture capitalists (VCs) play a critical role in sharing knowledge and might best be thought of as knowledge brokers. Indeed, in my mind, they are more important for their network of connections than for their money. Mark Suchman's chapter reveals how lawyers work this way, too.

Even at a more informal level, however—at parties, at restaurants, at sports events, at your kid's school—you discover whom you need to meet, who is worth working with, whom you should avoid, etc. Here's one reason why geography matters. The density of the region matters because it enhances serendipitous contacts. Couple this density of the Valley—caught as it is between the bay and the ocean to the east and west, and the cities of San Francisco and San Jose to the north and south—to the regional culture and you get a remarkable petri dish, as AnnaLee Saxenian's chapter shows. For the culture here is amazingly

open to novel ideas and radical ventures and emerging forms of entre-
tainment (entrepreneurship is a form of entertainment in the Valley).
All these are supported by a social fabric that maintains constant, ongoing conversations through which you can test and develop your
thoughts, find folks to work with, and turn ideas into action. As Stephen Cohen and Gary Fields argue, the Valley's social fabric is quite
distinct. It can also be quite casual. Benchmarking here takes on a new
dimension. It's not necessarily some formal process. Just go to lunch,
hear the buzz, and you'll quickly find out how you stand.

This dynamic that drives you, drives your competition, haunting
both of you. It haunts people, in particular, with the unsettling fear of
becoming a has-been. Things happen so fast that the step from being
ahead to being passé happens in the blink of an eye. It's not what
you've done, but what you've done *lately* that counts. So you made it
big, even really big, but that was three years ago and maybe it was just
luck. If it wasn't, why haven't you done something great since? Un-
nerving, yes. But still, very real. I actually hear billionaires who by anyone's standards would appear to be outstanding successes complain
about their fears along this dimension that leads to the Valley's van-
ishing point.

Let me get back to the knowledge *in* the various organizations and
institutions that make up the Valley. Undoubtedly, we live in a valley
of riches. We have two major research universities and many smaller
universities and colleges, and they all play multiple roles. Most obviously, they prepare students to work in the Valley. Here, I would point
particularly to the great business schools that have stayed ahead of the
curve despite the profound shifts that information technology has
brought to business practices. I also applaud the excellent engineering
schools that continue to push these technologies harder and faster. Together these institutions continue to provide a diverse and highly talented executive and technical workforce. But they do more than teach
students. They actively encourage their faculty to take what they know
and start companies. They also urge faculty to contribute their talents to
established companies in the area as consultants. These institutions are
then augmented by an excellent and omnipresent community college
system for rapidly assimilating immigrants into the workforce and
culture of the Valley. It's a mistake to see this traffic in knowledge as a
one-way street. These excellent schools feed the firms of the Valley, no
doubt. But as I note below, the firms in the Valley also help feed the ex-

cellence of the schools. Along with the schools, boundaries of research are continually pushed in the several major corporate research labs, such as PARC, that wittingly or unwittingly contribute to the Valley's flux of ideas.

These are the ingredients that go into what Homa Bahrami and Stuart Evans call the Valley's ecosystem, a system ideally situated for growing new firms and for learning from each other both through successes and failures. This is an image of the Valley that Duguid and I have used ourselves, talking of Silicon Valley as a "knowledge ecology," and it may be useful to elaborate on our view a little here. To us, a knowledge ecology has a dynamical structure that can help one understand how and where knowledge flows: how knowledge can leak *out* of a firm, presenting those who must defend IP with a constant worry. But the same understanding also reveals how, if that firm is an open participant in the ecology, knowledge can also flow back *into* that firm. A thriving ecology can turn these flows into feedback loops that serve to amplify the knowledge in the region.

Although it is popular to think that great ideas start with individuals, most knowledge gets produced in and by communities of practice (cops). These are teams of people that have worked together over a sufficient period of time to have evolved a deep ability to read each other, to communicate in highly condensed ways, and to know exactly when and when not to trust an opinion from one another. Within such entities, knowledge gets created, and when it does, it flows almost effortlessly. As we have detailed elsewhere, knowledge travels along the rails of practice. That's why it moves so easily within a community of practice. For the very same reason, it requires substantial work to move that knowledge to a community with different practices. Here there are gaps in the rails.

Since a corporation's value chain comprises a collection of quite different skills and practices and so different cops, radically new knowledge created in a corporation can easily stick where it starts (often in research). For example, to get an invention out of the lab, you first need to persuade the engineers. But why would a practically minded engineer trust the opinions of those wild-eyed guys in research and their off-the-wall notions? You can see why innovation is hard. It requires pushing an idea along that value chain. But along that chain, the implicit judgment, understanding, trust, and so forth that function within a cop have to be re-created across a variety of new and often suspicious contexts.

However, in an ecology of firms and universities, even if rails don't always run smoothly within a corporation, they will often run smoothly out of it. These rails link what we think of as networks of practice. For example, similar researchers in Sun, Apple, or Oracle are much more aligned to the thinking of PARC's computer wizards than are many Xerox engineers, even though the engineers are in the same company. As a consequence, knowledge may travel more easily around a network of practice that lies across several different firms than between two different communities of practice in the same firm. The mobility of labor in the Valley, the subject of David Angel's chapter, only accelerates the flows in these networks.

Start-ups usually don't have to deal with this problem. Since the start-up team is small, totally focused on the same goal, and working shoulder to shoulder, a rich and shared context for trust is easily created. The same is also true for specialty shops and boutique consulting firms, firms whose reputations in the Valley can replace the need for detailed legal contracts and whose reputations, earned through performance with many different customers, make them easy to trust at a technical level.

This helps to explain the flow of knowledge across an ecology. What I called the knowledge *in* a company may often flow out. As a result, there is a great deal of knowledge "in the air" in such regions, as the economist Alfred Marshall (who first analyzed the economics of clusters) put it. This is what I earlier called knowledge *about*—knowledge about what people are up to, where things are going, who is good at what, and so forth. It spreads across the larger networks of the Valley. But flow itself isn't sufficient to explain the drama of Silicon Valley. How, we all need to understand, does this dynamic lead to an ever-escalating regional advantage?

Let's take Stanford University as an example. Although Stanford is rightly recognized as a seat of knowledge creation and a key player in the Valley (as Timothy Sturgeon's chapter admirably shows), the flow of knowledge doesn't just go from inside to out. Knowledge also moves in from the rest of the region. Indeed, some of the most highly attended classes at Stanford are those taught by, or include lectures by, key figures in the Valley, carrying what they know back to the school. So as I look at Stanford University next door to me, I see flows of knowledge moving in and out along rails of practice that stretch across the region.

In the process, these flows develop feedback loops that amplify the knowledge both in the university and elsewhere in the Valley.

From this perspective, it's possible to see why copying the successes of the Valley to other regions may be very hard—a point that is made empirically in several of the essays in this book. Some people might think of planting an innovative firm to get a region growing. Others might choose to start with their university, encouraging that to flourish as a critical center of research. But either approach immediately faces the chicken-or-egg problem. Is it possible to build a great research university without dynamic, growing firms? Is it possible to have the firms without the university? And do both need the multiple other components in place in order to be able to feed off the environment as well as feed into it? Once all are in place, a natural, dynamic growth may develop. But it probably won't work to seed them one at a time. And it's very hard to seed them all at once. Bootstrapping an ecology, especially a knowledge ecology, is simply hard—very hard.

Moreover, nurturing seedlings is inherently a protective act. Yet thriving ecologies, as these essays again make clear, grow more robust through death. The death of a firm can happen quickly, and letting it die may be much more beneficial to the region than keeping it artificially alive. Its demise may fertilize new firms. Executives toughened by the experience of failure can be worth more than those who have had none. From the perspective of the region as a whole, then, we have an ecology of thriving species, failing species, and new species exploring untapped or abandoned ecological niches. It's a remarkable form of natural experiment which, given its interdependent complexity, may be hard to start, but which we have to hope, will also be hard to stop.

Contributors

David P. Angel is Laskoff Professor of Economics, Technology and the Environment at Clark University.

Homa Bahrami is a Senior Lecturer at the Haas School of Business, University of California, Berkeley.

Stephen S. Cohen is Professor of Regional Planning and Codirector of the Berkeley Roundtable on the International Economy (BRIE) at the University of California, Berkeley.

Stuart Evans is a Senior Associate at the Judge Institute of Management Studies, University of Cambridge, England.

Gary Fields is a Ph.D. student in the Department of City and Regional Planning and a Research Associate at the Berkeley Roundtable on the International Economy at the University of California, Berkeley.

Richard Florida is the H. John Heinz III Professor of Regional Economic Development in the H. John Heinz II School of Public Policy and Management at Carnegie Mellon University.

Martin Kenney is Professor in the Department of Human and Community Development at the University of California, Davis, and Senior Research Associate at the Berkeley Roundtable on the International Economy.

Stuart W. Leslie is Professor in the Department of History of Science, Medicine and Technology at Johns Hopkins University.

AnnaLee Saxenian is Associate Professor in the Department of City and Regional Planning at the University of California at Berkeley.

Timothy J. Sturgeon is Principal Research Associate at the Industrial Performance Center, Massachusetts Institute of Technology.

Mark C. Suchman is Associate Professor of Sociology and Law at the University of Wisconsin—Madison.

Urs von Burg is a Ph.D. student at the University of St. Gallen in St. Gallen, Switzerland.

The San Francisco Bay Area and Silicon Valley. (Silicon Valley is not a formal geographic area but encompasses much of San Mateo and Santa Clara counties, from San Carlos in the north to San Jose in the south.)

CHAPTER ONE

Introduction

MARTIN KENNEY

Over the last four decades, Silicon Valley firms have commercialized a number of the most important electronics and biomedical technologies developed in the second half of the twentieth century. Some of these technologies have changed the way we live in profound ways and in the process generated enormous wealth. It is difficult to think of any other region that has been able to commercialize so many significant new technologies in such a short period. Today, Silicon Valley firms have leadership positions in what might be the most powerful gale of Schumpeterian "creative destruction" of all, the Internet.

Despite the impact of these technological developments, Silicon Valley as a region or social system has received only sporadic scholarly attention. This book rectifies that situation by including contributions from many of the leading analysts of the region. From the outset it was understood that contributors would explain Silicon Valley in their own way. Rather than seeing that as a problem, I believe it is a virtue, because it provides the reader with multiple perspectives and exposes areas of agreement and disagreement. The various positions are ample evidence of the richness of thought and the difficulty of comprehensively explaining this complicated regional economy—as well as being a sign of how fascinating the region is as an object of study.

Silicon Valley is indeed a rich prize for social science theories. The contributors to this volume hail from five academic disciplines: business studies, geography, history, regional planning, and sociology. Despite these disparate disciplinary backgrounds, it is satisfying that none of the articles can be neatly circumscribed as the product of a single discipline. Each approaches Silicon Valley from a multidisciplinary perspective. As an editor, I did not favor any particular perspective or position, believing that it was preferable to allow the authors to advance their explanations from within their own paradigms. Affirmation of a particular perspective was not the intent; rather, the book is meant to provide readers with insights. My only editing bias was to encourage contributors to truncate long theoretical sections in favor of more empirical material.

Because of the focus on innovation and the formation of new firms, I have had to omit a number of other aspects of Silicon Valley's political economy, such as the role of immigrants into the Silicon Valley economy, which is discussed in great detail by Saxenian (1999). The concentration on innovation means necessarily that some of the negative features of the Silicon Valley region are not discussed. One that has received much interest is the antiunion bias of Silicon Valley firms and the lack of organized labor representation for manufacturing workers (see, for example, Siegel and Borock 1982, and, more recently, Benner 1998). There have been concerns expressed about the environmental impact of high-tech manufacturing and, once again, since they were not directly related to the innovation process, they are not examined here. Finally, many argue that the quality of life in the region is decreasing due to ever more expensive housing, spreading smog, and increasing gridlock on the area's roads and freeways; those issues too were beyond the scope of this book.[1] It is not our intention to minimize the importance of these issues; however, our rather tight focus does bypass them.

This volume is divided into three sections. The first comprises two papers about the early history of Silicon Valley. It creates the context for the phenomena tackled by the later papers. In the second section, four papers probe critical institutions and organizational routines for the region. The institutions studied are Silicon Valley law firms and venture capitalists; the routines examined are labor mobility and interfirm relationships. The final section consists of three papers addressing Silicon Valley as a complex of institutions and routines that cohere and are internally consistent. These papers draw upon the previous two sections by situating them in the development of the entire region, in which the various features operate symbiotically and, most often, synergistically to endow Silicon Valley with its extraordinary dynamism.

The History of Silicon Valley

The pursuit of historical origins is often frustrating, and exactly identifying the moment at which a region is born is necessarily a matter of ex post facto judgment. The recent recognition by economists that past events count and structure historical evolution with its inherent irreversibility has been formalized into a school of thought roughly grouped under the moniker of "path dependence."[2] The seminal thinkers in this line of theorizing are Paul David (1986) and W. Brian Arthur (1989, 1994), both of whom did their work at Stanford University.[3] Arthur (1994) explicitly argued that path dependence, based on agglomeration economies, provides an explanation for the clustering of high-technology firms in Silicon Valley. While his abstract model is inherently attractive, it does not provide much understanding of how specific institutions were created or evolved to serve the cluster. For these answers we need to turn to the archives and history.

Most scholars begin the history of Silicon Valley aptly enough with the foundation of Shockley Semiconductor in 1956 or, somewhat earlier, with the 1939 partnership between William Hewlett and David Packard (for first-hand reminiscences, see Packard 1995). In their path-breaking book, *Silicon Valley Fever*, Everett Rogers and Judith Larsen (1984) devote two pages to the region's industrial history before World War II. Similarly, in AnnaLee Saxenian's (1996) important book comparing Route 128 and Silicon Valley, the beginnings of modern Silicon Valley are traced to the establishment of Hewlett Packard (HP). Those authors judged that the prior activities were not critical to the current institutional arrangements. However in this book, Timothy Sturgeon and, to a lesser degree, Stuart Leslie contest that position. The reader will have to decide when the features currently considered to constitute the Silicon Valley business environment coalesced. No doubt these two papers will make that judgment more difficult.

Before the late 1960s, there had been little national attention to developments in what soon became known as Silicon Valley.[4] Industrial developments in the Santa Clara Valley became known to the general public only when the region was named, and the naming of Silicon Valley did not come from scholars, public relations executives, or local boosters. Rather, it came from Dan Hoefler (1971), a reporter for *Electronic News* who wrote a three-part series on the history of the semiconductor industry in the Bay Area. Hoefler detailed the dynamic by which the spinoff process got underway in the semiconductor industry and how it rapidly became an accepted practice. He used the term "Silicon Valley" in his series and it stuck. By the 1970s the region had begun to attract national attention. In 1974 Gene Bylinsky wrote a feature article in *Fortune* on the formation of new high-technology firms in Santa Clara County. Rather than simply focusing upon semiconductors, Bylinsky provided a far more comprehensive picture of the high technologies being developed in the region and celebrated Frederick Terman's catalytic role. By 1975 Silicon Valley's reputation had become fixed in the public imagination.

Timothy Sturgeon provides a comprehensive treatment of the development of the electronics industry in the San Francisco Bay Area and explicitly takes issue with those who date the origins of Silicon Valley to the period immediately prior to World War II.[5] He traces the development of a climate for electronics innovation, entrepreneurship, and spinoffs to the formation of the Federal Telegraph Corporation (FTC) in 1909. He documents a spinoff process at FTC, but also finds it in operation at a number of other firms. From this perspective, it is clear that Frederick Terman's activities encouraging entrepreneurship did not arise in a vacuum; rather, the milieu already contained successful venturers, such as Litton, and less clearly successful venturers, such as Farnsworth. For Sturgeon, Frederick Terman, credited by many as the founder of Silicon Valley, can be better understood as a catalyst and a booster in an already prepared environment. Terman's contribution was to bring in Stanford University's engineering departments, although, as Sturgeon points out, in 1909 the president of Stanford at that time, David Starr Jordan, had backed the start-up that would become Federal Telegraph. Clearly, Silicon Valley did not rise as a result of herculean efforts by a single great individual; the raw material out of which Silicon Valley would coalesce was already available.

The role of defense spending in the development of Silicon Valley is highlighted by Stuart Leslie. The importance of federal procurement for the early growth of the semiconductor industry has been noted before (Braun and MacDonald 1982; Borrus et al. 1988; Riordan and Hoddeson 1997), but Leslie's contribution broadens our understanding of other technologies, such as microwaves, that benefited from federal funding and that have played an important role in Silicon Valley's success. Leslie acknowledges Sturgeon's paper, which demonstrated the importance of military procurement even in the early days of Federal Telegraph, but he then goes further, arguing that there has been a pervasive military influence in Silicon Valley's development. In the tradition of Smith's work (1977, 1985) on the interaction between the military and technological development, Leslie provides ample evidence of the variety of ways by which military objectives and funding affected the development of Silicon Valley. So important was the military that he argues that it has been the biggest venture capitalist of all. Certainly, the list of technologies that were later commercialized in Silicon Valley and that had had, at least in their beginnings, some military funding is long; it extends even to the latest Silicon Valley investment darling, the Internet (Hauben and Hauben 1998). In effect, U.S. defense policy after World War II was an innovation policy, which greatly benefited Silicon Valley's high-technology firms by creating price-insensitive lead customers and by funding precommercial research, supporting universities, and training engineers and scientists.

These two historical chapters provide a rich basis for understanding the roots of Silicon Valley. The environment in which Terman and later Shockley operated was not an empty one. The authors force us to consider what are the features that make Silicon Valley so innovative, and when they coalesced into the current system. Their retrospective prepares us for understanding the situation there today.

Institutions and Practices

The infrastructure for any regional economy is a complex set of institutions and routines providing specialized goods and services.[6] This section examines two institutions and two distinctive routines that are central to the Silicon Valley "metabolism." Each contribution understands its subject as a constituent element of a complex regional economy, and thus does not fall prey to the imperialism of single-variable explanations. The first two articles focus on two critical institutions, law firms and venture capitalists. The next two papers examine the routines surrounding labor mobility and interfirm relations. Obviously, these papers explain only four salient features that function to create the region. Other important institutions deserving attention but that have not yet been studied include the investment banks, specialized marketing consultants, and commercial real estate developers, to name only a few of the most salient.

Institutional analysis provides a map of the structures that have emerged from the conduct of activity. But they do not provide an understanding of the routines, norms, and values that motivate the participants. Here the two papers examining labor mobility and interfirm relations provide insight into individual and firm routines that undergird the dynamics of Silicon Valley. On the one hand, for the law firms and venture capitalists to operate in the way they do, labor mobility is critical—the innovations must be extrudable from existing institutions, and trained personnel must be readily available to staff the start-ups, especially those growing rapidly. On the other hand, the availability of capital and legal assistance encouraged labor mobility both to form start-ups and to staff them. The availability of specialty suppliers and services, such as contract manufacturing, also assists in lowering entry barriers for new firms while assisting existing firms (Sturgeon 1999). This mutually reinforcing, interactive, regionally based system now has its own logic, which reinforces the current path.

Mark Suchman's contribution explicates the specialized legal practices that have evolved in Silicon Valley to facilitate the start-up of firms. These law firms have developed a multifaceted practice by undertaking multiple roles in advising new start-ups. The legal counselor–client relationship confers a central status upon the law firms in the start-up process. Silicon Valley law firms perform functions that go beyond their considerable talents in incorporating high-technology firms, in intellectual property and trade secret law, and in legal issues particular to venture investing. Their roles include actual involvement in dealmaking, through counseling entrepreneurs before their dealings with various entities, especially venture capitalists; gatekeeping, by deciding whether to take a new firm as a client; proselytizing, by encouraging certain types of behavior among their clients; and matchmaking, because an introduction from a highly regarded lawyer prompts venture capitalists to consider the fledgling firm's business plan seriously. These law firms have evolved into a nexus through which many crucial relationships necessary for new firm formation are coordinated.

Whereas Suchman examined the triangular relationship between venture capitalists, entrepreneurs, and lawyers, Kenney and Florida focus on the evolution of the Silicon Valley venture capital community. Bay Area venture capital is traced from its beginnings among investors using personal and family funds to federally chartered Small Business Investment Corporations (SBICs) and then to the current limited-partnership format. The growth of venture capital as an institution is linked directly to the extraordinary success of their investments. Repeated success meant that the venture capitalists were able to amass ever greater sums of capital, leading to an increasing number of investments and the wherewithal to take ever greater risks. Venture capitalists, though financial intermediaries, offer far more than capital. In recognition of their status as partners, they expect seats on the firm's board of directors, from where they participate in major strategic decisions; assist in recruiting key personnel; provide introductions to potential suppliers, customers, and partners; and even replace the founders. In effect, they have created a practice that is "hands-on" rather than "arms-length." This combination of the advisor and auditor role is meant to increase the investment recipient's probability of success, so much so that even firms not needing capital will recruit venture capital, largely for their know-how and know-who.

The existence of venture capital and the activities of the law firms are dependent upon entrepreneurs, most of who emerge from existing organizations. By definition, these individuals benefit from Silicon Valley's long-standing high labor mobility (Parden 1981). There are two distinct mobility patterns based upon the destination: the first pattern concerns the movement of managers and engineers from existing firm to existing firm in pursuit of more interesting projects, improved conditions, higher wages, better stock option packages, or any of a myriad of other benefits. Second is the movement from existing firms to establish a start-up. There have been two perspectives on the merits of this high mobility. In the late 1980s, some, such as Florida and Kenney (1990c), argued that very high rates of turnover were destructive for research teams and firms. For others, this interfirm mobility meant that the information and knowledge circulated rapidly, thereby upgrading the entire region's capabilities (Angel, this volume; Almeida and Kogut 1997). In more general terms, Carnoy et al. (1997) found that Silicon Valley pioneered the introduction of "flexible employment," which is a shift from the traditional pattern of individuals filling jobs in firms with career ladders and relatively stable employment, to a pattern in which jobs are filled on a relatively transient basis. In this regime of flexible employment an individual's knowledge and connections are critical.

In one sense, the chapter by David Angel is dated, in that it draws upon a survey conducted in 1987; however, it is one of the very few empirical studies of employment practices and labor mobility in an important Silicon Valley industry. Moreover, few would argue that his findings, with minor updating, are not as valid today as they were in the late 1980s. This study of semiconductor industry employees shows how their high mobility ensures a rapid circulation of knowledge and information among firms in Silicon Valley. In effect, the mobility is a knowledge-transfer mechanism that ensures an upgrading of the entire production complex. There can be little doubt that the pattern evident in semiconductors is more general to the other high-technology industries in the region. This has important implications, if competitiveness is considered not at the level of the individual firm but rather at the industrial-region level.

The contribution by AnnaLee Saxenian, the author of *Regional Advantage*, one of the few academic books on Silicon Valley, examines another important feature of Silicon Valley. She finds Silicon Valley's success is due to the loosely integrated interfirm networks that were a response to the market volatility experienced in the 1960s and 1970s. These interfirm collaborations draw upon specialist firms in the region. Out-sourcing was found to be more efficient than vertically integrating the entire production system. This organizational paradigm would be made famous by the 1992 book *The Virtual Corporation*, written by William Davidow, an important Silicon Valley venture capitalist, and Michael Malone, the author of a number of books about Silicon Valley. As in the case of David Angel's chapter, the empirical evidence regarding these collaborations is dated. However, the types of interactions and relationships then forged between firms can be found today in the new networking and Internet industries.

Each article recognizes that its subject is interwoven with and interdependent upon the other regional institutions and routines. Because of this, each contribution enriches comprehension without denigrating the myriad of reinforcing interconnections operating to create a coherent and reproducible system. This diversity of perspectives or slices into the Silicon Valley phenomenon provides a richness upon which the more comprehensive papers in the next section build.

Systemic Explanations

The maintenance, reproduction, and expansion of a system as complicated and rich as Silicon Valley is the result of the alignment of incentives and institutions on a variety of dimensions, including the political, economic, and social levels. And yet, it is a common fallacy to assume that the features and incentives remain constant. It is entirely possible that the features initially important for initiation and early growth can at later stages become much less important or even irrelevant. One example is the dramatic decline in the importance of military spending. Today, increased defense spending might paradoxically raise engineering wage costs and divert intellectual resources from Silicon Valley, thus inhibiting its growth. Another inhibitor is U.S. government control on technology exports, which lead to decreased sales. Thus a once important activity, defense spending, probably has evolved to being a burden rather than an accelerator.

The final three papers offer comprehensive explanations of the Silicon Valley phenomenon. Each paper explains it from a different perspective, though, not surprisingly, they often draw upon the same sources. They have significant points of agreement, especially on the proposition that any explanation must recognize the diversity of institutions that coexist and cooperate to make possible the new firm formation process. This indicates an important point of agreement among the three sets of authors—namely, they accept that an essential characteristic of Silicon Valley has been the ability to spawn new firms. And yet, within this agreement, each chapter has a different perspective and explanation. When taken together, they provide the reader with a stereoscopic perspective with which to comprehend the dynamics of the entire complex.

Explaining Silicon Valley as an interactive entity has a long history. For example, Schoonhoven and Eisenhardt (1988) termed Silicon Valley an "incubator region." Florida and Kenney (1988a) characterized the region as having a "social structure of innovation." Bahrami and Evans describe Silicon Valley as an "ecosystem" consisting of interdependent institutions, social norms, and communities that create an environment encouraging the evolution of existing firms and, especially, the creation of new firms. Picking up on David Angel's theme of labor mobility, they emphasize the constant recycling of human resources as older firms stagnate, lose top talent, and even fail. For them, the ability of Silicon Valley institutions to generate streams of new firms is important for regional evolution. And, most important, failure is highlighted as a critical phenomenon in recycling the region's human resources.

Stephen Cohen and Gary Fields critique the notion that Silicon Valley's *élan vital* can be understood through the concepts of "social capital" and "trust" distilled from studies of Northern Italian industrial districts. They dispute Robert Putnam's assertion that communities must be civic to become prosperous. For them, Silicon Valley, though having many small firms, is not predicated on small firms remaining small. In fact, the entire objective of Silicon Valley firms is to grow to be large firms as rapidly as possible—capital gains are the objective. In Silicon Valley social capital and trust are built through instrumental interactions among actors that have specific economic aims, and not through intense civic engagement. Trust and social capital accrue, because, to put it in the vernacular, the parties "get the job done." They argue that the direction of causality runs from performance to trust and not vice versa. For them, Silicon Valley is a community of performance; when a venture capitalist funds a set of entrepreneurs, they draw upon the venture capitalist's social capital, which is the promise of performance, not a selfless act of community-building.

Kenney and von Burg see the new firm formation process as the critical dynamic for Silicon Valley. They conceptualize Silicon Valley as an amalgam of two analytically separate "economies" in Silicon Valley. The first economy consists of the existing firms and institutions, which produce their expected outputs but also generate innovations that can be actualized commercially outside existing institutions. There is a second economy, whose institutions actually succeed by incubating firms to be sold to larger firms or to the public through a stock offering. The institutions that constitute this second economy are examined and their operation and interaction are detailed in the chapter.

These chapters explain the institutional and organizational mechanisms that make possible Silicon Valley's remarkable ability to find new, fast-growing economic spaces and fill them with new firms. They treat Silicon Valley systemically by integrating the immense variety of institutions, such as venture capital, specialty law firms, headhunters, marketing firms, and the myriad of other institutional actors that nurture and draw sustenance from these start-ups. Silicon Valley has created what now appears to be a self-regenerating and, currently, expanding ecosystem based upon the capital gains generated by start-ups.

The Future

This book provides readers with a variety of perspectives on how Silicon Valley came into being and the reasons for its continuing success. The historical chapters provide context that is often missing in discussions of Silicon Valley. The following four articles examine different routines and institutions. The three final chapters build more comprehensive explanations for the regional dynamics. At the outset of planning this book, I wished to assemble a collection of articles that did not necessarily agree, and that operated from different theoretical paradigms. My concern was to give different perspectives voice, while recognizing that any analysis of a region so turbulent and with so many experiments cannot be captured by any single analyst no matter how learned or brilliant. If it is true that the future is being created in Silicon Valley, then all the more reason that those predicting Silicon Valley's development must exercise care and humility.

This book is timely. From 1995 through 1998, perhaps the greatest wave of start-ups and initial public offerings in Silicon Valley's history was underway, centered on the commercialization of the Internet. Even as this Gold Rush puts all previous ones to shame, it should be recognized that it comes upon the heels of a very deep slump that began in the late 1980s and extended through the early 1990s. Many, including to some degree myself, believed in 1989 that the magic had finally ended. Obviously, we were wrong.

From a historical perspective, this leads to two observations: first, although the Silicon Valley high-technology complex has experienced secular growth since the end of World War II, it has regularly been beset by severe slumps, which have brought with them severe dislocation and pessimism regarding the future. These mood swings can be quite manic, moving from an incredible exhilaration to deep pessimism. It would be wiser to hesitate here (and by the time this book is published, Silicon Valley might already be falling into another of its down cycles). And yet, there is reason to believe that the institutions for new firm formation may have reached such critical mass that they can now recover from any temporary setback that might occur. Remarkably, after a hiatus a new technological wave invariably appears that is greater than the previous one. And it is possible that today's Internet wave is the most important of all. We may need to rename the region Networking Valley, no longer being driven by Moore's Law (postulated by Gordon Moore, a cofounder of Fairchild and Intel), which says that for the same number of transistors on an integrated circuit the price drops by one-half every eighteen months. The region now appears to be driven by variants of Metcalfe's Law (named after Robert Metcalfe, the inventor of Ethernet and founder of 3Com), which observes that the value of a network increases exponentially with the addition of every new user.

In a fundamental way, this book is an argument about the uniqueness of Silicon Valley. Therefore it is not our task to reflect upon the generalizability of the Silicon Valley model. However, one conclusion is that nearly all efforts to create Silicon Valley analogues have failed or, at best, been partial successes (see also Leslie and Kargon 1996). From this perspective it would be tempting to assume that the complicated environment or ecosystem encouraging the formation of new firms in Silicon Valley cannot possibly be cloned in other regions (except the Route 128 area in Massachusetts). This seems slightly too pessimistic. If it is true that we are entering a knowledge- or information-based economy, something that most persons would agree Silicon Valley is already in, then it seems quite feasible that many of the features and practices typical of Silicon Valley may find other congenial locations into which to spread. The ultimate result could be regions that, although possibly not as dynamic as Silicon Valley, might become self-reinforcing hotbeds of innovation, with their own set of institutions dedicated to new firm formation.

PART I

HISTORY

CHAPTER TWO

How Silicon Valley Came to Be

TIMOTHY J. STURGEON

During recent years the San Francisco Bay Area developed rather
suddenly into one of the major centers of electronics research and
industry in the United States. To those who knew the background it
seemed a natural evolution in a region that has been the scene of
radio and electronics pioneering since early in the Century.
    —Frederick Terman, from preface in Morgan 1967

The rise of Silicon Valley has garnered worldwide attention because it
seemed to offer the possibility that a region with no prior industrial
history could make a direct leap to a leading-edge industrial economy,
given the right set of circumstances, without the time and effort required to pass through any intermediate stages of development. Here
was "cowboy capitalism" in its most raw and dynamic form. The idea
that so much growth could occur in so short a time within such a small
geographic area sent planning bodies and government agencies from
Albuquerque to Zimbabwe scrambling to "grow the next Silicon Valley" in their own backyard (Miller and Côté 1985). Thus, the model of
Silicon Valley became the Holy Grail of economic development.
    Unfortunately, the full story of how Silicon Valley came to be has
not been told. Most accounts of the region's history begin in 1955, when
William Shockley, who had coinvented the transistor at Bell Laboratories in 1947, founded Shockley Transistor Corporation in Palo Alto. The
spinoff of Fairchild Semiconductor from Shockley Transistor and the
"Fairchildren" that followed are widely believed to be the stimuli that
set the Silicon Valley juggernaut in motion (Braun and MacDonald
1982; Morgan and Sayer 1988; Scott and Angel 1987; Scott and Storper
1987; Storper and Walker 1989).
    More careful accounts push the origin of Silicon Valley back a bit

further, to the formation of Hewlett Packard Company in 1938, and Varian Associates in 1948, within the incubator of Stanford University (Hanson 1982; Rogers and Larsen 1984; Saxenian 1983a, 1986, 1988a). The agglomeration of electronics companies around Stanford University is attributed, in this version of the Valley's genesis, to the vision of Frederick Terman, the dean of Stanford University's School of Engineering during World War II, and to the influx of military-financed research and development that he brought to the area (Saxenian 1985, 1989b).[1]

This chapter demonstrates that these accounts truncate Silicon Valley's history and divorce the region from the economic geography of the greater San Francisco Bay Area, within which it is situated (see the map of the region on the inside cover of this volume).[2] Hewlett Packard and Varian were not the first important electronics companies to arise near Stanford, and Fairchild was not the region's first "spinoff." Frederick Terman was as much a product of local ferment in electronics as he was its catalyst. While these revelations do not make the emergence of Silicon Valley any less important, they do change the basic premise of a widely held model for economic development, inviting reconsideration of both policy and theory (for the latter, see Sturgeon 1992).

This chapter shows that there has been a vibrant electronics industry in the San Francisco Bay Area since the earliest days of experimentation and innovation in the fields of radio, television, and military electronics. My aim is to undermine the myth of "instant industrialization" that has been so central to the story of Silicon Valley's development. What emerges instead is a portrait much more typical of studies in economic and historical geography: industrial development takes a long time to build up momentum, is profoundly structured by place and historical context, and acquires path-dependent characteristics that continue to influence outcomes far into the future.

One remarkable aspect of the material I present is that the characteristics of early Bay Area electronics companies closely match the structure of industrial organization so widely hailed in Silicon Valley today, albeit on a much smaller scale. A leading role for local venture capital; a close relationship between local industry and the major research universities of the area; a product mix with a focus on electronic components, production equipment, advanced communications, instrumentation, and military electronics; an unusually high level of interfirm cooperation; a tolerance for spinoffs; and a keen awareness of the region as existing largely outside the purview of the large, ponderous, bureaucratic electronics firms and financial institutions of the East Coast—all of these well-known characteristics of Silicon Valley were as much in evidence from 1910 through 1940 as they have been from the 1960s onward. In the jargon of the Valley, it seems that the key characteristics of Bay Area electronics, set in place so long ago, have proved to be readily "scalable" as the industry has grown in the region.

The Radio Industry Prior to World War I

To better understand the early days of electronics in the San Francisco Bay Area, the larger stage must first be set. While the roots of the electronics industry can be traced back to the rise of the telegraph, electric power, and telephone industries during the latter half of the nineteenth century, a more definitive ancestor is radio. Guglielmo Marconi transmitted the first radiotelegraph signals in 1895, but by 1910 the radio industry was still very much in its infancy. Commercial broadcasting had yet to be developed, and there were no in-home receivers available on the market.[3] Most early radio companies were established to compete with wire telegraph services, but due to problems caused by radio static and the resistance to radio by powerful telegraph companies, radio companies could hope to be competitive only in transoceanic circuits, where expensive submarine cables drove up costs. The radio application with the greatest immediate potential was shipboard communications, either to shore stations or ship to ship. Steamship lines and the internal shipping operations of companies such as United Fruit proved to be ready customers for early radio firms, but by far the largest user was the U.S. Navy, which recognized the advantages of radio communication over searchlight and flag signaling.

The earliest radio systems relied on crude "spark gap" transmitters to generate radio waves. Spark transmitters were so called because an electrical current was forced to jump across a gap between two poles, causing long radio waves to be emitted by the resulting spark. By opening and closing the electrical circuit, electromagnetic pulses, or "damped" radio waves, were emitted that were well suited to the dots and dashes of Morse code.[4] Reception was achieved with "crystal" detectors. The only way to transmit signals over greater distances was to build ever larger spark transmitters. The key technical problems were to develop a reliable way to generate "undamped" continuous (or carrier) radio waves better suited to voice transmission, and to improve reception, either by increasing sensitivity or by amplifying weak incoming signals.

Although the navy tried to award contracts to American firms whenever possible, the companies with the best radio communications systems at the time were Marconi, a British firm, and Telefunken, a German firm. Lee de Forest, an American inventor who founded the Radio Telephone Company (RTC) in New York City, had yet to produce a working radiotelegraph system, and the radiotelephones he was supplying to the navy were proving to be of "doubtful practicability." The National Electric Signaling Company (NESCO), founded by the Pittsburgh-based inventor Reginald Fessenden, was further advanced, but the alternator that he had invented to generate continuous waves was still under development at General Electric (GE). Further compounding the navy's problems was the constant litigation that these companies engaged each other in, to try to improve their patent positions. No single company held the patents for all the best technology needed for a complete, leading-edge radio system. For example, Marconi had the largest installed base and the most powerful spark transmitters, but NESCO had developed an improved means of reception called heterodyne (Howeth 1963).

In January 1909 the U.S. Navy requested bids for a new shore radio station in Arlington, Virginia, just outside Washington D.C., and radio equipment for two vessels. The navy's requirements intentionally exceeded prevailing technological capabilities in order to incite innovation. The system had to be capable of reaching ships at a distance of three thousand miles at all times of the day, in any weather, and during any season of the year. (Daylight and summer thunderstorms created static interference that severely hampered long-wave radio signals, especially over land masses; vacuum tube–based short-wave systems developed in the 1920s overcame this problem.) The system was also required to have wireless telephone capability within a range of one hundred miles. NESCO, with the lowest bid, won the contract over American Marconi, Telefunken, and RTC. Over the next two years, while the Arlington station was under development, NESCO built approximately 75 percent of the navy's radio equipment, the sales from which represented all the company's revenues except for a few systems sold to the United Fruit Company (ibid.).

In 1912 an engineer from a firm largely unknown on the East Coast arrived on the navy's doorstep with a system based on novel technology that proved to be far superior to the NESCO system, setting a pattern that, as we shall see, was to be oft repeated. The engineer was a Stanford graduate named Cyril Elwell; the company was Federal Telegraph Corporation, based in Palo Alto; and the radio transmission technology was the Poulsen arc, which generated continuous long radio waves with an electric arc operating in an atmosphere of hydrogen contained by a strong magnetic field. The system was so successful that FTC went on to design and install the world's first global-scale radio communications system, using ever-larger Poulsen arc transmitters.[5]

The role of FTC in the early radio industry has been widely overlooked (but see Aitken 1985) because the reign of the Poulsen arc occurred during wartime and was to be short-lived, as improved alternator—and shortly thereafter, vacuum tube—technology arrived on the scene at the war's end. However, FTC continued to be one of the key players in the early San Francisco Bay Area electronics industry through the early 1930s. Many of the luminaries of the local electronics scene, such as Leonard Fuller and Charles Litton, began their careers working at FTC. In the early 1920s a young Frederick Terman spent a summer there as an intern before temporarily moving to the East Coast to attend MIT.

The Birth of Federal Telegraph in 1909

In 1908, Elwell, recently graduated from Stanford, was working in Palo Alto on a spark-based radio telegraph system.[6] Elwell was unable to get the system to work with either a spark transmitter or an alternator, so he wired Dr. Vladimir Poulsen, the inventor of the arc transmitter, in Copenhagen about the possibility of acquiring its U.S. patent rights. Elwell had seen the arc demonstrated at an exhibition in Paris in 1900. Poulsen agreed and Elwell soon traveled to Denmark to inspect the system and negotiate a deal.[7]

On his return to Palo Alto in 1909, Elwell turned to David Starr Jordan, the president of Stanford, and C. D. Marx, the head of Stanford's Civil Engineering Department, to finance a new company to provide wireless telephone and telegraph services on the Pacific Coast using Poulsen arc technology. The company was initially called Poulsen Wireless Telephone and Telegraph. It is notable that the heavy involvement of Stanford's administration and faculty in the formation of

FTC came a full thirty years before Frederick Terman would help Hewlett and Packard to start their company.

Elwell built a small system and invited the public to demonstrations of wireless voice and telegraph communication between Stockton and Sacramento. At the time, wireless voice transmission was still extremely novel. The mayor of Sacramento, wealthy Chinese merchants, and local bank executives all tried the system. Beach Thompson, representing a group of San Francisco financiers including the Crocker family,[8] invested in the company. Beach Thompson became president, Elwell was named chief engineer, and the company was renamed the Federal Telegraph Company (Aitken 1985; Grass Roots Writing Collective 1969; Morgan 1967; Rosa 1960).

Arc transmitters were installed on the fleet of the San Francisco–based Pacific Mail Steamship Company, which offered San Francisco to Los Angeles service and transpacific service to Australia. A chain of stations was built for FTC's radiotelegraph service along the Pacific Coast, and Elwell installed a thirty-kilowatt radiotelegraph circuit between South San Francisco and Honolulu. While FTC's radiotelegraph service on the Pacific was profitable, stations that had been built in Phoenix, Dallas, Kansas City, and Chicago lost money because static problems made transmission unreliable.

Federal Telegraph's World War I
Navy Contracts

In 1912, Elwell convinced his backers to allow him to travel to Washington, D.C., to generate interest in the Poulsen arc at the navy. The twelve-kilowatt transmitter he brought with him impressed navy officials enough to win him a head-to-head comparison trial with the NESCO transmitter that was just undergoing tests at the Arlington station. The navy set the condition that the FTC apparatus be installed so that it could be removed without leaving any permanent marks on the station's floor, walls, or ceiling (Fuller 1976; Howeth 1963; Rosa 1960). The arc never was removed, because the small, nearly silent arc transmitter by far outperformed the NESCO unit, which had a spark discharge that could be heard a mile away. Contact was made with South San Francisco and then with Honolulu. The arc was able to maintain contact with outbound navy ships long after the transmissions from the

NESCO unit had faded to nothing as the vessels neared Key West, Florida (Rosa 1960). On the spot, the navy ordered ten thirty-kilowatt arc transmitters for shipboard use. Thus, FTC became known as "the navy's darling of the World War I period" (Howeth 1963).

The navy's demand for more powerful arc transmitters soon exceeded FTC's technical capabilities. On June 30, 1913, a one-hundred-kilowatt unit was requested for the Panama Canal Zone. This was to be the first station in a "high-powered chain" that was to extend southward from Arlington to the Canal Zone and westward to the Philippines. The contract specified the use of arc transmitters, sparking a storm of protests by East Coast radio companies who complained that the navy's Bureau of Equipment had written the specifications in a way that restricted competition (ibid.).

Elwell accepted the contract but refused to guarantee the system's success because the design team at FTC had been unable to increase the power of the arc beyond thirty kilowatts. The FTC team, which included Charles Logwood, a local amateur, or "ham," radio enthusiast who had assisted Elwell with the spark-based system, and Peter Jensen, an engineer who had come over from Denmark as part of the agreement between Poulsen and Elwell, had thus far increased the power of the arc from twelve to thirty kilowatts through the simple technique of "up rationing" the scale of the design drawings supplied by Poulsen (Fuller 1975, 1976).

The strength of FTC's design team was improved when Leonard Fuller was hired after a brief stint with NESCO in New York. Fuller knew about FTC because he had visited it in 1910 while on summer vacation from Cornell University, where he received his master's degree in electrical engineering.[9] Fuller, an avid ham radio enthusiast, was so impressed by the Poulsen arc transmitter that he built one on his return to Cornell. Innovations that he made with this small arc became the subject of his master's thesis. Fuller was hired as an engineer and led a research effort that soon increased the power output of FTC's arc transmitters to sixty kilowatts (and beyond) by tuning the magnetic field (Aitken 1985).

The Stanford High Voltage Laboratory was of great assistance to FTC's efforts to improve the Poulsen arc. Leonard Fuller, along with FTC employee Roland Marx (the son of Stanford professor and FTC investor C. D. Marx), collaborated with professors Ralph Beal and Harris Ryan on the development of antenna insulation. The Stanford lab had a better direct-current power supply than the FTC, and it was used for experimentation, continuing a pattern set by local electric power companies that had used the high-voltage lab at Stanford and U.C. Berkeley for the development of long-distance electric power transmission (Norberg 1976; Sturgeon 1992; Williams 1987, 1990). In return for the use of the lab, Fuller arranged for FTC to donate a twelve-kilowatt arc to Stanford. Ryan and Marx used this transmitter to investigate the insulation characteristics of porcelain, quartz, glass, redwood, and oak, and they published a paper in the *Institute of Radio Engineers Proceedings* in 1916 based on these experiments (Fuller 1976).

In December 1913 construction was begun on the navy's one-hundred-kilowatt Canal Zone station, using Fuller's improved designs. The commercial station in South San Francisco Station was upgraded as well, but for Elwell, commercial expansion was not proceeding quickly enough, especially in the realm of maritime communications; that was where Elwell believed the real opportunity to be (Aitken 1985). The economic failure of the Phoenix, Dallas, Kansas City, and Chicago stations had made the board of directors of FTC cautious about expanding too quickly. Frustrated, Elwell quit and moved to England, where he was hired as chief engineer for the Universal Radio Syndicate, a company that held the Poulsen patents for the British Empire.[10]

When the United States entered World War I, the entire radio industry was nationalized. FTC received orders for three hundred two-kilowatt shipboard transmitters from the U.S. Shipping Board, to be used aboard the Liberty Ships. The navy ordered thirty-kilowatt transmitters for "probably all" of their battleships, a twenty-kilowatt set for a cruiser, and a five-kilowatt set for a navy collier. The navy continued to push FTC's technical limits by demanding higher power transmitters as it extended its chain into the Pacific. With these large orders FTC outgrew its old facility, because the high-powered arcs required magnets too large for their building. The new facility, also located in Palo Alto, had increased office space, a large laboratory, a machine shop, an overhead crane, a stockroom, and a railroad siding. Orders for more shore stations for the navy flooded in, including a dual five-hundred-kilowatt station in Annapolis; a two-hundred-kilowatt station in Puerto Rico; a two-hundred-kilowatt set in Sayville, Long Island; another two-hundred-kilowatt set for San Diego; a transpacific five-hundred-kilowatt chain; thirty-kilowatt sets in Alaska; as well as a string of smaller stations around the Gulf and Atlantic coasts. The army ordered twenty-kilowatt and thirty-kilowatt sets for various army posts around the country (Howeth 1963). Employment at FTC surged from thirty to three hundred (Fuller 1976).

The war work at FTC culminated in installation of a pair of one-thousand-kilowatt transmitters at the Lafayette Radio Station, fourteen miles southwest of Bordeaux, France (ibid.; Howeth 1963; Norberg 1976). Work began in May 1918. The ground and antenna system, supported by eight 820-foot towers, was designed by Fuller. The workforce to construct the towers, largely brought in from the United States, consisted of six hundred riggers, steelworkers, bridgemen, and electricians. The only structure taller at the time was the Eiffel Tower. The war ended before the station was finished, but the French government paid to have the construction finished. Upon its completion in January 1920, the station was by far the most powerful in the world and had cost $3.5 million to build (Howeth 1963).

Early Vacuum Tube Developments

The end of World War I resulted in canceled orders at FTC, including a planned two-thousand-kilowatt station in Monroe, North Carolina.[11] With the success of large systems, Fuller believed that a five-thousand-kilowatt arc was possible. The problem with high-powered arcs was that they emitted strong harmonic radio frequencies that interfered with smaller stations. By contrast, the alternator emitted no harmonics and broadcast on a sharply defined frequency. But the reign of the alternator was to be even shorter than that of the Poulsen arc. During the war, vacuum tubes had been developed that could generate high-power, "short-wave" radio signals that overcame many of the static problems that plagued the long-wave systems of the day. In fact, by war's end, vacuum tubes had been improved to the point where they could be successfully applied to all aspects of radio communications: transmission, reception, and signal amplification. It was only a matter of time before they came to dominate the radio industry. Vacuum tubes played a role in the electronics industry of the pre–World War II period analogous to that of the transistor during the postwar period: they opened vast and unforeseen new market potential by increasing the capability and reliability of electronic systems while radically reducing their costs, power requirements, and size.

It is well known that Lee de Forest perfected a vacuum tube in 1912 capable of greatly amplifying the faint electrical signals from long-distance telephone and radio transmissions, a key innovation that is often said to have given birth to the "age of electronics." What is less well known is that de Forest developed this tube in Palo Alto, in the laboratory of FTC.

In 1910, Lee de Forest, who had earned a Ph.D. in electrical engineering from Yale in 1899, came to San Francisco to supervise the installation of wireless telegraph sets on two army transport ships. The receivers used a vacuum tube, the "audion," that de Forest had invented in 1906 and patented in 1907. This early vacuum tube, though unreliable, was a much more sensitive detector of radio signals than were the crystal detectors of the day. As the sets were being installed, de Forest continued his experiments with voice transmission in a makeshift laboratory in San Francisco. He was convinced that the vacuum tube technology he was developing could overcome reliance on Morse code by transmitting voice messages over the air (Morgan 1967).

While de Forest was working in San Francisco, his New York partners were arrested for mail and stock fraud because they had floated $1,507,505 worth of uncollateralized stock. A grand jury was called, and the company was shut down, leaving de Forest destitute in San Francisco (Lewis 1991; Morgan 1967). During his time in the Bay Area, de Forest had met some of the participants in the local radio scene, including Elwell, who convinced Beach Thompson to hire de Forest and provide him with a laboratory, two assistants, and free rein to develop his ideas. De Forest was taken aback at first by the lack of formal training of one of his assistants, Charles Logwood, but with time he grew to respect Logwood's inventiveness and willingness to try out new ideas.[12] When federal agents came to Palo Alto in 1912 to arrest de Forest in connection with the stock fraud scheme, Thompson posted $10,000 bail, allowing de Forest to continue his work (Lewis 1991; Morgan 1967).

At FTC, de Forest tackled the problem of amplifying the strength of incoming telegraph signals to the level at which they could be better received by FTC's "rotary ticker," which sent audible signals to the operator's headset. Within a few months, de Forest and his assistants had invented a three-element vacuum tube that greatly exceeded expectations in its ability to amplify faint signals. A few months later, the de Forest team found that the tube could also function as an oscillator, a device to generate continuous radio waves.[13]

By 1912, de Forest had developed vacuum tubes that could be applied to all three stages of wireless radio communications: signal generation (the oscillator), signal reception (the audion), and signal amplification (the amplifier). Because the amplifier could boost weak signals as much as a millionfold, high-power transmission eventually became less crucial, and the cost of long-distance wireless systems was radically lowered. But the three-element vacuum tube, which became known as the "telephone repeater," would have wider impact. In fact, it would be difficult to overstate its importance to the development of the nascent electronics industry. In 1931, Robert Millikan, then director of the Norman Bridge Laboratory of Physics and chairman of the Executive Council of the California Institute of Technology, gave a nationally broadcast speech, introduced by President Hoover, in which he noted the importance of the de Forest three-electrode amplifier.

The essential device, not only for the whole broadcasting art, and not only for most of modern long distance wire telephony, but also for all forms of speech reproduction and amplification, and this includes the greater part of the whole modern motion picture industry—not to mention picture reproduction at a distance in all its forms [television]—the essential underlying device for all this is simply one new instrument, the electron tube, telephone repeater or amplifier. The multiplicity of the new and wholly unforeseen practical uses which one new device or principle introduced into physics seems invariably to find always astonishes even the physicist who alone realizes how small and often simple is the fundamental scientific advance that has been made. Knock out that single instrument, the telephone repeater, and much of the whole structure of modern long-distance telephony, and practically all of radio and talking pictures, comes crashing to the ground. (Millikan 1931)

De Forest knew that his tube amplifier was an important development, and asked his friend John S. Stone to arrange a demonstration at AT&T's Bell Laboratories. The telephone system was rapidly expanding at the time, but it was plagued by signals that weakened over long distances. Because of such signal attenuation, telephone transmission over land wires was limited to about one thousand miles, and over submarine cables to one hundred miles. De Forest's amplifier made it possible to amplify signals at various "repeater stations" along transmission wire routes, allowing telephone messages to be sent over indefinite distances. In the spring of 1910, AT&T had embarked on a crash program to develop an amplifier that would make possible a long-distance telephone connection between New York and San Francisco in time for the opening of the Panama-Pacific Exposition in 1915 (ibid.).

Two years into the AT&T development effort, de Forest walked into Bell Laboratories in New Jersey with what appeared to be a solution to the problem. AT&T did not invite de Forest to join their effort but instead asked to keep his apparatus for testing while they arranged to buy the patent rights for $100,000. De Forest agreed because he felt that his new invention was covered by his 1907 patent for the audion. After a year of waiting back in Palo Alto, de Forest was approached by a lawyer representing an anonymous party, who offered him $50,000 for the rights to the audion. De Forest, characteristically impatient, agreed to the deal only to find out later that the purchasing party had been AT&T (Aitken 1985). With his $50,000, de Forest left FTC in 1913 to begin yet another company that was to fail, the Radio Telegraph and Telephone Company, located in the High Bridge section of the Bronx (Lewis 1991).

The de Forest team was very productive during its short tenure at FTC. Besides discovering the amplifying and oscillating properties of the three-electrode vacuum tube, they established an innovative wire-telegraph link between San Francisco and Los Angeles using a "duplex" system of telegraphy that allowed two operators to transmit simultaneously over a single set of wires. Telephone repeaters were used to boost the strength of the signal along the way (ibid.). While the development of the amplifier at FTC did little for the company in the short term, it became significant during the 1920s, when the increasing dominance of vacuum tube technology forced FTC to make the changeover from Poulsen arc– to vacuum tube–based systems.

The Rise of RCA

In those days, the Radio Corporation was such a monopoly that if they'd blow their fetid breath at you, you were supposed to fall over. And they blew their fetid breath at us, but we didn't fall over.
—Heintz 1982

The patent situation in the radio industry immediately after World War I remained fragmented. GE had just perfected the Alexanderson alternator and was seeking to recoup $1 million in development costs by putting the alternator up for sale. When Marconi offered to buy twenty-four alternators from GE for $3 million, including rights for exclusive use, the secretary of the navy asked President Wilson to oppose the sale, which he did. Radio had proven to be such a strategic asset during the war that it was decreed that no foreign company would be allowed to hold more than a 20 percent interest in any radio station on United States soil (Fuller 1976). By government order GE acquired American Marconi for $9.5 million, creating a new company called the Radio Corporation of America (RCA). Owen Young of GE was named chairman of the board; Edward Nally, who had been vice president and general manager of American Marconi, became president; David Sarnoff, Nally's right-hand man, became general manager; and Rear Admiral W. H. G. Bullard of the U.S. Navy took a seat on the new company's board of directors.

Westinghouse acquired NESCO in 1919, including Fessenden's patents on heterodyne reception, but continued to rely on outmoded spark transmission technology inasmuch as AT&T held the key de Forest vacuum tube patents. In 1921, Westinghouse asked FTC to supply arc transmitters, but before the deal could be consummated Westinghouse joined in an elaborate patent sharing arrangement with GE and RCA, along with AT&T and United Fruit (ibid.). The formation of the "radio group," as it came to be known, left FTC completely out in the cold. RCA had essentially been granted monopoly control over the key radio patents for radio transmission, amplification, and reception by the U.S. government, which had orchestrated the deal. RCA acted as the marketing and systems operation arm for the group, while GE, Westinghouse, and AT&T manufactured equipment and components.

Because Marconi managers were installed to run RCA, the company inherited the monopolistic and predatory characteristics of Marconi corporate culture (Howeth 1963). Aggressive, litigious, and monopolizing, RCA emerged as the dominant force in the industry, ready to sue, buy out, or collect steep license fees from any fledgling electronics company in its path. While these traits were inherited from Marconi, RCA became vastly more powerful than its predecessor as electronics began to pervade more and more aspects of society. Commercial broadcasting had been almost completely unforeseen, but the number of in-home radio receivers grew from five thousand units in 1920 to twenty-five million units in 1924. The "radio craze" was on, and RCA was in a unique position to profit from it. By 1925, RCA's commercial wireless revenues were about $4 million, while sales from home radio sets and related equipment were about $46 million—and the gap was widening. As thousands of home-grown companies grew up in every major U.S. city to supply this burgeoning market, RCA moved aggressively to enforce its patent monopoly.

As we shall see, the early electronics industry in the San Francisco Bay Area labored under constant threat of RCA litigation. At the same time, the Bay Area was far enough from the dominant industry centers in the East for many of its activities to go unnoticed, at least initially. A few Bay Area companies were persistent thorns in the side of David Sarnoff, and some were able to beat him in court. Many others were small enough and far enough away to simply fly under RCA's radar. If the cooperative nature of Bay Area electronics companies during the 1920s, 1930s, and 1940s had any one source, it was opposition to the domination of the field by RCA. It is also likely that the dominance of RCA influenced the region's product mix as well. As we shall see, early Bay Area electronics companies largely eschewed consumer electronics to specialize in electronic instruments, military electronics, advanced communications technologies, electronic components, and production equipment, just as Silicon Valley's firms do today. This pattern may well have been set by the structure of the radio industry in the 1920s. As Frederick Terman put it during an interview in 1978:

I think they were "every man for himself" much more back [east]. . . . [East Coast] manufacturers would never cooperate [on standards for vacuum tubes], partly because of the patent situation. RCA dominated the patents and you couldn't leave RCA out, and if RCA was brought in, it wanted to boss everything. The group out here was involved in military production, instruments, and specialized stuff, where RCA patents weren't such a dominating feature. RCA wasn't trying to build a monopoly in the instrumentation business, for example. (Terman 1978)

Tube Production at Federal Telegraph

The sudden cessation of navy contracts after World War I, the shift to vacuum tube–based transmission, and the rise of RCA left FTC in significantly reduced circumstances. To generate new business, FTC tried to build a transpacific circuit for the Chinese government. This was strongly resisted by RCA, which argued that it had a right to a monopoly in long-distance radio traffic. The navy came to FTC's defense and the deal was approved, but the political tensions that grew with the rise of Chiang Kai-shek meant that the stations would never be built (Howeth 1963). Although some attempts were made at FTC to improve arc technology by using focused beams of higher frequency radio waves, the research team was never able to transmit further than forty to fifty miles using this technique (Heintz 1982). As it became obvious that the heyday of the Poulsen arc was past, FTC returned to the business of commercial radiotelegraph service, and Fuller left to help found the Kennedy Radio Company in San Francisco, to manufacture high-end home radio receivers under license from RCA (Fuller 1976). In the mid-1920s FTC was acquired by the Mackay interests, which controlled Postal Telegraph and Commercial Cable.[14] Mackay had good wire telegraph circuits in the Pacific and in South America; FTC's radio circuits in these regions were purchased to augment Mackay's cable business. In 1928, Mackay was purchased by ITT, giving FTC a new parent.

Federal Telegraph functioned as the manufacturing facility for Mackay's radio equipment and needed to make a transition to vacuum tube–based short-wave systems. A major stumbling block was that Westinghouse and GE would not sell vacuum tubes to FTC, since Mackay was perceived as a threat to RCA's near monopoly on long-distance radio communications. FTC brought in Ralph Heintz, a local expert in short-wave radio and vacuum tube manufacture, as a consultant to help them determine what would be required to manufacture tubes. Heintz reminded FTC management that they held "shop rights" to manufacture vacuum tubes covered by de Forest's patents because he had made his discoveries while under the employ of FTC. This allowed FTC to manufacture vacuum tubes for internal use without paying royalties. FTC officials immediately went to William Crocker, then the company's president, to obtain funding to establish a tube manufacturing facility (Heintz 1982).

Fuller returned to FTC, this time as vice president, to help organize vacuum tube production. While FTC's shop rights allowed them to produce vacuum tubes for reception and amplification, they still had to devise means to circumvent a host of additional RCA patents, particularly for large, high-powered, water-cooled transmission tubes. According to Norberg (1976), "They attacked the problem in a very structured manner. ITT's patent department provided information on all sorts of patents. The group at FTC analyzed the data and returned schemes to circumvent the patents. The patent lawyers then forwarded an opinion as to whether the device would withstand an infringement suit."

Federal Telegraph's Spinoffs

FTC generated some important spinoff companies, including Magnavox, Fisher Research Laboratories (FRL), and Litton Industries. Spinoffs are common in many industries and in many locations, but the FTC spinoffs are worth mentioning because of the importance that has been placed on spinoffs in the dynamic process of new firm formation in Silicon Valley's post-Fairchild era. Firm spinoffs are a central feature of the "Silicon Valley Model" of economic development. The examples provided in this section, as well as in later sections, show that the spinoff process—including the proverbial garage start-up—has been alive and well in the San Francisco Bay Area since 1910, when Magnavox spun off from FTC.

MAGNAVOX

Only one year after its founding, FTC produced its first spinoff. The two Danes who had come to America to help Elwell commercialize the Poulsen arc, Jensen and Albertus, along with FTC employee E. S. Pridham, who had earned a degree in electrical engineering from Stanford, left FTC in 1910 to start a research and development firm in a garage in Napa. By 1913 they had patented the "moving coil" loudspeaker, which was a vast improvement over existing speakers (standard texts state that this technology was invented by Ray Kellog in 1915). By 1917 they had perfected a design that most loudspeakers are still based on today. They named their company Magnavox, Latin for "big voice" (Morgan 1967).

During World War I, Magnavox built public-address systems for destroyers and battleships that allowed the captain to address all personnel on board. The company also developed an antinoise microphone for the navy that was installed on all of their four-motored Navy Curtiss seaplanes, allowing the crew to communicate with one another over the loud drone of the engines. The company received a national medal for its war efforts. After the war Magnavox built public-address systems for factories, hospitals, and sports stadiums nationwide. Magnavox built the first public address system used in a presidential speech; in September 1919 a Magnavox system was used by President Wilson to speak to fifty thousand people in San Diego.

Because Magnavox produced complete systems, they required powerful amplifiers to drive their loudspeakers. RCA had its own line of loudspeakers, however, and they refused to supply Magnavox with vacuum tubes for their amplifiers. The company was forced to produce tubes in-house, and they turned to Ralph Heintz for designs that would not infringe on RCA tube patents. The chief engineer for Magnavox was Don Lippincott, who went on to become an important San Francisco patent attorney who worked closely with local electronics companies on their patent difficulties with RCA.

Eventually, Jensen split off from Magnavox to form a company to produce loudspeakers only (Heintz 1974). Magnavox, now a subsidiary of the Dutch electronics giant Philips, went on to manufacture a full range of consumer electronics products and released the very first home video game system in 1972, the Magnavox Odyssey.

THE SINGLE-DIAL RADIO TUNER

In 1925, an FTC draftsman-cum-research engineer named Harold Elliot, who had a prominent role at FTC working on various features of the arc transmitters, began experimenting with designs for a single-dial radio tuner for broadcast receivers. Home receivers of the day required users to manipulate four or five different knobs. One knob, controlling the local oscillator, had to be moved at a constant difference to the others, which was too complicated for the average user (MacLaurin 1949).

By 1927, Elliot had worked out detailed engineering and manufacturing specifications for a single-dial tuner. After carefully researching various radio manufacturers, he brought the device to the attention of the Victor Phonograph Company. Victor, well known for its phonographs, had a license from RCA and was on the brink of entering the market for home radio sets. The company bought the rights to Elliot's device, which they dubbed the "microsynchronous tuner." Just as the company completed the design for the new receiver and was ready to go into production, Victor was acquired by RCA. The set went into production as the "Victor Microsynchronous Receiver," the first single-dial receiver on the market. In 1978, Frederick Terman said, "I believe probably more sets of that microsynchronous model were sold than any other single chassis built up to that point." Terman met with Elliot in 1938, shortly after the completion of the San Francisco–Oakland Bay

Bridge and the Golden Gate Bridge. Elliot told Terman that, in terms of retail price, the dollar value of all the Victor Microsynchronous Receivers sold was more than enough to build both bridges (Terman 1978).

FISHER RESEARCH LABORATORIES

Gerhard Fisher came to FTC in 1926 from New Jersey, where he had worked for de Forest. At FTC Fisher worked as an assistant to Frederick Kloster, who had developed an electronic direction finder for the navy during World War I. After the war, Kloster came to FTC to develop this technology for commercial shipping applications (Howeth 1963). In 1928, Fisher invented the first metal detector in his Palo Alto garage. He called the device the "Metaloscope," or "M-scope." The M-scope found wide acceptance, becoming standard equipment for water and gas companies across the country that used it to locate buried pipes. Miners and treasure hunters soon began using the device as well. In 1929, Fisher developed airborne navigation aids that improved on designs from Kloster's radio direction finder. In 1936, Fisher opened Fisher Research Laboratories in Palo Alto to manufacture a variety of electronics products, including radio telephones and marine radios (Morgan 1967). Today, FRL is located about eighty miles southeast of San Jose in Los Banos, where it still designs, manufactures, and sells metal detectors and related underground detection devices for industrial and hobby applications.

LITTON INDUSTRIES

In 1928, Charles Litton, who had just graduated from Stanford at the age of twenty-three, was hired by Fuller to manage FTC's in-house vacuum tube manufacturing department (Fuller 1976; Heintz 1982; Morgan 1967). Litton had built his first ham radio set at the age of ten and soon made his own vacuum tubes, which he sold to other hams. He operated his homemade radio set through two one-hundred-foot antenna towers at his parents' house in Redwood City; with it he was able to establish voice communications with stations as far away as Australia and New Zealand (Morgan 1967). According to Alexander Poniatoff (1974), Litton's father said that his son began operating a foot-pedal-driven metal lathe when he was so small that he had to pump the pedal by hand and then jump up on a chair to cut metal. Litton attended the

Lick-Vilmerding High School in San Francisco (later known as the California School for the Mechanical Arts), which had an amateur radio club on campus. While at Stanford, Litton continued experimenting with vacuum tubes for his ham sets, constructing most of the Communications Laboratory's vacuum tube manufacturing and test equipment from surplus parts scavenged from FTC's yard (Fuller 1976). At FTC, besides creating original designs for high-power vacuum tubes, Litton built innovative equipment for the entire tube manufacturing process, including glass-blowing lathes, radio-frequency electric furnaces, bake-out ovens, vacuum pumps, and test setups (ibid.; Norberg 1976).

In 1931, because of the depression, ITT decided to consolidate Mackay's manufacturing facilities, including FTC, in Newark, New Jersey. Both Fuller and Litton had clauses in their contracts stating that they would work only on the West Coast. Fuller left the company to take a position as professor of electrical engineering at U.C. Berkeley, where he later became department chairman.[15] Litton stayed on at FTC as chief engineer to manage the transition. The vacuum tube factory in Palo Alto was kept in operation to ensure a steady supply of tubes for Mackay's radio network. A testament to the degree of expertise needed to run this operation is found in the fact that it took two years, with Litton's active consultation, to get the new facility in Newark running satisfactorily (Fuller 1976).

With the departure of FTC to New Jersey in 1932, Litton formed Litton Engineering Laboratories to design and manufacture vacuum tube production equipment. Litton's glass-blowing lathe was able to mass produce glass tube blanks of uniform quality, a huge improvement over the hand-blown blanks of the day (Morgan 1967). These machines were unique and were used for mass production by virtually all major vacuum tube makers, including GE, Westinghouse, and RCA (Fuller 1976).

In 1940, Litton began manufacturing large, high-powered "magnetron" vacuum tubes for ground-based radar systems that were available from no other source. Although these tubes, some of which stood four feet high, were highly sought after by the U.S. military, Litton began by fabricating them from scratch in his backyard. According to Fuller, Litton "could do the seemingly impossible with metal and glass" (quoted in Morgan 1967). During World War II, tube production expanded, and, as Litton said, "I woke up one day, and out of the clear blue sky . . . found myself the sole owner of a million-and-a-half-dollar concern" (ibid.). In 1946, Litton separated the tube business from his research laboratory and machinery business.

In 1953, Litton sold his tube business to "Tex" Thornton and moved his laboratory to Grass Valley, east of the Sierra Nevada Mountains. Thornton saw "the opportunity for a new type of company: one that was technologically oriented and could develop and apply these high technologies, primarily electronics, to different types of products and industries" (O'Green 1989). The plan was to grow the company, initially dubbed the Electro Dynamics Corporation, into a diversified giant through the acquisition of small, innovative electronics companies. The company's first acquisition was Litton Industries, which reached $3 million in sales from Litton's state-of-the-art magnetron tubes in the first year. When he found that the name of Charles Litton carried a great deal of weight with the navy, Thornton changed the company's name to Litton Industries (ibid.). By 1980, Litton Industries had grown to $4.2 billion in annual sales.

Philo Farnsworth Develops Electronic
Television in San Francisco

Philo Farnsworth was an inventive prodigy. In 1924, at the age of fourteen, Farnsworth, studying on his own in his native Utah, combined the concepts of the photocell (for the camera) to the cathode ray tube (for the picture tube), thereby conceiving a full-blown system for electronic television (Everson 1949; Fisher and Fisher 1996).[16] Until the 1920s, the television systems under development had used a mechanical scanning disk to translate images into electrical impulses. Farnsworth continued to work on the theoretical details of his system but lacked the money to build a prototype. In 1926 he met a businessman from San Francisco, George Everson, and impressed him with a confident and enthusiastic description of his idea. Everson provided Farnsworth with seed money and eventually arranged for him to meet William Crocker in San Francisco. Farnsworth's enthusiasm and depth of knowledge proved impressive, and Crocker agreed to back the venture (Everson 1949; Fisher and Fisher 1996; Morgan 1967).

Farnsworth was installed in a crude laboratory at 202 Green Street in San Francisco, at the base of Telegraph Hill. Farnsworth's brother-in-law, Cliff Gardner, although he had no training as a glass blower, developed an extraordinary talent for fabricating the oddly shaped tubes that Farnsworth needed for his electronic scanner, which he called an "image dissector." RCA was also working on a television system at the time. In 1931, as news of Farnsworth's progress began to filter back to the East Coast, David Sarnoff sent Vladimir Zworykin, who was heading up RCA's research effort, to visit Farnsworth's laboratory (Sarnoff visited personally in 1931, but his offer to buy the company for $100,000 was rejected). Zworykin was very impressed with what he saw, particularly with Gardner's oddly shaped tube envelopes, which glass blowers at RCA had told him were impossible to fabricate. Farnsworth's work convinced Zworykin that an electronic method of image scanning was possible, and on his return to RCA he set out to develop his version of an electronic scanner, which he called the "ionoscope."

Farnsworth achieved the first all-electronic transmission of a television image in 1927, and he was able to win a solid patent on the system in 1930, thanks to the help of his patent attorney Donald Lippincott. Farnsworth's strong patent position eventually prevailed in court, and RCA was brought to heel for the first time when an agreement to pay continuing royalties to use the ionoscope was signed in 1939 (Fisher and Fisher 1996). Still, Farnsworth's activities in San Francisco during the 1920s remain little known, and Zworykin is widely considered to be the inventor of electronic television (perhaps the work of Fisher and Fisher [1996] will help to remedy this). Ralph Heintz (1982) put it very succinctly: "Phil was so frustrated, because they gave Zworykin credit for his invention. The press was loath to give credit to a poor little guy like Phil Farnsworth. Zworykin, of course, was a big shot, he was a Ph.D. and he was at Westinghouse, and they just snowed Phil under."

In 1931, Farnsworth's television system had been perfected to the point where commercial production seemed feasible. The San Francisco backers, eager to see some return on investment, sold the company to Philco, then the largest home radio manufacturer in the United States. Farnsworth and his team moved to Philadelphia to continue the development of the system (Fisher and Fisher 1996; Morgan 1967). According to Fisher and Fisher (1996), Farnsworth's team did not fit in well into Philco's more conservative corporate culture. The team from California refused to wear suits, vests, and long sleeves as they toiled in their stifling laboratory. As a result, William Grimditch, director of Philco's research department, referred to them as "animals," and they became known by the rest of the Philco staff as "those mavericks from the West." Tensions reached the breaking point when RCA threatened to withdraw Philco's license to manufacture radio sets if Farnsworth's laboratory were not shut down. In 1933, Farnsworth left Philco and struck out on his own. Despite a series of landmark victories in his patent litigation, Farnsworth's company was never able to compete with the R&D, marketing, and political muscle of David Sarnoff and RCA. In 1949, Farnsworth's still struggling company was sold to ITT, where Farnsworth became vice president in charge of research and advanced engineering (ibid.).

In San Francisco, Farnsworth had drawn heavily on local talent for the research effort. Russell Varian, an electrochemist recently graduated from Stanford, worked on the project for four years (Russell Varian would go on to found Varian Associates with his brother in 1948). Varian experimented with new phosphors for the picture tube and with new oscillators for transmission. Farnsworth was visited and encouraged regularly by local electronics luminaries including Leonard Fuller, Frederick Terman, and Ralph Heintz (Morgan 1967). Heintz, whose activities are discussed at length below, worked with Farnsworth "from the very beginning," visiting his laboratory "several times a week." "I helped them and they helped us" (Heintz 1982). Gardner was provided with a great deal of coaching and equipment by Bill Cummings, head of the glassblowing shop at the University of California at Berkeley (Fisher and Fisher 1996). Throughout his career, Farnsworth's ties to the electronics and financial communities of the San Francisco Bay Area remained strong. The television laboratory in San Francisco remained in operation as a branch laboratory through the 1930s. When Farnsworth invented the cold cathode ray tube, or "multipactor," in 1934, the first public demonstration was conducted by Ralph Heintz in South San Francisco (Everson 1949; Fisher and Fisher 1996).

Ralph Heintz: Short-Wave Radio Pioneer

As has already been mentioned, one of the leading figures in Bay Area electronics during the 1920s was Ralph Heintz, a Berkeley ham radio enthusiast who had attended Lick-Vilmerding High School in San Francisco and both U.C. Berkeley and Stanford. During World War I, Heintz developed an early radio-controlled missile guidance system for the British military. After a brief stint as a chemical engineer with Standard Oil after his graduation from Stanford in 1920, Heintz opened a small shop to repair scientific apparatuses in San Francisco. At the time radio broadcasting was just beginning, and Heintz built most of the early radio stations in the area. He also worked for the army, installing a radio station in Mazatlan, Mexico, and a system to relay telephone messages from British Columbia, where the wires stopped, to military bases in Alaska (Heintz 1982).

In 1924, the British Marconi Company announced successful experiments with long-distance communication using short-wave radio, prompting Heintz to begin to experiment with the technology. In 1925 Heintz installed a set on a private yacht, the first short-wave radio system to be installed on any ship in the Pacific (Morgan 1967). During this period Heintz also built five short-wave transmitters for the San Francisco–based Hearst newspapers, allowing them to disseminate news worldwide (Heintz 1982).

Heintz became a leading figure in the development of short-wave radio systems for aircraft. In 1927 he equipped the airplanes participating in an Oakland to Honolulu race sponsored by James Dole, the pineapple magnate, with short-wave radios, likely the first ever to be installed on aircraft. In 1928 he equipped the first successful flight from Oakland to Sydney, Australia. By this time Heintz had improved his systems to send and receive both long- and short-wave signals. Included in this equipment were waterproof distress transmitters that raised their aerials with either a kite or a gas balloon. In 1929, he built all the radio gear for Admiral Byrd's pioneering flight over Antarctica. Besides the system installed on Admiral Byrd's plane, the ground stations and the dog sled rescue teams were also equipped with Heintz's short-wave sets (Morgan 1967).

In the late 1920s Heintz was approached by William Boeing's son-in-law, Thorpe Hiscock, to design and manufacture a short-wave radio telephone system for Boeing's fleet of aircraft carrying mail between Seattle, Portland, and Chicago. The company was beginning to carry passengers with increasing regularity and needed extra safety measures. Western Electric, AT&T's manufacturing arm, controlled the patents rights for the manufacture of commercial radio systems, but they refused to build the system because they believed that air passenger travel would not develop into a significant business. Heintz built a prototype set for one of Boeing's airplanes and a series of ground stations that worked well. When officials at Western Electric heard of it, they agreed to build the system if Boeing would cease all relations with

Heintz. The equipment was sold back to Heintz at ten cents on the dollar, and he in turn sold the used components to ham radio enthusiasts in the area (Heintz 1974, 1982).

In the course of developing his airborne radio systems, Heintz fulfilled the increased power requirements necessary for the larger and more powerful radios he was installing by perfecting an innovative ac polyphase electric alternator that was about one-sixth the weight of the dc systems then in use. Heintz wrote some technical papers on the subject and had been flying them since 1925, but no one took his ideas seriously until Warren Bowten of Douglass Aircraft contacted Heintz in the early 1930s. Bowten questioned Heintz about the system and Heintz readily shared information about the system with him (Heintz 1982).

Soon afterward, Heintz learned that Bendix, Douglass's alternator supplier, had been awarded a large contract by the Air Force to manufacture ac polyphase power systems that closely matched his designs. Heintz traveled to Washington and threatened the Air Force that he would ask his congressman to "bring before the people what is happening to the poor lonely inventor who brings out something new." The Air Force agreed to split the contract between Bendix and Heintz. When the prototypes were finished the Bendix system failed, so Bendix bought the project out for $150,000 (ibid.).

Bendix insisted that the deal include the services of Heintz, and he agreed to a two-year contract since his other business was slow during the early years of the Depression. Heintz brought people with him from the Bay Area that he knew and trusted and set up what was effectively a separate engineering division within Bendix. Heintz lasted about as long as Farnsworth had at Philco, apparently for similar reasons. After two years, Bendix tried to get Heintz to extend his contract and stay in New Jersey, but Heintz refused. "I didn't want to, because I didn't like their outfit. Their engineering stank. So, I had to tell them. 'There's no use. I'm going home. I'm a Californian. I can't live in this atmosphere'" (ibid.).

Heintz & Kaufman Develop the Gammatron Tube

In 1926, Heintz, along with his partner Jack Kaufman, had started working on ship-to-shore radio communications systems for the Dollar Steamship Company. In 1928, Dollar acquired majority share of Heintz and Kaufman (H&K) to create a subsidiary to manufacture the short-wave communications equipment needed for its fleet of steamships. H&K moved to a larger facility in South San Francisco, where they employed twenty to forty people. Heintz retained a one-third share in H&K, and Heintz and Kaufman, Inc., was incorporated as a separate company, leaving Heintz free to work on outside contracts (many of which were discussed in the preceding section). At the same time, Globe Wireless was incorporated to manage the operation of the radio network. Jack Kaufman was named manger of Globe Wireless, and Heintz remained president of H&K (Heintz 1982). By the time the Globe system was completed, in the early 1930s, H&K short-wave equipment was installed at shore stations in Los Angeles, Long Beach, Portland, Seattle, New York, Hawaii, Manila, Guam, and Shanghai, as well as on 160 merchant ships (Heintz 1974; Morgan 1967).

Because RCA, GE, and Westinghouse perceived H&K as a competitor, they refused to sell them vacuum tubes. Tubes from England were extremely expensive, and H&K was thus forced to manufacture tubes in-house. In the course of developing the Globe system, Heintz developed a two-element, electrostatically controlled tube that he dubbed the "gammatron." This tube did not infringe on RCA's patents because it was based on expired patents and other unpatented technology and used tantalum elements (Norberg 1976).[17] Charles Litton, who knew the specifications for tube blanks available from Corning Glass in New York, assisted H&K in getting started in tube production by helping them pick out glass tube blanks and buy Pyrex stock for glass-blowing. Local ham radio enthusiasts William Eitel and Jack McCullough were hired to help develop the tube operation. When the Globe system was complete, H&K reverted to production of replacement tubes (Heintz 1974, 1982).

Dollar would not let H&K sell tubes on the open market because a patent suit brought by RCA in 1929 had made the company cautious. The sole reason that Dollar was in the electronics business was to supply its ships and Globe Wireless with radios. However, during the Depression internal demand almost disappeared, and Heintz convinced Dollar to let him sell on the outside to keep the business functioning. H&K began to sell gammatron tubes to ham radio operators, and, according to Heintz, they "got a tremendous reputation right off the bat because the hams would run them white hot . . . just beat the tar out of them." For ham radio applications, H&K gammatrons were better than anything available on the market at that time (Heintz 1974, 1984).

The animosity between RCA and Globe Wireless was quite strong. As Ralph Heintz put it: "We [Globe Wireless] were a monkey on [RCA's] back, because we had a mechanism of handling [radio] traffic across the Pacific that they seemed unable to stop. They tried to harass us by having Western Union refuse our traffic in every conceivable way" (Heintz 1982). In 1937, RCA again filed suit against Globe Wireless for patent infringement. Heintz, fed up with RCA harassment, constructed a series of "breadboard" demonstration sets to compare various vacuum tube technologies that could be used to send and receive radio signals. One set was based on the de Forest patents, which RCA controlled. The other sets were based on technology that RCA did not own the patents on, including those owned by Larson (Norway), Vreeland (U.S.A.), Simpson (U.S.A.), and Goddard (U.S.A.). These patents, plus others held by Heintz, covered the technology on which Globe's system was based.

Heintz asked his friend and classmate from Stanford, Frederick Terman, to appear in court as a technical expert. Donald Lippincott provided legal advice. When the day in court came, the request to have Heintz's "breadboard" sets entered as evidence was accepted by the judge. When the six RCA patent attorneys realized that losing the case could jeopardize RCA's entire patent position, the attorneys immediately approached the bench and asked that the suit be withdrawn (Heintz 1982).

Eitel and McCullough Establish High-Volume Tube Production

In 1934, when tube production for the Dollar system began to increase, Dollar demanded that H&K stop selling gammatrons on the open market. They agreed, but Eitel and McCullough became frustrated and struck out on their own to form a company to supply the ham market (Heintz 1984; Norberg 1976). At first they simply used the same vacuum tube technology that had been developed at H&K. When Heintz was asked during a 1974 interview why he chose not to sue them, his response strongly echoes the tolerant attitudes found in modern-day Silicon Valley by Saxenian (1989a, 1994):

I didn't have any desire to sue. They were nice fellows and my partner [Kaufman] was very burnt up. I was more amused than burnt up and what amused me was that they went to the Dollar Company and said, "Look, we can supply you with what you need for your communication system cheaper than H&K." They were immature at business. . . . They could be forgiven, because they were highly successful after that. Very innovative and very, very industrious and they're good friends of mine. (Heintz 1974)

Eitel and McCullough set up shop in an old meat-packing plant in San Carlos. Aiming at the amateur radio market, they advertised their tubes in *QST*, a national magazine for ham radio enthusiasts, and sold them through small distributors nationwide (Norberg 1976). Their tubes were so much more durable than anything else available on the market that the abbreviated company name printed on each tube, "Eimac," became known worldwide. By 1940, the company had grown to about twenty employees and moved to San Bruno (Morgan 1967).

In early 1941, Eitel and McCullough unexpectedly received an order from the U.S. military for $500,000 worth of tubes. To their surprise they learned that their tubes had been used in army and navy radar experiments for more than four years (Norberg 1976). War tensions were increasing, and the military was ready to go into mass production with its newly perfected radar system, for which it needed tubes. After the bombing of Pearl Harbor and the official U.S. entry into World War II, the company was ordered to build a new plant in Salt Lake City, away from potential bomb targets. By 1942, the company had eighteen hundred employees working three shifts to produce four thousand tubes each day (Morgan 1967).

After the war, these high production levels came back to haunt Eitel and McCullough. Just as the military orders abruptly ended, the market was flooded with surplus Eimac tubes selling below cost. The company survived the postwar transition by developing new military and commercial markets for their tubes. They built large "klystron" tubes for airborne radar, tubes for aviation, nuclear resonance, radio and television broadcasting, telephone systems, oceanography, factory automation, and early computers. By 1959, when the company moved into a large facility in San Carlos, Eitel and McCullough was the largest merchant manufacturer of vacuum tubes in the world (ibid.). In 1999, Eitel and McCullough still existed in San Carlos as the Eimac Division of Varian Associates.

The vacuum tube industry in the San Francisco Bay Area, while certainly smaller than the captive operations of the large East Coast firms, was nevertheless an important one. The activities of Elwell, Fuller, de Forest, Farnsworth, Litton, Heintz and Kaufman, and Eitel and McCullough reveal an unbroken lineage in leading-edge electronic component design and production in the San Francisco Bay Area that precedes the birth of the region's semiconductor industry by nearly four decades. It is clear that—from the dawn of the radio industry to the present day—San Francisco Bay Area companies have played a central role in developing and commercializing many of the key technologies that have served to drive the "electronics revolution" forward. Indeed, it may be the uncanny ability of Bay Area companies and entrepreneurs to successfully identify and make the leap from one underlying technology to the next that best explains the region's ongoing success.

Dalmo-Victor Develops an Airborne
Radar Antenna

While a student at Mt. Tamalpias High School in Marin County, located across the Golden Gate from San Francisco, Tim Moseley was the foreman of the school's machine shop. In 1921, when he was nineteen, Moseley established his own machine shop in San Francisco, the Dalmo Manufacturing Company. He often improved on the designs he was given by his customers and was soon inventing his own products (ibid.).

In 1934, Moseley hired an immigrant Russian Ph.D. research engineer named Alexander Poniatoff to help with the development work. Poniatoff had come to San Francisco by way of Shanghai, where he had worked at a power station. He then worked for three years for GE in Schenectady, New York, as a research engineer and for four years for PG&E in San Francisco. Bored with his work at PG&E, Poniatoff quit his secure job and approached Moseley, stating that he would work on a trial basis for no pay. Moseley agreed. Poniatoff's first assignment was to fix a problem with a hair-styling machine that Moseley was building for a local distributor. They patented the improved design, sold it to the distributor, and Moseley shared half of the proceeds with Poniatoff (Poniatoff 1974).

Poniatoff worked for Moseley until 1939, when the company was bankrupted by a patent infringement suit brought by the Schick Company for an electric shaver they had developed. Poniatoff went back to work for PG&E until 1944, when Moseley asked him to help with work on a prototype airborne radar antenna for the navy. According to

Poniatoff, Moseley said to him, "Do you know anything about radar?" Poniatoff replied, "I don't, not a damn thing." "Neither do I," Moseley said, "but the contract says the unit must be completed in 100 days, so you can't waste time" (ibid.). In the Dalmo shop in San Carlos, they worked for a hundred days without a break, often sleeping in the shop. Surprisingly, they won the contract. At a banquet in their honor, a navy admiral told them this story (as related by Poniatoff during an interview in 1974): "This contract was issued to Westinghouse, GE, and another company. Then this Moseley arrived, out of the woods, nobody knew who he was. He wanted the contract. When the models were brought in, we studied all of them. Moseley's model was so obviously ahead of the others we told the other companies good-bye" (Poniatoff 1974).

Westinghouse offered to manage the contract, arguing that high-volume production would be too difficult for a small company like Dalmo Manufacturing. Moseley agreed, and the company, now Dalmo-Victor, moved to a larger facility in Belmont to produce the unit (ibid.). By the end of World War II, Dalmo-Victor had emerged as the leading manufacturer of airborne radar antennas. By 1966 the company was also producing 90 percent of the nation's submarine antennas and was building antenna systems for NASA's lunar missions (Morgan 1967). Dalmo-Victor was eventually acquired by the General Instrument Defense Systems Group, which in turn was acquired in 1991 by Litton Industries Applied Technologies Group, headquartered in San Jose. The Dalmo Victor Division is still located in Belmont and has manufacturing operations in Grants Pass, Oregon.

It is worth commenting on the role of gifted mechanics and ham radio enthusiasts in the development of the Bay Area's early electronics industry. It seems that the best results were achieved when such practical mechanical brilliance was wedded to advanced technical training and theoretical knowledge. Such combinations existed in the development teams that paired Charles Logwood with Lee de Forest, Philo Farnsworth with Russell Varian, and Tim Moseley with Alexander Poniatoff. Even more potent, perhaps, were the instances where this mixture of tacit ability and formal training were embodied in individuals. Leonard Fuller, Ralph Heintz, and Charles Litton built on their boyhood fascination with ham radio by studying electrical engineering at Cornell, U.C. Berkeley, and Stanford, thus gaining a theoretical understanding of what they already knew so well empirically.

Perhaps the strongest thread that runs through the Valley's past and present is the drive to "play" with novel technology, which, when bolstered by an advanced engineering degree and channeled by astute management, has done much to create the industrial powerhouse we see in the Valley today. Indeed, the caricature of the "ham" radio enthusiast—the shy but intelligent teenage boy who, bent over his homemade radio set in his bedroom late at night, taps into a secret world known only to him and his far-flung community of fellow hams—bears a striking resemblance to that of the "computer geek," "code hacker," and "web surfer" of more recent vintage.

Ampex Develops the Tape Recorder

Key components of Dalmo-Victor's radar antenna system were two small precision electric motors to aim the device and a tiny generator to supply power. Motors and generators of this sort were unavailable on the open market at the time. In late 1944, Moseley asked Poniatoff to form his own company to manufacture them. Poniatoff was initially shocked at the suggestion, but after a few days of thought he agreed, adding $5,000 of his savings to $25,000 invested by Moseley to capitalize the startup. Poniatoff also got a loan from the First National Bank, and he set up shop in an attic above Dalmo-Victor. Poniatoff called his new company Ampex, using his initials (he was known as "Dr. AMP" around the Dalmo shop) plus "ex" for excellence (Poniatoff 1974).

As Ampex expanded with wartime production, the company moved into a larger facility in San Carlos. Most of the military work went to supply the Pacific theater, particularly antennas for the airplane known as the "black widow." The news of Japan's surrender in August 1945 was almost immediately followed by telegrams from the military canceling all orders. Although some advised Poniatoff to close his company and quit while he was ahead, Poniatoff decided to develop home high-fidelity sound systems. A forty-thousand-dollar order for ten thousand precision motors from a Berkeley furnace manufacturer kept the company afloat as they developed their new product (ibid.).

As the development of the hi-fi system progressed, it became clear to the team that the weakest link was the phonograph disk player. It was then that a key Ampex engineer attended an Institute of Radio Engineers meeting in San Francisco, where he witnessed a demonstration of a German tape recorder called "The Sound Mirror."[18] Poniatoff perceived the tape recorder as "the missing link in the hi-fi system" and set on a program to reverse-engineer the German unit. Although Ampex's technology for small, precision electric motors was well suited for tape recording, the technology involved with the magnetic tape heads was entirely new to them. A representative from 3M Company, who had heard of Ampex's development efforts, came to San Carlos with a sample of the new magnetic tape they were developing. The two companies worked together to improve the quality of magnetic tape, clearing up a crucial development problem for the team at Ampex (ibid.).

When it was learned that Bing Crosby was shooting a film in San Francisco, a just-completed Ampex tape recorder was brought to him for a demonstration. On hearing the quality of the recording, Crosby ordered twenty units for $3,000 each and negotiated a deal for Crosby Enterprises to become sole distributor for the product. Soon Jack Benny, Bob Hope, and Michael Todd, the developer of Cinerama, became Ampex customers (ibid.). Ampex abandoned the development of a complete system and switched production exclusively to tape recorders, but it continued to receive orders for precision motors. Poniatoff encouraged an employee named Walter Cabral to start his own company to produce them. "I said, 'Why don't you start your own company like Moseley [helped] me [to do?]' I talked him into it. 'Supply it,' I said. 'Here is the order'" (ibid.).

Through many of the lean times, Poniatoff was able to secure loans through First National Bank in San Francisco. When First National was sold to Wells Fargo Bank, Poniatoff was told of a "very remarkable consultant to new companies" at Wells Fargo who "has had a lot of experience helping struggling young companies like yours." This was Stanfield Rayfield, who set up a meeting between Poniatoff and Henry McMicking, a wealthy investor with interests in the Philippines. McMicking invested $365,000 in Ampex, forming a fifty-fifty partnership with Poniatoff. McMicking brought in an IBM salesman from the Philippines named Kevin Mallen to be general manager. Mallen set up new distribution channels, breaking the exclusive distribution contract with Crosby. McMicking was well connected in Washington, D.C., and helped to secure contracts from the National Security Agency.

McMicking set a five-year plan for the company to grow to $11 million in annual sales, a target well beyond Poniatoff's imagining but which the company greatly exceeded. McMicking drastically reorganized the marketing structure of Ampex but held to a strict policy not to interfere in any way with engineering. By 1957, Ampex had fifteen hundred employees and a wide range of products for professional recording, commercial aviation, and the U.S. government (ibid.). Ampex later went on to develop multitrack recording in 1954 and the first video tape recorder in 1956.[19] It become a major force in the field of tape backup drives for large computer systems. In 1999, the company was still in operation in Redwood City.

The approach that Rayfield, McMicking, and Mallen took to Ampex's development bears a striking resemblance to the role that modern venture capitalists have played during the post-Fairchild era. It is likely that Rayfield, in particular, played a wider role in the Bay Area electronics industry during the 1940s and 1950s, and research into his activities would be a fascinating study. Based on the current work, however, it can be said that William Crocker, the banker and railroad magnate's son from San Francisco, was Silicon Valley's first true venture capitalist.

Conclusion

The confusion over Silicon Valley's beginnings is deep-seated. There is a plaque (California State Historic Landmark #976) at 367 Addison Ave. in Palo Alto entitled "The Birthplace of Silicon Valley." It reads:

This garage is the birthplace of the world's first high-technology region, "Silicon Valley." The idea for such a region originated with Dr. Frederick Terman, a Stanford university professor who encouraged his students to start up their own electronics companies in the area instead of joining established firms in the East. The first two students to follow his advice were William R. Hewlett and David Packard, who in 1938 began developing their first product, an audio oscillator, in this garage.

Just a few blocks away, on the southeast corner of Emerson St. and Channing Ave., there is another plaque (California State Historic Landmark #836), entitled "Electronics Research Laboratory." It reads:

Original site of the laboratory and factory of Federal Telegraph Company, founded in 1909 by Cyril F. Elwell. Here, with two assistants, Dr. Lee de Forest, inventor of the three-element radio vacuum tube, devised in 1911–13 the first vacuum tube amplifier and oscillator. World-wide developments based on this research led to modern radio communication, television, and the electronics age.

The founding of FTC predates Hewlett Packard by nearly forty years, but when busloads of visitors come to Palo Alto to pay their respects to the birthplace of Silicon Valley, they stop at the first plaque, not the second. The argument of this chapter is not only about establishing precedent and assigning credit where it is due. The shadows of Frederick Terman and William Shockley loom large, not just in Silicon Valley, where they have honored places as the region's founding fathers, but also in countless other localities throughout the world that are trying to emulate the region's success. Development schemes derived from Silicon Valley include the incubation of "sunrise" technologies (following the William Shockley theme), the encouragement of cooperation between universities and industry in high-tech commercial ventures (following the Frederick Terman theme), and the provision of high-tech industrial parks (an extension of the Terman theme following the model of Stanford Industrial Park). As economic development tools these schemes have met with very limited success (Malecki 1981; Saxenian 1988b; Taylor 1983). However, they continue to absorb the resources of planning agencies and universities in countless locations (Engstrom 1987).

Stripped of its tabula rasa antecedents, Silicon Valley retains its millionaires, its legacy of boom and bust and cowboy entrepreneurialism, its record of astonishing urbanization and skyrocketing land values, its polluted air and groundwater, its daily traffic snarls, and its reputation as the hearth of innovations that have transformed the way humans relate to nature and to each other. What is lost is the notion that *anyplace can be Silicon Valley*.

The fact that the San Francisco Bay Area's electronics industry began close to the turn of the twentieth century should lay to rest the notion that industrialization and urbanization on the scale of Silicon Valley can be quickly induced in other areas. Silicon Valley is nearly one hundred years old. It grew out of a historically and geographically specific context that cannot be re-created. The lesson for planners and economic developers is to focus on long-term, not short-term, developmental trajectories. Silicon Valley was the fastest growing region in the United States during the late 1970s and early 1980s, but that growth came out of a place, not a technology. Silicon Valley's development is intimately entwined with the long history of industrialization and innovation in the larger San Francisco Bay Area.

CHAPTER THREE

The Biggest "Angel" of Them All:
The Military and the Making
of Silicon Valley

STUART W. LESLIE

For nearly forty years, Silicon Valley has symbolized American high-technology competitiveness. Where other regional high-technology clusters have faltered, Silicon Valley has adapted successfully to new technologies and new competitors.[1] Yet as the lackluster records of so many subsequent Silicon Forests, Silicon Mountains, and Silicon Beaches (which at least makes some sense, technically!) suggest, identifying the crucial ingredients of Silicon Valley—a strong research university with close links to industry, entrepreneurial corporate and academic cultures, aggressive venture capital markets, supportive government institutions, a pleasant climate, a technology park—has turned out to be far easier than combining them into a successful recipe for regional economic prosperity.[2]

If Silicon Valley has been more often imitated than equaled, it still remains an attractive and influential model for regional development, though certainly not the only one. Some localities, following the lead of the Research Triangle, designate technology parks on the theory that if you build it, they—branch plants of multinational corporations—will come, and bring high-paying research and manufacturing jobs with

This chapter is based on Stuart W. Leslie, "How the West Was Won: The Military and the Making of Silicon Valley," which appeared in *Technological Competitiveness: Contemporary and Historical Perspectives on the Electrical, Electronics and Computer Industries,* ed. William Aspray (New York: Institute of Electronics and Electrical Engineers), 75–89. ©1993 IEEE.

them.[3] Others try to grow their own, by setting up technology incubators of one sort or another.[4] Still others set out to copy what they interpret to be the Silicon Valley model, only to scale down their ambitions in the face of unexpected difficulties.[5] But as the very names of many of these high-technology developments suggest, Silicon Valley continues to be the ultimate yardstick of success.[6]

Yet for all the scholarly attention paid to Silicon Valley in recent years, there seems to be little agreement on its larger lessons. Should it be understood as a unique example of American entrepreneurship? Or can it provide a model for regional development in other places? Are its biggest success stories merely "accidental empires," as business journalist Robert Cringely (1992) insists? Or has the popular image of "Silicon Valley Fever," "the new alchemists," and "the big score" obscured a more complex story (Hanson 1982; Malone 1985; Rogers and Larsen 1984)?[7]

Missing in virtually every account of freewheeling entrepreneurs and visionary venture capitalists is the military's role, intentional and otherwise, in creating and sustaining Silicon Valley.[8] For better and for worse, Silicon Valley owes its present configuration to patterns of federal spending, corporate strategies, industry-university relationships, and technological innovation shaped by the assumptions and priorities of Cold War defense policy. Indeed, the name Silicon Valley itself may be something of a misnomer, ignoring as it does the crucial role of microwave electronics and aerospace in providing this archetype for the American high-technology industry. For most of its history, Silicon Valley's largest single employer has been Lockheed Missiles and Space (now Lockheed-Martin), with a peak of twenty-eight thousand workers at its Sunnyvale production facilities and its Palo Alto R&D laboratory. And even with recent cutbacks, Silicon Valley remains one of the leading recipients of defense contracts in the country, whether measured by total dollars or by dollars in prime contracts per worker, with four times the national average and twice (per worker) what Los Angeles, itself at the heart of the military-industrial complex, receives (Gray et al. 1999). Certainly, defense contracts no longer dominate the local economy as they once did. In the early 1960s the Polaris (for which Lockheed Missiles and Space was the prime contractor) and Minuteman missile systems absorbed virtually the entire region's output of integrated circuits. Only in 1967 did the military's share of the integrated circuits market drop below half (Braun and MacDonald 1978: 113–18).

Yet Silicon Valley firms, led by Lockheed-Martin and Ford Aerospace, still rank disproportionally among the country's five hundred largest prime defense contractors. In the military buildup of the Reagan years, Santa Clara County approached $5 billion a year in prime contract awards, although that figure has now dropped to $3.4 billion. Even companies better known for their commercial products, such as Sun Microsystems, are nonetheless significant defense contractors, while the commercial semiconductor manufacturers that gave Silicon Valley its name still sell a substantial share of their product to defense contractors, generally a fifth, and firms specializing in military electronics often sell three-quarters or more of their output to defense contractors (Gray et al. 1999).

So it may not be too much of an exaggeration to say that the Department of Defense was the original "angel" of Silicon Valley—a relationship that Sturgeon (in this volume) shows goes back to before World War I. Military contracts put companies like Varian Associates and Watkins-Johnson in business, and helped companies like Hewlett Packard to expand their businesses. Military contracts encouraged established East Coast companies such as General Electric, Sylvania, and Zenith to set up outpost laboratories and production facilities in Santa Clara County, just as foreign firms would later come to Silicon Valley looking for ways of tapping into local expertise and connections. Personal contacts and a proven market encouraged spinoffs, especially when, as was often the case, Eastern companies found it difficult to adjust to a distinctly Western high-technology culture. At a time when six-figure venture capital investments were still considered risky by West Coast standards, a start-up company such as Varian Associates could routinely attract million-dollar-plus contracts from the U.S. Air Force or Navy. Even better, from a corporate point of view, defense contracts generally meant a production contract along with an R&D contract, and so a guaranteed market. Add in the additional incentive of cost-plus contracts, virtually eliminating risk, and it is not hard to understand why so few start-ups saw the need to pursue traditional venture capital or public stock offerings, at least in the beginning.[9]

Radio Days

For all its isolation from the centers of East Coast industry, the Santa Clara Valley played a surprisingly significant role in the early days of radio and electronics (see also Sturgeon, in this volume). Broadcasting pioneer Federal Telegraph (later bought by ITT) got its start in Palo Alto under Stanford graduate Cyril Elwell, with financial backing from Stanford's president and several faculty members.[10] Audion inventor Lee de Forest worked there for a time, developing more powerful arc transmitters, and in the process he made the crucial observation that an audion could generate continuous waves (Aitken 1985: 233–46). Charles Litton, another Stanford graduate, joined Federal's vacuum tube department following a stint at Bell Laboratories, then quit to go into business for himself when Federal moved the laboratory back East in 1932. William Eitel and Jack McCullough similarly left Heintz and Kaufman (cofounded by yet another Stanford graduate, Ralph Heintz) in 1934, to design and build their own tubes for the amateur radio market (Norberg 1976: 1318–19; Eitel-McCullough, Inc. 1960).

Under Frederick Terman, Stanford University became the leading academic center for radio research on the West Coast. Son of an eminent Stanford psychologist, Terman grew up on campus, took his undergraduate degree there, and then headed off to MIT for graduate training in electrical engineering. He returned to Stanford in 1925 with his doctorate and promptly launched an aggressive, commercially oriented program in radio electronics.[11] Taking a lesson from MIT, he talked Pacific Telephone and other companies into donating the equipment, and drew his research problems directly from industry—for instance, investigating ways of increasing the number of radio stations able to broadcast on a single frequency. To keep his students up to date, he arranged field trips to local electronics companies (a few, like Heintz and Kaufman, founded by Stanford graduates), and invited their engineers to give campus seminars. David Packard, then a graduate student in the radio laboratory, recalled these tours as a course highlight: "Here, for the first time, I saw young entrepreneurs working on new devices in firms which they themselves had established. One day Professor Terman remarked to me that many of the firms we had visited, and many other firms throughout the country, had been founded by men who had little formal education. He suggested that perhaps someone with a formal engineering education and a little business training might be even more successful."[12] Shortly thereafter, Terman got an opportunity to prove his point by helping Packard go into business with another graduate student, William Hewlett. In 1939 they started their own company to build resistance-tuned oscillators (an idea they'd heard about from Terman) and began their climb to the top of the electronics industry. Walt Disney Studios bought the first batch of oscillators for the *Fantasia* sound track. This began a long relationship between the Bay Area electronics industry and the Los Angeles–based entertainment industry.

Even Terman's textbooks reflected his commercial bent. His *Radio Engineering* became an immediate best-seller, primarily because, like his courses, it placed real-world problems at the center, with an elegance and simplicity that especially appealed to working engineers. Interestingly, Terman never took a sabbatical to write this or any other textbook. Instead, he set himself the deceptively easy goal of writing one page a day, and actually managed to turn out a shelf full of books that way.

Stanford also played a key role in fostering the klystron, perhaps the most important electronics innovation developed on the West Coast before World War II. In 1937 the Varian brothers, working with several Stanford physicists, invented the klystron, an original and extremely flexible microwave receiver and transmitter. Under an unusual contract with the university, the Varians were granted access to faculty, laboratory space, and modest funding for materials in return for a half-interest in any resulting patents. A subsequent agreement between the university and Sperry Gyroscope Company provided substantial corporate funding for klystron research and development at Stanford and gave Sperry an exclusive license to make, use, and sell any microwave equipment developed in the university laboratory.[13] To follow up its investment, Sperry set up a small development and production facility in nearby San Carlos (Bryant 1990).

The War Years

None of the West Coast companies grew very large before World War II. To survive in an industry still dominated by Eastern laboratories and patents, they had to exploit technical niches, either by creating new products, as Hewlett Packard did, or by improving the performance and reliability of traditional ones, as did Eitel-McCullough (Norberg 1976). Wartime orders gave the infant West Coast industry a chance to show what it could do. RCA, GE, Westinghouse, and the other East Coast giants won the lion's share of the defense electronics contracts, but even relatively small orders could make a big difference for the West Coast start-ups. Hewlett Packard, spurred by massive orders for its line of electronic measuring instruments, jumped from nine employees and $37,000 in sales in 1940 to one hundred employees and $1 million in sales just three years later (*Microwave Journal* 1959b). Eitel-McCullough, on the strength of huge subcontracts from Western Electric and GE, grew even faster, churning out one hundred thousand tubes a week at the peak of wartime production (ibid. 1960). At the same time, it proved that it could still beat the competition in quality as well, mass-producing tubes that more established firms like GE could never seem to get right, even as prototypes (Terman 1953b). Sperry, recognizing the dangers of too widely separating its research and development from production, moved the entire Stanford klystron group out to its Long Island laboratories for the duration.

Terman spent the war directing the Radio Research Laboratory (RRL), a spinoff of MIT's famous Radiation Laboratory housed upriver at Harvard and devoted to radar countermeasures. As director, Terman had responsibility not only for developing new radar jamming and countermeasures devices but also for teaching industrial contractors such as RCA, GE, and Bell Labs how to manufacture them. Terman brought along a number of Stanford students and colleagues—thirty in all served tours of duty at RRL—and together they received a practical education in the art of microwave engineering. Writing to a colleague back at Stanford, Terman said:

I have learned a tremendous amount, for I had never before realized the amount of work required to make a device ready for manufacture after one had a good working model, such as the number of drawings, the amount of detailed design that is involved to turn out a good job, the problems of how to get stuff to meet specifications, testing and standardization problems, etc. (Terman 1944a)

Postwar Growth of the West Coast Industry

Terman returned to Stanford in 1946 with a new title, dean of engineering, and a new vision of Western industrial leadership:

The west has long dreamed of an indigenous industry of sufficient magnitude to balance its agricultural resources. The war advanced these hopes and brought to the west the beginning of a great new era of industrialization. A strong and independent industry must, however, develop its own intellectual resources of science and technology, for industrial activity that depends upon imported brains and second-hand ideas cannot hope to be more than a vassal that pays tribute to its overlords, and is permanently condemned to an inferior competitive position. (Terman 1947: 10)

Yet Terman and his colleagues recognized that the war had advanced more than hopes. By introducing new kinds of tubes and by opening up an entirely new range of the electromagnetic spectrum, it had revolutionized electronics. And since most of that new knowledge had been created under government sponsorship, and would therefore be available to anyone, the East Coast industry would no longer be able to control the field through patents as it had done before the war. More than ever, they all realized, in the postwar world the secret of success was going to be research. Terman did not expect the fledgling Western electronics industry, despite its rapid growth during the war, to overtake its Eastern rivals right away. Rather, he believed that the first step toward invigorating the industry was strengthening the university's programs in selected areas of electronics. As he explained to the university's president: "Government-sponsored research presents Stanford, and our School of Engineering, with a wonderful opportunity if we are prepared to exploit it. . . . We failed to take advantage of a similar opportunity presented by the research activities of the war. We are fortunate to have a second chance to retrieve our position. It is doubtful if there will ever be a third opportunity" (Terman 1944b).

Terman and the core of electronics veterans he had brought back with him from RRL were especially well positioned by their wartime contacts and contracts to exploit the most recent advances in microwave electronics. Stanford's traveling-wave-tube (TWT) program exemplified the new style of Stanford electronics. Perfected at Bell Laboratories during the war by a team that included recent Stanford graduate Lester Field, the TWT offered significant improvements in bandwidth and tuning over other microwave tubes, making it ideal for electronic countermeasures applications. Terman knew about Field's work, recognized its implications, and convinced Field to continue his research back at Stanford. With strong military support, Field quickly established himself as one of the best researchers in one of the most competitive specialties of postwar electronics. Although on a shoestring budget compared with industrial efforts at Bell and RCA, Field and his students, including such future industry leaders as Dean Watkins and Stanley Kaisel, kept pace with the giants, developing new kinds of TWTs, increasing their power, and reducing their noise level.[14]

The Sperry klystron group also came back to the West Coast after the war determined to go into business for themselves. Some, like Marvin Chodorow and Edward Ginzton, joined the university faculty. Others, including Russell Varian, took temporary jobs as research associates. In 1948 they founded Varian Associates to design and manufacture klystrons and other advanced microwave tubes. The company literally got its start at Stanford. Its first board meeting was held on campus, its board of directors included several faculty members, and its first successful product, a tiny reflex klystron for guided missiles, was designed by a faculty consultant.[15]

The Korean War transformed Varian and other fledgling electronic enterprises into big business. The sudden demand for microwave tubes for radar, electronic countermeasures, and communications gave these companies the inside track in securing defense contracts, especially the invaluable research and development contracts that could position them for the lucrative production contracts ahead. California's share of prime military contracts doubled during the course of the war, from 13.2 percent to 26 percent. From 1951 to 1953 California received some thirteen billion dollars in prime contracts, overtaking longtime defense contract leader New York State (Clayton 1965). That windfall represented not so much savvy political maneuvering, as some New York congressmen charged, but rather the success of California aerospace and electronics companies in anticipating and cultivating the military market. Most of that money went to Southern California aerospace contractors in Los Angeles and San Diego, but Santa Clara County companies won their share, and before the end of the decade Santa Clara was contending with San Diego for second place.

"Varian's growth during the first decade or so was rapid, primarily military based, and tied in closely with the growth of the aerospace industry," the head of its tube division recalled (Varian 1973: 15). Its product line expanded into a full range of klystrons, from low-power models for airborne radar and guided missiles through medium-power versions for mobile communications and radar jamming to very-high-power tubes for radar transmitters—all but a tiny fraction destined for the defense industry. To expand its output, Varian arranged a sizable loan through the Defense Production Administration, plus an additional $1.35 million from the air force for a new small-tube manufacturing plant (Varian 1951, 1952). Meanwhile, Varian's sales climbed from $200,000 in 1949 to $1.5 million two years later, to $25 million by the end of the decade, with military tubes accounting for all but a small fraction. Employment soared from 325 in 1951 to 1,300 by 1958 (Varian 1951, 1973: 14). Varian strengthened its ongoing ties to the university by signing on as the first tenant of the Stanford Industrial Park, negotiating a long-term lease on university-owned land just south of campus for its research laboratories and its expanding tube department.[16]

Litton's growth paralleled Varian's. Litton did a good business before the war designing and building machinery for manufacturing power vacuum tubes, and, like other tube-related companies, grew dramatically during the early war years. Charles Litton himself spent the war back at Federal Telephone's New Jersey plant making radar tubes. Afterward, he returned to California and reorganized Litton Industries into a power tube manufacturer with a reputation for delivering high-quality magnetrons at prices that bigger companies lost money on (Terman 1953a). He then sold the company in 1953 to an aggressive group of Hughes expatriates led by Charles "Tex" Thorton, who dramatically expanded the operation to meet the sudden demand for tubes in the national air defense program. In just three years the new managers tripled sales (to $6.2 million) and backlog (to $36 million), and quadrupled employment (to 2,115) (Litton Industries 1957). Like Varian, Litton Industries aimed almost exclusively at the military market, with such products as pulse magnetrons and tunable klystrons for radar and tunable continuous-wave magnetrons for jamming and missile guidance systems.

Eitel-McCullough, though more commercially diversified than either Varian or Litton, also rode the wave of defense appropriations. It supplied high-power klystrons for virtually every major air defense project—the Dew Line, White Alice, and Pole Vault—tubes for missile tracking, and a truly giant klystron, the X626 (with 1.25 million watts of peak power) for ballistic missile detection. On the strength of those contracts, the company grew to 2,600 employees and $29 million in sales by 1959 (*Microwave Journal* 1960).

Stanford's laboratories continued to spawn innovative startup companies looking for opportunities to commercialize the latest microwave technologies being developed there. Huggins Laboratories got its start in 1948 when founder R. A. Huggins, a former research associate at the university, put the first traveling-wave tube on the market. With a boost from government R&D contracts, Huggins continued to expand, diversifying into backward-wave oscillators, low-noise TWTs, and electrostatic-focused tubes, all based on research done at Stanford.

By 1961, Huggins was doing $3.5 million of business a year and was among the leaders in the TWT field (*Microwave Journal* 1961a). Ray Stewart, after a peripatetic early career with Litton and Dalmo Victor, joined Lester Field's group in the late 1940s as a technician, building some of the earliest TWTs. Although essentially self-taught, Stewart decided to try his luck in the market, first with vacuum tube furnaces and vacuum pumps, and then in 1952 with the first commercial backward-wave oscillator (Paine 1962a). William Ayer, a graduate student in Stanford's Radioscience Laboratory, cofounded Granger Associates (with former RRL and Stanford Research Institute [SRI] researcher John Granger) in 1956 to produce ionospheric sounders and military communications equipment based on designs pioneered at the university. By 1962, Granger Associates was doing $5 million a year in sales (Simon 1960). In the meantime, Ayer and another Granger engineer spun off Applied Technologies to concentrate on electronic countermeasures and land-range detecting and monitoring equipment (*Microwave Journal* 1961b). Its 1961 sales topped $1 million. Stanley Kaisel, yet another Field student, spent two years working on TWTs for RCA, returned to Stanford during the Korean War to run a tube laboratory on a classified countermeasures contract, and then took a job with Litton. Convinced that he could make more long-lived and reliable TWTs than what were currently on the market, he and another Litton engineer broke away in 1959 to form Microwave Electronics Corporation (MEC). Initially specializing in low-power, low-noise TWTs for electronic countermeasures, MEC built up a $5 million a year business with four hundred employees by the time it sold out to Teledyne in 1965. Like Granger and Applied Technologies, MEC relocated in the Stanford Industrial Park to cement its academic connections (Paine 1962c; *Microwave Journal* 1963).

Watkins-Johnson was undoubtedly the most financially successful of the new Stanford spinoffs. A former student of Lester Field, Dean Watkins had gone on to Hughes, then essentially swapped places with his mentor in 1953. At Stanford, Watkins led the Stanford TWT research to national prominence over the next few years, especially for work on low-noise TWTs. In 1957 he and former Hughes engineer Richard Johnson cofounded Watkins-Johnson to develop and manufacture microwave tubes for surveillance, reconnaissance, countermeasures, and telemetry, all directly based on the TWT technology Watkins had been perfecting at Stanford. Watkins-Johnson secured its initial financing from the Kern County Land Company, a large real estate and oil hold-

ing company looking for profitable investment outlets.[17] Watkins-
Johnson immediately started returning money on that investment,
turning a profit its first year. Sales rose from $500,000 in 1958 to $4.6
million in 1961, $9.5 million in 1963, and $16.8 million in 1966, with con-
sistently strong earnings (Terman 1957; Watkins-Johnson Company
1964). Watkins-Johnson later acquired both Stewart Engineering and
Granger Associates. By the early 1960s a third of the nation's TWT
business, and a substantial share of the klystron and magnetron business as well, was located in the Santa Clara Valley, most of it a stone's
throw from Stanford.

Response from the East Coast
Industrial Establishment

That kind of success naturally attracted the attention of established
East Coast companies ready to cash in on the burgeoning military electronics market. By East Coast standards, the West Coast startups were
still puny. Industry leaders GE and RCA posted 1956 sales of $725 mil-
lion each. Admiral, Sylvania, Philco, Zenith, Westinghouse, and a
dozen other companies had sales of over $100 million. But with half of
all electronics sales going to the military that year—$3 billion a year in
all—and an increasing share of that going for high-technology equipment for missiles, avionics, and the like, even the most myopic component maker could read the writing on the wall (Harris 1957). On average, military electronics was about equally as profitable as commercial
business, or slightly less so—about 10 percent on sales. But as *Fortune*
pointed out, military electronics nonetheless represented "a whale of a
good business," both because the defense market was generally stead-
ier than its commercial counterpart and because military R&D contracts
offered an inexpensive entry into new fields and enticing prospects for
commercial spinoff.

Sylvania, primarily a manufacturer of television and radio tubes,
got its chance to break into the military market in 1953 when the Army
Signal Corps offered it a contract to construct a new laboratory for missile countermeasures. The Signal Corps had been considering some
kind of facility for "quick reaction capability" (QRC) in electronic warfare since 1949, and, forced into action by the Korean emergency, it offered Stanford a $5 million contract in 1952 to develop "engineering test

models" of guided missile countermeasures. (All of the missiles in the U.S. and Soviet inventories in those days used radio guidance.) Concerned that any new contract might overwhelm its already taxed resources, Stanford begged off (Harris 1952; U.S. Army 1952). So the next year, following a formal competition, the Signal Corps awarded Sylvania a $3 million initial contract for studying and designing prototype electronic countermeasures against surface-to-target missiles and proximity fuses, two-thirds of the money for R&D and the rest for quick reaction tasks. The army would equip the laboratory and fund the research, while Sylvania would provide the land and the building and recruit the staff. For the company, the contract represented a quick, and very inexpensive, entry into the military electronics business. For the army, the laboratory represented an important step toward parity with the air force and navy in the missile race.

Although Stanford would not manage the laboratory directly, it nonetheless played a significant role in determining the laboratory's eventual location and research priorities. Sylvania's central research laboratory was then in Bayside, Long Island, New York. The army, however, insisted on a site that would not present such an obvious target. Sylvania knew all about Stanford's expertise in electronic countermeasures. Moreover, the company already had a small tube plant in nearby Mountain View. So Sylvania built its new Electronics Defense Laboratory (EDL) there, close to prospective Stanford faculty consultants and newly graduated engineers. The Signal Corps similarly recognized the advantages of putting the laboratory within Stanford's orbit, where subcontracts for search receivers, converters, special tubes, and other electronic warfare equipment developed by university researchers could more easily be arranged (Urhande 1953).

Over its first decade, EDL grew into one of the largest electronics enterprises in the valley, with some thirteen hundred employees (including more than five hundred scientists and engineers) and annual contracts of $18 million (it currently has thirty-five hundred employees). From a "captive" Signal Corps laboratory dedicated to missile countermeasures, EDL branched out into tactical countermeasures (against surface-to-air missiles and artillery fuses), and into electronic intelligence (intercepting and interpreting missile telemetry and guidance signals) for all the defense agencies. By 1964 electronic intelligence accounted for two-thirds of the laboratory's revenues. EDL also earned a reputation for its QRC work, notably the spread-spectrum communications gear built, on a month's notice, for the Berlin crisis (Perry 1991; Scholtz 1982; Schulman 1964).

As anticipated, EDL drew extensively on its Stanford connections. It recruited heavily among both research associates and recent graduates. It hired several top faculty members as consultants, including Terman himself. And it became the first participant in the honors cooperative program, Stanford's pioneering effort to encourage more formal collaboration between high-technology enterprise and the university. Local companies, starting with EDL and Hewlett Packard, sent their best young engineers back to school part-time for advanced degrees. EDL got better trained people, plus a direct pipeline to Stanford ideas. By the early 1960s EDL was sending ninety-two people a year to the program.

Along the way, EDL spun off several laboratories devoted to specific technologies. In 1956 Sylvania set up an independent Microwave Physics Laboratory for advanced research on ferrites and plasma. The next year it established the Reconnaissance Systems Laboratories, specializing in satellite detection and other air force priorities, first in a converted supermarket in downtown Mountain View and later in its own facilities next to EDL. Four EDL engineers broke away in 1956 to form Microwave Engineering Laboratories, initially concentrating on solid-state microwave devices for the military market. And in 1964, EDL director William Perry, frustrated with what he considered home office exploitation of the laboratory, defected, along with a half-dozen senior managers, to found Electronic Systems Laboratories (ESL, Inc.) as a direct competitor in electronic intelligence (Leifer and Sernuik 1991; *Microwave Journal* 1959a; Paine 1962b, 1963).

General Electric moved west in 1954, looking for ways to enlarge its already considerable share of the defense electronics business by tapping Stanford expertise. GE's Electronics Division had recently established an advanced radar laboratory in Ithaca, New York (on Cornell University land) to assist its heavy military electronics group in Syracuse. At Stanford, it saw a similar opportunity to cash in on academic research in high-power klystrons, TWTs, and other exotic hardware. In 1954 it opened what it called the General Electric Microwave Laboratory at Stanford in the Industrial Park. Like Sylvania, GE hired a number of recent graduates and research associates outright, including coupled-cavity TWT pioneer Erwin Nalos (a former Chodorow student), signed up several faculty consultants, and sent dozens of its most promising engineers to the honors cooperative program. Sixteen of its forty top scientists and engineers had been at one time either graduate students or faculty members at Stanford (Enochs 1958: 34; Nalos 1991; Terman 1955).

At first the laboratory concentrated almost entirely on elaborating concepts originally developed at the university. Gradually, however, it established its own reputation as a center for work on high-power klystrons and TWTs (for radar systems) and on low-noise TWTs, including the first metal ceramic designs (for electronic countermeasures systems). By 1956 it was bringing in two-thirds of its annual research budget in independent military contracts. It supplied the TWTs for GE's Rainbow, the first frequency diversity radar, the klystrons for the Nike-Hercules radar, the mammoth klystrons for Westinghouse's missile defense system, and the small, low-noise TWTs for Sylvania's countermeasures systems. The laboratory doubled in size after its first two years, doubled again a few years later, and then doubled once more, to 336 employees and a $5 million annual budget, by 1958 (Lob 1991; Nalos 1955: 20; Terman 1958).

Following Sylvania's and GE's lead, other East Coast companies established outposts in the area. Sensing the shift in the market, the Chicago-based television and radio giant Admiral, which had been supporting a small color television laboratory in Palo Alto since 1952, opened a new laboratory in the Stanford Industrial Park in 1955 for research on radar, guided missiles, and air navigation and communications systems. It later won large air force and navy contracts for designing and manufacturing automatic decoders for identification, friend or foe (IFF) systems. In 1956, Zenith set up a research laboratory nearby, under one of Terman's former group leaders at RRL (Terman 1958, 1963).

The Aerospace Connection

Lockheed Missiles and Space came to the valley in 1956 looking to break into the missiles and space market by breaking out of a corporate culture dominated by airplane enthusiasts. It opened a major manufacturing facility in Sunnyvale and a complementary laboratory complex in the Industrial Park. Significantly, in selecting the Stanford location, Lockheed's president stressed the university's reputation in electronics rather than aeronautics. With the increasing complexity and sophistication of guidance and communications systems, Lockheed felt it could no longer rely on outside electronics expertise and would have to develop its own. "To handle these big defense systems involving billions not millions of dollars and covering a multitude of sciences, we must broaden and deepen our competence into fields related to ours," Lockheed's president stressed. "The one I think of as most logical and natural is electronics" (Jessup 1957; Schoenberger 1996).[18]

Lockheed's investment paid off immediately and spectacularly. Lockheed Missiles and Space won the Polaris submarine missile contract (initially worth $62 million) from the navy, and the first reconnaissance and surveillance satellite contracts from the CIA and the air force (York and Greb 1977). On the strength of those projects, Lockheed's employment soared from two hundred in 1956 to nine thousand in 1958 to twenty-five thousand in 1964 (with twelve hundred in the research laboratories alone), making Lockheed, by an order of magnitude, the biggest employer in the valley.

Lockheed provided a crucial catalyst for further high-technology growth. Lured by the prospects of lucrative subcontracts for the ground support and tracking network for the air force satellite programs, Philco broke ground for its multimillion-dollar Western Development Laboratories (WDL) in Palo Alto in 1957. About 90 percent of its sales in the early years came from air force contracts for satellite tracking and command systems. WDL later won a Signal Corps contract for Courier, the first active-repeater communications satellite, a $31 million army contract for a worldwide teletype and high-speed digital data communications system, and a $25 million contract for a Department of Defense (DOD) communications satellite network. These and other contracts pushed WDL employment to twenty-five hundred by 1960. Ford, frankly looking for a toehold in the defense and space business, bought Philco the next year and made WDL the core of its new aerospace division. Under Ford, WDL continued to be a major player in the satellite business, winning additional large contracts for communications satellites, antenna systems, and the NASA flight control center in Houston.[19]

The aerospace industry offered opportunities for smaller companies as well. Four local scientists founded Vidya in 1959 to conduct supersonic wind tunnel tests on the Polaris nose cones. Itek, the Massachusetts-based antenna manufacturer, bought out Applied Technology to give it a West Coast presence. Link Aviation, the Binghamton-based flight simulator manufacturer, shifted its advanced engineering laboratory to Palo Alto in 1957, adding a line of simulators for guided missiles. Kaiser Aerospace relocated to the Industrial Park a few years later. Even local tape maker Ampex found a booming new market for its recording systems in reconnaissance satellites and guided missiles.

When Fairchild Semiconductor was still just Robert Noyce and two dozen bright young engineers, the Under Secretary of Commerce was calling Santa Clara County the "microwave capital" of the world (Enochs 1958: 30). Indeed, by 1960 it had already become the center of an aerospace complex rooted in microwave electronics technology for reconnaissance, communications, and countermeasures, with its main trunk at Lockheed Missiles and Space and the adjoining Air Force Satellite Control Facility (or the Blue Cube) and its branches extending in all directions (Schultz 1983). Electronics Defense Laboratory director William Perry caught something of how the corporate components of this complex intertwined:

We are continually demanding microwave tube performance beyond the state of the art. We were one of the companies pushing that industry to get more and more bandwidth, more and more power, more and more ease of tuning. So there were an amazing set of technical developments going on in tubes at that time and they were being driven by electronic countermeasures companies. (Perry 1991)

Similarly, Watkins-Johnson bought low-noise tubes from GE's microwave laboratory, reverse-engineered them, and then brought out its own. Those tubes and others like them went into the systems that Sylvania was building for Lockheed's satellites and into the communications and tracking gear being designed by Philco's Western Development Laboratories. Microwave tubes provided the "linchpins" for virtually every contemporary military electronics system, from radar to electronic warfare. And not just anyone could build them. The biggest cost upward of $200,000 each and took such skill to manufacture properly that insiders liked to say that to get one right "you pray over it, you nurse it, you make love to it" (Lob 1991).

Hard Times in the Valley

The aerospace complex prospered in the post-Sputnik defense boom, but at the cost of increased isolation from the commercial world outside. GE's Microwave Laboratory never really found a place for itself in the larger corporation. Other divisions, lacking experience in the microwave tube art, could never satisfactorily duplicate TWT's and other tubes based on the laboratory's designs. From the perspective of GE's power tube division, the laboratory's corporate parent, high-power microwave tubes offered limited commercial possibilities. So rather than using the laboratory to break into new high-technology markets, upper management turned it instead to "putting out fires for other manufacturing divisions" (Terman 1966). Dissatisfied with that role, many of the best engineers left for more promising opportunities elsewhere, some of them right next door. By 1965 the GE Microwave Laboratory staff was down to 170, less than half its peak strength.

Sylvania similarly failed to capitalize on EDL. Although the division itself remained profitable, it developed only the most tenuous connections with the rest of the corporation. GTE bought out Sylvania in 1960, in part to acquire a central laboratory for its telephone business. Despite some attempts to spin off commercial technologies, including electronic security systems, testing devices for telephone headsets, industrial lasers, and even a Sociosystems Products division, GTE Government Systems (as it was renamed) remained too specialized and too expensive to compete in the civilian world. "The government doesn't train us to do things cheaply," one senior scientist explained (Blachman 1991). While continuing to do 90 percent or more of its business with the military, GTE also tried to set up a separate commercial laboratory in Palo Alto, a "miniature Bell Telephone Laboratories for serving the GT&E system, and financed at least in part from telephone revenues," and, surprisingly enough, hired the recently retired chief signal officer to organize and run it. GTE's operating divisions, convinced that such an enterprise was unlikely to contribute much to their mission, immediately backed out and put their money into the old Bayside laboratories instead (Terman 1962; Voakes 1978).

One by one, the transplants to the valley shut down or sold out. Admiral closed its Palo Alto laboratory in 1964 and sent the one hundred remaining researchers back to Chicago, as did Zenith. Sylvania sold off its TWT division to Microwave Electronics and its ferrite components division to MELabs to concentrate on its core defense business. Varian, looking to make up lost ground in the TWT market, bought up what was left of the GE Microwave Laboratory in 1966 and merged it with its tube division (Terman 1964).

With the conspicuous exception of Hewlett Packard, which had always concentrated on commercial technologies, the remaining microwave electronics companies never really cracked the civilian market.

Varian diversified into analytical instruments and medical electronics, as did a few of its local competitors, but none of them managed to break their essential dependence on defense contracts, or on the culture of classified projects and security clearances that sustained those contracts. Like Lockheed itself, which virtually abandoned the civilian market altogether, they staked their futures on the procurement policies of the national security establishment.

The microwave electronics industry set the pattern for the sort of horizontal structure and collective learning that would become characteristic of Silicon Valley. Companies such as Hewlett Packard and Varian Associates forged the technical and cultural links between the microwave and the microelectronics industries and served as models for a subsequent generation of start-ups and spinoffs. In designating an old garage on Addison Avenue in Palo Alto, where Hewlett Packard got its start in 1939, as "the birthplace of Silicon Valley," the state of California was only recognizing what industry insiders had long understood.[20] Hewlett Packard and Varian not only entered the microelectronics and computer business themselves—Hewlett Packard with conspicuous and long-lasting success—they also designed the crucial testing, measuring, and processing equipment that opened the market to other firms. David Packard, convinced that the continuing health of his own company depended on the economic strength of the region, cofounded the northern branch of the West Coast Electronics Manufacturing Association and the Santa Clara County Manufacturing Group to advance the interests of the local electronics industry. The "H-P Way," with its decentralized corporate structure and informal management style, its emphasis on teamwork, shared responsibility, and entrepreneurship, became the very hallmark of Silicon Valley (Saxenian 1994).

The Silicon Valley Model?

Back in 1965, as Silicon Valley was just beginning to take off, Bell Laboratories president James Fisk cautioned against placing too much confidence on this model of industrial competitiveness. Thanks to "intense federal subsidy of electronics, space vehicle and guidance operations, communications and computer programs," places like Silicon Valley and Route 128 (in Massachusetts) appeared to be seedbeds of innovation. But the innovations spawned there, however important for the national defense, would not necessarily translate into "the sort of enduring, economically productive high employment industries which are the backbone of this nation," he warned. "We believe it would be inaccurate and probably eventually dangerous to persist in the presumption that this is the way to start and maintain important industrial innovation." What America really needed to compete were policies aimed at strengthening and revitalizing older industries as well as creating new ones. And that could not be done by following a model of industrial development that "depends so heavily on federal subsidy as do these classic spinoffs from the universities" (Fisk 1965).

In the short run, Fisk was wrong. If few of the original electronics companies in the Valley succeeded in breaking their dependence on federal subsidy, second- and third-generation companies often did, sometimes in spectacular fashion. But even they could not always master the "missing consumer connection" dividing the high-tech world of Silicon Valley from the larger world of consumer electronics, no doubt in part because that connection had never been an integral part of Silicon Valley.[21]

Yet Fisk appreciated, as many would-be imitators of Silicon Valley did not, just how important the military connection had been in the making of Silicon Valley. To this day, Stanford remains near the top of the list of university recipients of defense contracts, as does SRI, a contract research institute spun off from the university in the wake of student antiwar protests in 1970. SRI is nearly as defense dependent as it was when it was still part of Stanford, with about three-quarters of its funding from defense agencies. Likewise, Lockheed-Martin wrestles with Boeing for the top spot among corporate defense contractors, with Ford Aerospace not far behind.

Even Frederick Terman, the acknowledged "father of Silicon Valley," could forget how important military money had been in turning both Stanford and its surrounding industrial community into high-technology powerhouses. After he retired as provost in 1965, Terman became a highly sought after consultant for other regions whose business and political leaders hoped he might be able to teach them the secrets of Silicon Valley's success. As it turned out, he couldn't, despite some sizable investments by business groups and state agencies in New Jersey, New York, Texas, and Oregon. Like many successful entrepreneurs, academic and otherwise, Terman did not fully comprehend his own achievements. As a lifelong academic with little direct experience in the world of business (though he had served on the boards of several

Silicon Valley companies and astutely invested in many others), he overemphasized the university's value in the Silicon Valley equation, a common pitfall, as subsequent efforts at high-technology regional development would show.[22] He tended to assume that what was good for Stanford was good for Silicon Valley, and vice versa, without fully considering how much that symbiosis owed to a mutual dependence on the special circumstances of the early Cold War. "Stanford Industrial Park succeeded not only because of its exemplary design and its devotion to high-tech industry," urban historian John Findlay rightly concludes, "but also because it was in the right place at the right time" (Findlay 1992: 118). And what was true of the Industrial Park was generally true for the entire region. Without massive federal investments (mostly for defense) in Stanford's academic programs and in the surrounding industrial community, neither the university nor the region could have grown as strong as quickly. Terman and his industrial counterparts took full advantage of those resources, but they did not create them. In advising other regions on how to profit from his experiences, Terman encouraged them to follow an already outdated political economy (Leslie and Kargon 1996). Silicon Valley's strengths, as well as some of its limitations, are very much the legacy of a Cold War era that pumped (and continues to pump) billions of defense dollars into Stanford and into the high-technology companies that grew up around, and in part depended on, it. Those dollars encouraged further investment in the region by established electronics companies and encouraged local entrepreneurs to try their own hand in the defense business. Those dollars also lured some of the best minds in the business to the Santa Clara Valley, as graduate students, faculty members, and most significantly in terms of numbers, as corporate engineers. Technically and culturally, the microwave industry laid the foundation for the success of the microelectronics industry, and in the process turned what would later be called Silicon Valley into the gleaming buckle of "the Gun Belt."[23]

PART II

INSTITUTIONS

Dealmakers and Counselors: Law Firms as Intermediaries in the Development of Silicon Valley

MARK C. SUCHMAN

Lawyers are a critical but often overlooked constituent of the Silicon Valley political economy. This chapter examines three interrelated empirical puzzles posed by the role of lawyers in the recent history of the region. The first puzzle centers broadly on the question of how new organizational communities coalesce out of previously open environmental space (cf. Astley 1985). This could be called "the community structuration problem." The second puzzle focuses more narrowly on the prominent role of law firms in Silicon Valley life, asking whether the dynamics of community development somehow privilege lawyers, relative to other organizational actors. This could be called "the legal prominence problem." Finally, the third puzzle concerns the ongoing difficulties that many San Francisco law firms have faced in penetrating the Silicon Valley legal market, despite the success of the Valley's own indigenous firms. This could be called "the legal parochialism problem." This introductory section will briefly examine each of these three problems.

Today's Silicon Valley exemplifies a phenomenon that organizational researchers have termed, variously, an "organizational field" (DiMaggio and Powell 1983), a "societal sector" (Meyer and Scott 1983), or an "organizational community" (Astley 1985): "organizations that, in the aggregate, constitute a recognized area of institutional life: key suppliers, resource and product consumers . . . and other organizations that produce similar services and products" (DiMaggio and Powell

1983: 148). What defines an organizational community such as Silicon Valley is its high level of internal interaction and interdependence, its distinctive normative and behavioral style, its collective identity, and, more generally, its pervasive sense of "entity-ness." As one local chronicler observed, somewhat hyperbolically: "[M]ore than any industry in history, [Silicon Valley] is a self-contained, living entity. . . . It has defined boundaries, is self-perpetuating and reproducing and has predictable behavior—including the instinct for self-preservation. Even in the electronics industry, there is a tendency to speak of 'Silicon Valley' as though it were a sensate being" (Malone 1985: 8).

Although several of Santa Clara County's leading industrial firms date back to the 1930s or earlier, the region has only recently developed these crucial community attributes of structure, culture, and identity. Until the advent of the microcomputer era, few local residents had a sense of participating in a distinctive industrial phenomenon. As recently as 1950, the area that was to become Silicon Valley still touted itself more modestly as "the Prune Capital of America." Less than 0.25 percent of Santa Clara's population (eight hundred workers) held manufacturing jobs, and half of those were in canneries and food-processing plants (Rogers and Larsen 1984: 28). Although a number of electronics companies already operated in the area, neither their numbers nor their product lines distinguished them from electronics manufacturers in other parts of the country (see Sturgeon in this volume for a somewhat different perspective). In public discourse, the activities of the region were identified by their particular geographic locales—Palo Alto, Sunnyvale, Santa Clara County—rather than as part of a larger social system.

By the 1970s, however, the population of interrelated spinoff firms had blossomed, and previously isolated startups were beginning to perceive themselves as participants in a common endeavor. In 1971, *Microelectronics News* coined the phrase "Silicon Valley" to describe this new regional entity. In the national press, references to "Silicon Valley" increased substantially faster than references to the individual electronics industries of the region's constituent communities from 1975 until at least 1985. This heightened sense of commonality corresponded with a marked increase in intracommunal business relations and with a progressive standardization of local business practices (Bygrave and Timmons 1992; Saxenian 1994; Suchman 1994).

In the lexicon of organizational sociology, Silicon Valley's experience over the past twenty-five years falls under the ungainly rubric of "community structuration." Structuration refers to the development of coherent and consistent social relations—shared meanings, stable interaction patterns, consensually defined roles—within a group of previously isolated firms (DiMaggio and Powell 1983: 148). Increasingly, researchers have identified this transition from quasi-randomness to systematicity as a crucial "phase change" in organizational life. Among other things, the trajectory that an organizational community follows in its early history often determines the fate of new technologies (Van de Ven and Garud 1989) and "locks in" many industrial characteristics for years to come (Arthur 1989; Rosenkopf and Tushman 1994; Stinchcombe 1965). Unfortunately, current understandings of how viable organizational communities coalesce over time remain only partial, at best. Silicon Valley's economic success, coupled with the community's central place in contemporary policy discourse (Malone 1985; Miller 1987; Hall and Markusen 1985), makes it a promising site in which to seek answers to this "structuration problem."

The second puzzle centers on the unexpected prominence of the legal sector in Silicon Valley. The unusually high profile of local attorneys is an empirical reality in Silicon Valley life: for example, a recent issue of the weekend magazine from the *San Jose Mercury News* (Holub 1990) featured a cover photograph of Larry Sonsini, the leading partner in the region's leading law firm, over the headline "Silicon Valley's Secret Weapon—Superlawyer Larry Sonsini: The Entrepreneur's Best Friend." Another local commentator (Mitchell 1991) lists "knowledgeable attorneys" as both a key factor that "made Silicon Valley" and also a crucial ingredient that eludes many "Silicon Valley wannabes." Similar themes recur throughout discussions with members of the region's industrial and financial communities, who frequently refer to one attorney or another as "the most powerful man in the Valley," or "one of the people who brought this place together."

Considering the general antipathy toward lawyers in contemporary America, these sentiments are at least mildly surprising. What makes them truly puzzling, however, is the fact that Silicon Valley largely lacks the factors that analysts have traditionally credited with producing legal prominence elsewhere. Legal practice in Silicon Valley is hardly a case of the hypertrophied team-lawyering that Galanter (1983) calls "mega-law": matters tend to be minor and thinly staffed, with relatively junior associates single-handedly covering the basic legal needs of many small companies. Further, the prominence of Silicon Valley attorneys does not seem to be driven by the existence of any noteworthy body of refined professional arcana (see, e.g., Abbott 1981): In the early years of the community (and even to a large extent today) the legal doctrines surrounding central local activities—for example, laws regarding electronic intellectual property and venture capital finance—were hazy and rarely invoked. Indeed, in most Silicon Valley transactions, the economic risks have traditionally dwarfed the legal risks: litigation has been relatively rare, and, in any case, transactional partners tend to be small, tenuous, and judgment proof. In short, Silicon Valley lawyers rarely participate in gargantuan cases or gargantuan deals; they rarely serve as sacred guardians of potent mysteries; and, in their formal legal activities at least, they rarely mediate key sources of organizational uncertainty. Given this, their prominence becomes a puzzle of significant proportions.

The third empirical puzzle centers on the remarkably indigenous composition of the Silicon Valley legal sector. As the following discussion details, as recently as the mid-1970s, the local bar was essentially indistinguishable from that of any other affluent American suburb. In 1975, the largest Palo Alto law firm had twelve attorneys and operated in the shadow of a major national legal center, barely thirty miles away in San Francisco. San Francisco attorneys represented virtually all of the region's leading corporations, and there was little indication that this would ever cease to be the case. By the late 1980s, however, the situation had changed dramatically. The largest indigenous Silicon Valley law firm had grown to over 150 attorneys, and several other indigenous firms had expanded almost as significantly. Virtually all of the region's new industrial leaders patronized local law offices, and the share of Silicon Valley legal business being performed in San Francisco had dwindled to negligible proportions. Further, while a handful of San Francisco law firms had opened successful Silicon Valley branches, an equally large number of San Francisco firms—as well as several other national heavyweights—had discontinued or sharply curtailed their ineffectual efforts to penetrate the Silicon Valley market.

In light of the new industrial community's burgeoning resources and its demonstrable appetite for legal services, the dramatic disparity between the fates of local lawyers and the fates of their more prestigious and more organizationally sophisticated San Francisco colleagues is a puzzle worthy of note. Clearly, something about the new industrial community, or the local law firms, or the interaction between the two, produced a result that few would have predicted. The challenge to organizational theorists is to formulate an account that explains this occurrence.

Theoretical Orientation

To understand these puzzles, one must begin with a theoretical framework capable of situating legal practice in a changing matrix of interorganizational relations—encompassing not only law firms but also various populations of clients, collaborators, and competitors. To date, the two most prominent accounts of such organizational "communities" come from organizational ecology (e.g., Astley 1985; Baum and Singh 1994; Hannan and Freeman 1977, 1989) and institutional theory (e.g., DiMaggio and Powell 1983; Meyer and Rowan 1977; Meyer and Scott 1983; Powell and DiMaggio 1991).

Organizational ecology stresses the competitive constraints that underlie the differential survival of varying organizational forms. Drawing on the work of biological ecologists, theorists in this school argue that organizational populations, like biotic species, face external resource pressures that produce differences in survival and mortality rates. Over time, populations of organizations consequently converge on forms that are optimally fit with respect to environmentally determined niches. Thus, looking at Silicon Valley, organizational ecologists would see an "ecological community"—a stable system of competition, predation, and symbiosis arranged around internally consistent populations and mutually reinforcing food chains.

Where organizational ecology stresses adaptation to material constraints, institutional theory emphasizes construction of cultural models. Borrowing from the work of social phenomenologists (e.g., Berger and Luckmann 1967), institutional theory highlights the cultural forces—norms, roles, scripts, and rituals—that promote conformity and isomorphism among organizations, often independent of the dominant form's functional utility. Institutional theorists see organizational life as reflecting taken-for-granted cognitive and normative frameworks that channel firms into predetermined roles governed by widely recognized behavioral scripts. Research in this tradition consequently stresses the definitional processes by which society delineates organizational types and the labeling processes by which society assigns individual entities to specific categories. Thus, looking at Silicon Valley, institutional theorists would see an "institutional field": a stable system of roles, performances, and accounts arranged around internally consistent typologies and mutually reinforcing rituals.

Although commentators have often viewed organizational ecology and institutional theory as competing formulations (Singh and Lumsden 1990: 182; see, e.g., DiMaggio and Powell 1983; Scott 1992), the two are in reality complementary: organizational ecology focuses almost exclusively on flows of *operational resources* (the raw materials that support organizational survival), while institutional theory concentrates primarily on flows of *constitutive information* (the basic rules that determine organizational structure). This duality between operational resources and constitutive information suggests the importance of constructing a more comprehensive "institutional ecology" that melds organizational ecology and institutional theory into a unitary whole (Suchman 1988): in the growth and structuration of actual organizational communities, resources and information generally appear as intricately coevolving flows, not as isolated exogenous constraints. If one wishes, ultimately, to understand the complex interplay of institutional and ecological processes, one must identify the real-world conduits that mediate these two flows, and one must examine how these conduits are themselves enmeshed in ongoing processes of selection and construction.[1]

In the institutional ecology of Silicon Valley, local law firms serve as precisely such conduits. By examining the relations between these firms and their industrial clients, the present analysis attempts to construct a coherent picture of Silicon Valley lawyers' roles in the world of nonlegal decision-makers. The study also attempts to delineate a number of factors, both at the level of individual organizations and at the level of the organizational community, that might expand, contract, or otherwise reconfigure that role. The fundamental premises of this enterprise are (a) that law firms participate actively and consequentially in the interorganizational network; and (b) that, at certain stages of community development, the work of corporate lawyers often has as much to do with managing, constructing, and mediating the informal "taken-for-granteds" of the local normative environment as it has to do with interpreting, invoking, or evading the formal sanctions of the legal system as a whole. Furthermore, law firms are creations as well as creators of this shifting community structure, simultaneously shaping and reflecting surrounding flows of resources and information in a complex coevolutionary dance.

The Institutional Ecology of Silicon Valley Legal Practice

THE GROWTH OF SILICON VALLEY
LEGAL PRACTICE

In 1975, at the dawn of the microcomputer era, Silicon Valley's legal community was small and rather parochial—not unlike the legal communities of other affluent suburbs throughout the country. In total, thirty-five Palo Alto law offices listed biographies in the 1975 edition of the *Martindale-Hubbell Law Directory*.[2] Fully 40 percent of these contained only one lawyer, and none were branches of firms headquartered outside Santa Clara County. The largest law firms in Palo Alto at the time—Wilson, Mosher and Sonsini, and Ware and Friedenrich—had only twelve lawyers each. Wilson's partner-associate ratio stood at 1.4:1; Ware's, at 1:1. Neither appeared to be undergoing or anticipating substantial growth. If clients desired the resources of a large law firm, they had to drive thirty miles north to San Francisco (Cox 1988b).

By 1988, Palo Alto's legal community had almost doubled, to sixty-nine firms. At the same time, the mean firm size had climbed from 3.75 to 9.10, and, according to one estimate, the number of lawyers per capita had come to rival that of midtown Manhattan and Washington, D.C. (Friedman et al. 1989). Further, ten law firms from outside Silicon Valley had opened branch offices in town,[3] and although most of these remained relatively limited operations, two San Francisco firms boasted Palo Alto staffs of thirty or more: Cooley, Godward, Castro, Huddleson and Tatum (thirty-two), and Brobeck, Phleger and Harrison (thirty-three).

Equally important, three of Palo Alto's indigenous law firms had ridden the microcomputer semiconductor wave to national prominence: With over 120 lawyers, Wilson, Sonsini, Goodrich and Rosati had become the widely acknowledged leader of the Silicon Valley legal community. Not far behind were Ware and Friedenrich, with sixty-six attorneys, and Fenwick, Davis and West, with fifty-nine. Interestingly, the three firms' growth rates followed fairly stable, generally similar trajectories until approximately 1980.[4] Although all three outpaced the expansion of Palo Alto's legal community as a whole, the size-ordering changed almost annually during this early period, and there was no clear hierarchy among the firms. In the early 1980s, however, the situation changed: each firm experienced a dramatic up-tick in growth, but the pace of this growth varied across the three, and substantial size differentials developed. The general image is one of increasing differentiation and growing stratification.[5]

THE ELEMENTS OF SILICON VALLEY
LEGAL PRACTICE

In addition to fueling the expansion of Palo Alto's law firms, the growth of Silicon Valley also shaped their practices.[6] Needless to say, the major legal players in the Valley are all well versed in the intricacies of "computer law"—particularly the patent, copyright, and trade secret doctrines surrounding the protection of intellectual property. To survive, a high-tech corporation must balance the benefits of participating in technical information networks against the costs of divulging its own exclusive knowledge (von Hippel 1986); the legal tools for controlling such information flows are an important stock-in-trade for Silicon Valley lawyers (see, e.g., Cox 1988c; Friedman et al. 1989; Rogers and Larsen 1984: 90–94).

At the same time, however, many aspects of "high-technology law" are *consequences*, rather than causes, of the growth of Silicon Valley's legal community. As one attorney noted in a recent interview:[7] "In the early '80s, the lawyers were quite unsophisticated in high-technology legal matters. I wouldn't blame the lawyers as much as the fact that the law just wasn't all that developed. There really was no developed body of intellectual property law that applied to computer hardware, software, [and] biotechnology" [062601.6]. Given this doctrinal vacuum, it seems somewhat implausible to trace the rise of Silicon Valley law firms to their mastery of a particular body of uniquely relevant legal knowledge. To a large extent, the legal community emerged first, and the law second.

Under these circumstances, general business counseling, not intellectual property practice, drove the growth of Silicon Valley's law firms in the early years. Clients came disproportionately from the region's emerging high-technology industries, but the services that the legal community provided often had more to do with the generic problems of entrepreneurship than with either technology or law. And despite a rise in litigation and an increase in attorney specialization, general business counselors continue to form the core of most Silicon Valley law firms today. As one partner at Wilson Sonsini puts it: "Our philosophy has been: (1) to focus on the high-tech client, and to try to anticipate the needs of that client; (2) to act not only as a legal advisor but as a business advisor; and (3) to take very much a hands-on approach to clients" [070801.4]. A prominent attorney in the Palo Alto office of a leading San Francisco firm confirms this assessment: "Business lawyers in this area—at least the ones who are quite successful—tend to be counselors in the broader sense. I think Larry Sonsini is the best example. Larry is a director of more and more companies, and I think it shows the fact that he's gone beyond just being a lawyer into being something of a business advisor" [071502.10–11].

In the daily life of Silicon Valley, this advisory role displays several distinct facets. Most local attorneys have, at one time or another, served as dealmakers, as counselors, as gatekeepers, as proselytizers, and as matchmakers. The following sections examine each of these roles in turn. The first and second sections, below, outline two major types of activity—"dealmaking" and "counseling"—that, together, form the core of the Silicon Valley law firm's contribution to community life. The third section then extends this discussion to examine a number of "mixed effects" that arise when lawyers conjoin elements of dealmaking and counseling into three additional "combined" roles: the role of "gatekeeper," the role of "proselytizer," and the role of "matchmaker." Since matchmaking is the most complex of these three, the discussion of mixed effects closes with a fairly detailed examination of how new companies can be shaped by the venture-capital "marriages" that their attorneys help to arrange.

The Silicon Valley Lawyer as Dealmaker

No American law school teaches a course in "dealmaking," and that activity has never occupied a particularly prominent place in either the academic literature on the legal profession or the popular conception of lawyering. Nonetheless, the dealmaking role is fairly straightforward, and it holds a central position in many Silicon Valley legal practices: as dealmakers, Silicon Valley attorneys draw on their connections in the local business community, in order to link clients with various transactional partners. In the words of one study: "Business luncheons, afterwork drinks, cocktail parties, and other social occasions are the stuff of which a high-tech lawyer's career is built. Their Roladex [*sic*] card-files are as indispensable as their law books" (Rogers and Larsen 1984: 81).

Perhaps unsurprisingly, this dealmaking role is most pronounced in those transactions that are most distinctively "Silicon Valley creations"—particularly venture capital financings. The region's law firms "look upon venture capital start-ups as our bread and butter" [070801.1], and in representing such clients, local attorneys often go beyond simply assisting with legal mechanics, to actively facilitate the funding search itself. Silicon Valley is, in many ways, a small town ("It looks like a big city, but it isn't," says one CEO), and resources can prove frustratingly inaccessible to outsiders: "It's a very cliquish community, so for the younger entrepreneur it's hard to break in. You feel like you're right in the middle of it, but how do you get *in* it? The clubby-ness of it is hard" [070101.21]. In this environment, prominent attorneys can provide the contacts and recommendations that ease entrance into the venture capital market.

While the overall significance of this dealmaking activity is hard to quantify, some press accounts have suggested that the Wilson Sonsini law firm, alone, may control access to as much as 60 percent of all Silicon Valley venture capital (Cox 1988a: 48). And even if these figures are substantially overstated, few community members would dispute the prevalence of the underlying phenomenon. As an associate at the Wilson Sonsini firm observes:

Clients choose us because we know a lot of people in the venture capital community. A lot of our partners are invested in these funds. Our top partners can get leading venture capitalists on the phone and say, "Hey, I've got this great business plan, take a look at it." Clients are looking for that "in." Venture capitalists get flooded with business plans, and they need some way to sort out the wheat from the chaff. They try to read them all, but most venture capital operations tend to be thinly staffed, with a high demand on general partner time. [060301.9]

Venture capitalists confirm the value of such introductions: "We see six or seven hundred proposals a year. We probably actively work on 120 and we make 8 to 12 new investments. So it's a pretty selective process. How do we find them? A lot of it comes through the law firms. We work closely with Brobeck, with Wilson Sonsini, with Ware Friedenrich. That's been quite a good source of deals for us" [070901.15].

Significantly, the law firm's dealmaking role affects investors as well as entrepreneurs. Indeed, some venture capitalists seem almost as concerned about whether lawyers will refer deals *to* them as entrepreneurs are about whether lawyers will give them an entré into the financial community. As a general partner in one of the region's newer funds puts it:

In Silicon Valley, lawyers tend to get involved fairly early. In fact, we just did mailings to all the lawyers in Silicon Valley, so they wouldn't think we were some odd-ball firm in the hinterlands. Lawyers can act as a detriment if they don't know who you are and you don't have the relationships with them. They're an important part of this whole network of deal-flow for us. [070101.19–20]

Admittedly, most venture capitalists are quick to point out that many deals come from sources other than law firms, with referrals by executives of portfolio companies being the most frequently cited alternative. Few investors, however, dispute the general proposition that law firms provide an important link between the region's financial and industrial communities—particularly for new entrepreneurs who may lack contacts with the senior management of more established companies.[8]

Notably, although venture capital financings offer some of the most important venues in which lawyers play a dealmaking role, similar activities occur in other areas of community life, as well. Fairly regularly, attorneys introduce their clients to various suppliers, licensees, joint venturers, and other transactional partners—and some law firms even go so far as to assist in filling out top management teams with appropriate personnel. Thus, rather than being an idiosyncrasy of the venture capital process, dealmaking appears to represent a more general interorganizational role: in their capacity as dealmakers, Silicon Valley law firms mediate the flow of a wide range of scarce resources within the local business community.

Although it is hard to tell exactly how exclusive these referral relationships have become, this system of lawyer dealmaking holds the potential to exert a considerable influence on the ecology of the community as a whole. At the extreme, if law firms were to act as separate "watering holes," each uniting a distinct stable of possible exchange partners, interorganizational competition would become increasingly localized and segmented, rather than operating homogeneously throughout the community as a whole. In such a segmented regime, client companies would disproportionately compete among themselves for the favors of the law firm dealmaker—while at the same time, the clusters of companies centered around each law firm would compete with one another at the clique level for opportunities in external consumer and supplier markets. Under these conditions, each law firm would enjoy substantial incentives to coordinate the activities of its various clients, so as to maximize its own viability by maximizing the performance of its clique. Admittedly, this degree of segmentation and intragroup coordination represents a relatively extreme scenario, and there is little evidence that such conditions have materialized as yet. Nonetheless, even in today's more open regime, it seems clear that law firm dealmakers have gained substantial wealth and influence by providing the crucial "brokerage" glue that binds together the Silicon Valley network (Marsden 1982; Nohria 1992).

The Silicon Valley Lawyer as Counselor

In itself, dealmaking might be enough to explain the power and prominence of attorneys in today's Silicon Valley. After all, resource control lies at the core of most sociological theories of power, at both the interpersonal and the interorganizational levels (e.g., Blau 1964; Emerson 1962; Hickson et al. 1971; Pfeffer and Salancik 1978; Thibaut and Kelley 1959; Thompson 1967). However, without something more, one might be hard put to explain how law firms acquired this dealmaking role in the first place. The interview evidence suggests that this missing ingredient may lie in the second (and, arguably, the more important) half of the Silicon Valley lawyer's core activities: counseling.

In itself, the assertion that lawyers act as counselors should come as no surprise. What distinguishes Silicon Valley practice from the image of large law firm practice in much of the recent literature, however, is the fact that in Silicon Valley, successful attorneys see themselves as offering general business advice, rather than purely legal guidance. Repeatedly, and across a wide variety of contexts, Silicon Valley lawyers describe an advisory role that closely resembles the work of more conventional business consultants.

Unable to afford specialized consulting firms, small companies often turn to their attorneys for guidance and perspective on troubling business decisions. Sometimes, entrepreneurs' questions revolve around quasi-legal issues, such as contractual terms or stock purchase rights. Almost as often, however, they reflect much broader business concerns.

As one Wilson Sonsini associate notes:

People definitely look for a lot of advice about how to set up the corporate structure, about valuations, about what type of stock options are appropriate—all of those kinds of issues related to the organization of the company. People also want you to evaluate the adequacy of offers, and of term sheets. Unless you are dealing with somebody who has been through it a few times, they generally have no clue what's going on. There's a lot of non-legal advising that goes on. I think that's something that really is expected of us. [060301.10]

While a number of considerations promote the attorney's counseling role, the impetus for this activity lies primarily in the law firm's privileged structural position within the developing organizational community. Unlike most industrial organizations, law firms enjoy regular contact with a large number of companies facing similar sets of operational challenges. This exposure allows lawyers to monitor wide ranges of client strategies and to formulate coherent accounts of the determinants of success and failure. Such summary accounts then become the business attorney's stock-in-trade and the target of client inquiries. As one senior partner puts it:

Good lawyers are a wonderful resource for business advice, because the problems that growing companies encounter are similar, and even if a problem is new to an entrepreneur who's never been president of a company before, the outside counsel has seen various ways people have dealt with it. So, the business lawyer is a repository of experience with a lot of different companies. [070301.11–12]

Entrepreneurs and venture capitalists echo these views. An executive in a rapidly growing biotechnology firm, for example, describes his own company's use of lawyers as follows:

I think you learn largely by making mistakes and it helps to have people who have had the experience of making those same mistakes so they can guide you. The lawyers put very important brakes and safeguards on the entrepreneurs. The entrepreneurs always want to charge ahead and just dive in first and then find out how deep it is. The lawyers kind of go, "Watch out for the rocks."

The lawyers have been through this before. For the entrepreneurs, it's often pretty much the first time, but the lawyers give pointers along the way: "If you've got this kind of problem, well, we had a client who handled it this way." There's a wealth of experience that goes in there that the entrepreneur doesn't necessarily have. The lawyers know how to get these things done. That's invaluable. [061301.1–2]

In short, in their role as counselors, Silicon Valley law firms employ their broad vicarious experience base, in order to formulate and promulgate compilations of general business knowledge (Suchman 1996). Here, rather than mediating flows of operational resources, lawyers appear to be mediating flows of constitutive information—of basic rules about how to set up and operate a viable organization.

Like dealmaking, counseling exerts a profound influence on the surrounding organizational community. At the simplest level, summaries of constitutive information have obvious value to individual clients, many of whom come from engineering or academic backgrounds and lack solid understandings of basic business activities. Lawyers clearly offer one way for new companies to fill this experience gap. Although the frequency and intensity of lawyer-client contact varies, the comments of a former entrepreneur who recently launched a venture capital fund are typical: "We treat our lawyers as confidants. Our attorney is considered part of our firm, just like he would be considered part of the entrepreneur's firm if he was their lawyer. A lawyer is very, very important and, in our case, our attorney is an extraordinarily talented guy and we use him as a sounding board for our ideas" [070101.20].

In addition to assisting individual companies, however, counseling exerts a more global influence as well. The anecdotal character of respondents' accounts should not obscure the fact that, cumulatively, law-firm efforts to summarize and codify basic constitutive information can place significant pressures on the macro-structure of the emerging organizational community. As clients come to embody the models compiled by their attorneys, the diversity of organizational forms falls, and interorganizational relations become more consistent, more highly typified and, ultimately, more taken for granted. This process is reflected, for example, in one local attorney's comments about the emergence of standardized venture capital financing agreements:

If there's a transaction with one of the other Silicon Valley law firms, there's very little argument or negotiation about the agreement. Very often, they've adopted our contract forms or vice versa. Usually, the forms that are used representing the investor are the same as were used representing the company, because they follow well-defined molds. I remember one attorney at another firm saying that a couple years ago he had this whole set of negotiating responses to my firm's forms. But in the last few deals that I did with them, their forms were virtually identical to ours, and there wasn't anything to argue over. [060701.1]

As this description suggests, the cumulative effects of law firm counseling tend to render the organizational community both more isomorphic and more institutionalized over time. As socially scripted enactments (Weick 1979) replace outcome-driven experimentation, people simply stop asking "why?"

As one attorney notes, this aspect of community structuration has its costs: "I think there are law firms out there that have three cookie cutters, and they just ask: 'Is it A, B, or C?' They're going to force these things into one of those cookie cutters, and just ignore the fact that you may not fit the profiles. They'll just pretend you do, and they'll just cram you into the structure" [071502.15]. Other comments, however, suggest that strong normative assumptions may have beneficial effects, as well. In particular, routinization facilitates and normalizes otherwise problematic transactions, stabilizing the community and freeing resources for more productive uses. In the words of an attorney who had moved to Silicon Valley from a more traditional San Francisco firm: "When I came here, secretaries were doing the things that I had been doing as a third- or fourth-year associate in San Francisco. Doing it just as well or better. Those kind of institutional things—form documents and other stuff—all really institutionalize efficiency and allow us to do the work cost-effectively" [060701.5].

Further, as DiMaggio and Powell (1983) have observed, mimetic isomorphism—the imitation of successful role models—can become particularly important when organizations face otherwise paralyzing uncertainties. Discussing what distinguishes Silicon Valley from other communities, a venture capitalist raised in Michigan notes how the availability of institutionalized models has fostered Silicon Valley's entrepreneurial climate:

I think in other areas people don't have that sense of their ability to make this happen. In the Midwest maybe one person gets that idea and that fire, but then they get picked to death. There's a way to shoot holes in almost any deal you can find. But around here, you sort of learn by example. If it's not broken, you don't have to fix it and you don't have to invent. There's a way to do this—so just do it. It's not like this is the first time a new company has been created. So, just execute. Go like hell. [070901.17]

In their capacity as counselors, Silicon Valley lawyers play an active part in shaping and disseminating such scripts for action. By virtue of their privileged structural position, lawyers develop a wealth of vicarious experience—not only with legal issues but with business issues as well. In providing this know-how to new entrepreneurs, attorneys become "information intermediaries," helping to spread basic constitutive information throughout the larger community. As these rules and definitions diffuse, community life becomes both more structured and more institutionalized.

Mixed Effects

Although the preceding discussion portrays dealmaking and counseling as wholly separable roles, in reality Silicon Valley law firms often mediate both resources and information at once, in single sets of behaviors. This blending of dealmaking and counseling produces a number of "mixed" activities, the most significant of which are gatekeeping, proselytizing, and matchmaking. As gatekeepers, Silicon Valley lawyers use their dealmaking powers to construct and defend moral boundaries, guarding against interlopers who might disrupt emerging community understandings; as proselytizers, Silicon Valley lawyers use their counseling powers to explain and promote particular types of transactions, indoctrinating converts into emerging community norms; and as matchmakers, Silicon Valley lawyers use both their dealmaking and counseling powers to discern and categorize recurrent situations, pairing transactional partners in accordance with emerging cultural typologies.

THE SILICON VALLEY LAWYER
AS GATEKEEPER

In its purest form, the dealmaking role described above would simply involve facilitating the search for transactional partners by alerting would-be buyers to a list of would-be sellers, would-be lenders to a list of would-be borrowers, and so forth. Law firms would act merely as clearinghouses—reducing search costs, and perhaps (if each firm's listings were sufficiently distinct) segregating competition patterns, but not significantly affecting the ultimate nature of completed transactions. In reality, however, law firms both accept and refer clients selectively, and as a result, the "introduction" system not only channels resources but also reinforces and institutionalizes emerging community norms. As attorneys take on increasingly central positions in the deal-flow network, their ability to act as agents of social control increases apace. Over time, a gatekeeping system seems to be emerging, in which law firms use their influence on resource flows to screen out entities that challenge Silicon Valley's structural or behavioral taken-for-granteds or that otherwise threaten community cohesion. One member of Wilson Sonsini's Legal Practice Committee touches on an example of such exclusionary power:

Historically, attorneys in the firm have been very much encouraged to go out and take on any and all business. But now that we are bigger, we are starting to be more selective—in part because clients are coming through more and more on the basis of the firm's reputation and the perception that somehow we can enable transactions that might not otherwise be possible. So at this point we are encouraging attorneys to take into account whether the reputation of the client will create problems with other clients, and whether the proposal of the client is so outlandish as to be unreasonable. For example, we want to know whether they're litigious. Frequently, the lawyer carries the ball for the client, in terms of opening up connections and introducing the client to the business world. We want to make sure that we're not making an introduction that will ultimately backfire on us. [070801.6–8]

Efforts such as these increase the stability and cohesiveness of the community, albeit perhaps at the risk of stifling structural innovation.

THE SILICON VALLEY LAWYER
AS PROSELYTIZER

A second mixed role that Silicon Valley attorneys often play is that of proselytizer. In essence, this set of behaviors consists of counseling activity directed toward encouraging certain types of deals and discouraging others. Although lawyers sometimes simply employ their experience base to evaluate the legal implications of proposed contracts, proselytizing efforts more often involve educating clients about the larger, less formal aspects of Silicon Valley's normative order. Thus, like missionary educators, Silicon Valley law firms perceive themselves as possessing a "moral charter" to ease their clients into the lifeways of the civilized world. One prominent attorney, for example, describes his firm's Newport Beach office as follows:

In Southern California I've encountered many entrepreneurs who could hardly believe that venture capitalists weren't really "vulture capitalists"— that they weren't just good guys to stay away from. I felt like our office in

Newport Beach had a sort of missionary mode—to at least encourage the entrepreneurs to consider that venture capital could be an alternative, because some of the other options are really awful. Some of the things that they think they want to do are really bad news stuff. [070301.15]

As this quotation suggests, the proselytizer role is particularly salient in the case of venture capital transactions. Indeed, much of the Silicon Valley attorney's contribution to the financing process simply involves explaining the activities of local investors to inexperienced entrepreneurs. Such tutelage has at least two advantages for the community. First, lawyers inculcate a worldview that depicts venture-capital transactions as being natural, or even desirable, rather than as being "evil" (in the words of one entrepreneur-turned-venture-capitalist) and adversarial. As a senior attorney observes:

It is not an adversarial process. People who view it properly, who have a lot of experience in venture financing, realize that they are creating a very long term partnership between the venture capitalists on the one hand and the entrepreneurs on the other. So it's important that it be very fair, that parties can live with each other for a long time. [070301.4]

In addition to suppressing antagonism in individual transactions, however, the proselytizing efforts of Silicon Valley attorneys also promote the smooth operation of the capital market as a whole. Sometimes, this contribution takes the form of counseling about the range of "reasonable" terms and valuations, with lawyers subtly moving clients toward negotiating positions that comport with prevailing community norms. This is particularly true when an entrepreneur is relatively inexperienced or when a deal is relatively novel. At other times, lawyers ease communications between entrepreneurs and investors by explaining conventions and by translating responses. In the words of one prominent attorney:

We're one of the forces that makes the fundraising market more efficient. We help clients to refine their business plan to the point where it meets the standards and the criteria that venture capitalists expect. Then you get that out and get feedback, and you read those tea leaves. There is, in fact, a lexicon that you have to understand: What are they saying to you? What does this mean? What should I expect? [071502.10,14]

THE SILICON VALLEY LAWYER

AS MATCHMAKER

Beyond such conscious efforts to impose norms on the organizational community, law firms may also foster structuration by acting as interorganizational matchmakers, particularly in the financing process. As suggested above, Silicon Valley culture stresses the importance of cooperative relationships between entrepreneurs and venture capitalists; given this, finding the right mate takes on heightened importance. In this climate, law firms often help to facilitate "good marriages." This organizational matchmaking role has three parts, much like traditional romantic matchmaking: First, matchmakers (both romantic and organizational) winnow out "ineligible" clients, who are so deviant either ethically or structurally that representing them would besmirch the matchmaker's reputation; here, the matchmaker acts primarily as a gatekeeper. Second, matchmakers formulate typologies of clients and encourage those who are seeking partners to conform to certain culturally approved models; here, the matchmaker operates much like a proselytizer. Finally, and most distinctively, matchmakers employ cultural "rules of compatibility" to sort their clienteles, arranging matches between "likes" and discouraging contact between "unlikes."

This sorting process is fairly well recognized within the Silicon Valley community. In the words of one venture capitalist:

Very early on, the entrepreneur gets in touch with a lawyer—probably before he gets in touch with a venture capitalist—in order to form the corporation, discuss methods of financing and so forth. And very frequently the attorneys will aim the entrepreneur into a certain group of venture capitalists. There are law firms that do a lot of that. Wilson Sonsini is a good case in point. [062501.14]

Indeed, the role of lawyers in channeling start-ups to "appropriate" venture capital funds is so well established that some Silicon Valley law firms actually incorporate this matchmaking function directly into their formal structure, through standing committees that specialize in "brainstorming on who we think would be good people to look at a particular proposal" [070301.5].

As the preceding discussion suggests, in addition to stabilizing the flow of operational resources within the Silicon Valley community, matchmaking also structures the pool of constitutive information—both by creating sanctions against deviance and also by promulgating typologies of community participants. This institutionalizing effect goes beyond a simple restatement and codification of widely diffused knowledge, however. In a developing organizational community, matchmaking, like counseling, allows lawyers to impinge on the *local* flow of constitutive information even before any more *global* understandings have emerged.

Unlike counseling, however, matchmaking shapes the flow of information only indirectly, through the law firm's decisions about how to pair start-ups and venture capitalists. Simply put, these indirect effects arise because venture capitalists provide "more than money" for the new enterprise (Timmons and Sapienza 1991). The typical Silicon Valley investment fund exploits its experience with large numbers of portfolio companies to support the same kinds of counseling, connection-making, and norm-building services provided, in other contexts, by lawyers. In addition, venture capitalists often possess extensive first-hand industry experience of their own, coupled with a substantial stake in the start-up and a significant degree of direct coercive control. Consequently, the selection of an investor can exert a profound impact on the start-up's character and survival chances.

Through matchmaking, then, lawyers can affect the transmission of operational resources and constitutive information "at one remove," so to speak: here, the *primary* locus for the transmission of norms is not the lawyer-client encounter itself but rather the consequent pairing of entrepreneur and venture capitalist. Like the traditional marital matchmaker, the attorney-matchmaker reads the landscape of eligible partners and attempts to unite "ideal couples"; and like the traditional matchmaker, the attorney-matchmaker judges potential pairings based on typologies of actors and accounts of relevance. Perhaps unsurprisingly, in both cases, the content of these cognitive constructs can significantly influence both the shape of a community's social structure and the composition of a community's future generations.

The Style of Silicon Valley Legal Practice

As suggested earlier, Silicon Valley law presents a puzzle of legal parochialism: the growth of Palo Alto's legal elite seems at least mildly odd, given the preexisting presence of well-established and nationally prominent law firms in nearby San Francisco. Dealmaking and counseling help to shed some light on this puzzle, since both activities are facilitated by a law firm's participation in the local business community. Even before community structuration began, however, other less substantive aspects of legal practice may have favored Palo Alto's local law firms over their San Francisco competitors. This section offers a brief exploration of such stylistic issues. The focus here is not on what Silicon Valley lawyers do but rather on how they do it. As organizational ecologists might predict, selection pressures appear to have played a central role in excluding many San Francisco law firms from Silicon Valley during its formative years. The following pages discuss some of these pressures and demonstrate how they may have exerted a differential impact on Palo Alto's "small town lawyers" and San Francisco's "big city attorneys" (Landon 1988, 1990)

The first significant contrast between San Francisco and Silicon Valley law firms resides in the differing strategic postures required by their distinct client bases. Having evolved within a stable organizational community dominated by large corporations and established legal specialties, San Francisco's leading law firms often lack the opportunistic flexibility needed to exploit Silicon Valley's more fluid environment. In contrast, for suburban firms adapted to dealing with small, high-mortality clients, a rapidly evolving community poses few problems.

Nowhere is this truer than in the area of law-firm finances. Start-up clients can rarely afford legal services on a pay-as-you-go basis, and to succeed within Silicon Valley, lawyers must often defer billing or accept stock in lieu of payment. These practices come naturally to a small-town law firm that got its start representing gas stations and restaurants. As one Wilson Sonsini attorney puts it:

Normally, we will take on start-up companies and make an effort to keep the billable hours down, without compromising the legal issues involved. Frequently we will hold, delay, or suspend billing until financing can be obtained. In effect, we become partners with the start-up client. I think that's part of the reason why we're able to bring in small clients that aren't able otherwise to afford the rates that lawyers charge. [070801.8–9]

Among San Francisco's more traditional firms, by contrast, such contingent-payment schemes are often viewed with mistrust. One Palo Alto attorney recounts a case in which the branch office of a prominent San Francisco firm accepted a "funky," "fast-paced" client, pending approval from the firm's New Business Committee in the city:

In the middle of the afternoon they got a call from San Francisco saying, "Hey, we can't approve this client, because what you guys are saying here is you'll discount your time by 50%, and you're going to let them pay it over six months in installments. Installments? We don't believe in installments. And you'd be taking stock in the company? The implications! We haven't even thought about the tax issues, the conflict of interest issues. . . . And then the statement at the bottom of the memo that the law firm may never get paid back at all??? We're not in the business of extending credit."

In addition to operating under more flexible (and less pricey) billing structures, Silicon Valley firms are often less punctilious about the strictures of professional ethics, as well. At times, this involves a law firm's sharing the risks of its clients' transactions (Suchman and Cahill 1996). A local attorney, for example, tells of an instance in which a rival firm had refused to draft a contract containing standard language (a "representation") regarding the validity of the client's intellectual property rights:

The representation was drafted with an unusual number of hedges, and it raised a flag. So the lead venture capitalist has the typical VC reaction to that, which is to fly off the handle. He calls up the entrepreneurs, and they call up their lawyer, and the lawyer says, "Well, I've got to write my opinion letter, and my letter's based on what your representations say, so there have to be all these qualifications." And now the entrepreneurs are really getting upset, because they're sensing that this guy may not be willing to go out on a legal limb for them.

So they ended up dumping him and coming here, because we'd been saying, "Gosh, we deliver that opinion all the time. Yes, we understand the risk involved in giving an opinion that might not be totally 100% right; but weighing the costs and the benefits, we'd be willing to give you that opinion." [062601.13]

At other times, Silicon Valley law firms may exhibit similar flexibility in their interpretation of the ethical guidelines governing the provision of legal services to parties with opposing interests. In the words of a partner in the Palo Alto office of a San Francisco firm: "Larry Sonsini is able to work through what historically would have been very difficult conflict of interest issues, and to get his clients to go along. Larry has a tremendous facility to get clients to say, 'That's fine. We'll waive any conflicts. You can represent us both.' He is, in a sense, transforming the law on that, although not single-handedly" [071502.11]. As the industrial community has grown, these conflict-of-interest "innovations" have enhanced the ability of local firms to preserve the multiple contacts that facilitate dealmaking and counseling.

In addition to these differences in financial and ethical flexibility, the very prestige of San Francisco's legal community may have produced an organizational population poorly suited to Silicon Valley practice. According to Abbott (1981: 819), intraprofessional prestige is largely a function of intellectual purity; yet, in the early years of the microcomputer industry, structures adapted to maintaining and displaying such purity often proved to be competitive liabilities: "[B]lue-jean clientele demand down-to-earth advice. Arcane legal discourse . . . does not go down well with the young and the restless" (Cox 1988a: 48). In contrast to their San Francisco counterparts—and in keeping with small-town attorneys elsewhere (Landon 1988)—Silicon Valley lawyers embrace a "pastoral" prestige structure, centering on community engagement rather than on professional purity. From this perspective, the blending of legal and business concerns is a sign of practical relevance, not of extraprofessional contamination. An attorney in a leading Palo Alto firm captures the difference between the two models when he notes:

Large New York, Los Angeles or San Francisco law firms tend to represent established institutions with proven track records, and they tend to focus almost exclusively on legal issues, as opposed to business issues. This firm is different, in that it tends to represent a lot of engineers and scientists who don't really have much experience in running businesses. They come here in search of advisers who are going to tell them how you start a business. A fatal mistake down here would be to put the legal issues in front of the business issues—to be too much of a lawyer. [062601.1, 11]

Silicon Valley's indigenous law firms thus seem to differ from their San Francisco counterparts not only in substance but also in style. Under the pressures of the surrounding organizational community, Silicon Valley lawyers have developed distinctive billing structures, distinctive ethical principles, distinctive prestige hierarchies, and distinctive cultural outlooks.[9] While many of these distinguishing features appear to have been in place well before Silicon Valley became a self-aware organizational community, the structuration process of the 1970s and 1980s increased their relevance and altered their survival value. As Palo Alto's flexible, opportunistic law firms were shaping the region's broader organizational community, the changing structure of that organizational community was shaping the region's population of law firms as well.

Discussions and Conclusions

The preceding pages suggest that Silicon Valley's business lawyers play several important roles in the developing organizational community; the evidence, however, also suggests that these roles often extend well beyond the "official charter" of the legal profession per se. At the most general level, local law firms use their distinctive structural positions to mediate crucial flows of operational resources and constitutive information within Silicon Valley's larger interorganizational network. As dealmakers, lawyers link their clients to potential transaction partners (and other pools of operational resources), facilitating the survival and growth of individual companies and structuring patterns of access, symbiosis, and competition within the community as a whole. At the same time, as counselors, lawyers link their clients to potential role models (and other pools of constitutive information), facilitating the consolidation and legitimation of individual companies and structuring patterns of imitation, categorization, and identity-formation within the community as a whole. Further, beyond these pure archetypes, the mediation of resources and the mediation of information also blend together—when lawyers act as gatekeepers to withhold community resources from inappropriately constituted deviants; when lawyers act as proselytizers to promote community transactions among uninitiated novices; and when lawyers act as matchmakers to sort and steer transaction-seekers according to community typologies. In each of these activities, the Silicon Valley bar benefits from organizational structures and professional styles that reflect its small-town past: flexible billing structures, pragmatic ethical postures, and pastoral prestige hierarchies.

At the outset, this paper highlighted three interrelated empirical puzzles emerging from the recent history of Silicon Valley: (a) the community structuration problem, (b) the legal prominence problem, and (c) the legal parochialism problem. Through the voices of Silicon Valley's lawyers, entrepreneurs, and venture capitalists, some answers to these puzzles begin to emerge, shedding light on both the development of new organizational environments and the activities of corporate lawyers.

The community structuration problem is the broadest of the three. At its core, the evidence presented here depicts the structuration of Silicon Valley as a gradual building of (a) conceptual and material *connec-*

tions, linking initially disparate groups of organizations; (b) descriptive and prescriptive *models,* identifying which situations are alike and which are distinct; and (c) instrumental and ritual *decision rules,* delineating which attributes are beneficial, proper, and appropriate for specific organizations in specific situations. One particularly noteworthy feature of this unfolding process is the fact that, in Silicon Valley at least, organizational reproduction and community structuration appear to be closely intertwined: Rather than constructing each start-up from scratch, founders often turn to established populations of intermediary organizations (such as law firms and venture capital funds), who act as interorganizational "pollinators," providing new companies with preprocessed infusions of relevant know-how. The presence of these intermediaries not only eases the birth of individual organizations but also shapes the larger course of community development: at the community level, mediated reproduction both facilitates and domesticates the diffusion of innovative competences—accelerating the flow of constitutive information but segregating and homogenizing it according to prevailing cultural typologies. In effect, as interorganizational pollinators, Silicon Valley's law firms and venture capital funds serve to perceive, to promulgate, and to institutionalize the community's emerging normative order. They foster community structuration by systematizing organizational reproduction.

The linkage between mediated reproduction and community structuration helps to answer the legal prominence problem, as well. The American model of legal practice places Silicon Valley lawyers in a distinctively advantageous structural position within the emerging community, endowing them with the threefold advantages of (a) exposure, (b) access and timing, and (c) trust (Burt 1992). First, law firms routinely encounter large numbers of clients facing similar challenges, and this broad exposure helps to ensure that lawyer-dealmakers will be a reliable source of referrals, and that lawyer-counselors will be a reliable source of advice. Second, law firms routinely encounter new entrepreneurs at the most preliminary stages of the start-up process,[10] and this early access helps to ensure that lawyer-dealmakers will be able to "sign the freshest talent," and that lawyer-counselors will be able to impart advice while companies are still malleable and receptive (Freeman 1982; Hannan and Freeman 1984). Finally, law firms benefit from a substantial degree of trust, on the part of both community insiders and start-up clients: lawyer-dealmakers are "reputationally bonded" by their ongoing need to preserve a good name within the organizational community; and lawyer-counselors are symbolically sanctified by prevailing institutional accounts of the attorney as personal champion. To put it epigrammatically, your lawyer is yours in a way that your venture capitalist, your EPA inspector, and your auditor will never be yours.

Together, these attributes give law firms access to a privileged niche within the institutional ecology of the emerging organizational community. In the early stages of the structuration process, lawyers find themselves well situated to monitor wide ranges of organizational behaviors, to convey the results of these observations to new companies at times of maximum permeability, and to have this advice received with relatively little skepticism or suspicion. As a result, law firms tend to become interorganizational pollinators and referees of developing community norms, functioning both as trusted advisers to their clients and as authoritative repositories of reputational information about other community members.[11] Over time, as the body of reputational information grows, the law firm's role broadens to include not only counseling and proselytizing but gatekeeping, matchmaking, and dealmaking as well. In conjunction, these activities eventually foster a milieu in which prominent attorneys and core law firms come to hold substantial amounts of intracommunal power—both *material* power, based on control over essential resources, and *cultural* power, based on control over central definitions. Legal prominence, then, reflects the structural advantages of a distinctive network position.

Turning finally to the legal parochialism problem, the failure of San Francisco law firms to capture the Silicon Valley market highlights the fact that intermediary organizations are not exogenous actors in the structuration process, but are, themselves, subject to the pressures of competitive selection and social construction. In many ways, the leading law offices of San Francisco and of Palo Alto compose distinct organizational populations. Like many big-city law firms, San Francisco's dominant legal actors are relatively large, formal entities, adapted to operating within a stable "climax" community. Oriented toward a Fortune 500 clientele, these firms often lack the perceptual apparatus needed to "see" (and the flexibility needed to serve) the kinds of small start-ups that emerge in less structured environments. In contrast, Silicon Valley's indigenous law firms more closely resemble traditional suburban practices: in suburban settings, even the most prominent law firms interact regularly with small, high-mortality organizations, and a client who does business from a garage or a kitchen table poses no particular cognitive challenges. Further, prestige in suburban firms rests primarily on involvement in the local business community rather than isolation in the legal stratosphere. Speaking regularly to the Rotarians counts for almost as much as speaking regularly to the Court of Appeals. Finally, the internal structures of suburban firms tend to favor the rapid, flexible exploitation of new opportunities, rather than the reliable, efficient exploitation of existing clienteles.

Overall, the evidence from Silicon Valley suggests that, in the birth of new organizational communities, the fates of flagship industries and the fates of ancillary service providers can become intimately intertwined. Although Silicon Valley's indigenous law firms could never have risen to prominence without the impetus of a thriving business community, that business community took its shape, at least in part, from the dealmaking, counseling, gatekeeping, proselytizing, and matchmaking activities of its law firms. Over time, Silicon Valley lawyers have successfully parlayed their initial assets of exposure, access, and trust into an important and lucrative linking-pin role in the institutional ecology of organizational reproduction and community structuration. But in the process, the practices of these lawyers have also come to reflect Silicon Valley's unique configuration of industrial, financial, and legal forces. The story of the Silicon Valley bar may be only one subplot in the larger history of the region; however, it is a part that both recapitulates and integrates the whole. In building a stable niche for itself, the Silicon Valley bar has also constructed a lasting foundation for the industry around it, and in shaping its environment, the Silicon Valley bar has ultimately reshaped itself.

CHAPTER FIVE

Venture Capital in Silicon Valley: Fueling New Firm Formation

MARTIN KENNEY AND

RICHARD FLORIDA

> Very few people understand why what works here and in Boston works. It's very difficult to clone those environments. Too many people think that the criticality in the environment is the money. For me the criticality in the environment are the entrepreneurs.
> —Donald Valentine (1988), venture capitalist
> and founder of Sequoia Capital

For the last two decades, the San Francisco Bay Area has been home to the largest concentration of venture capital in the world and the recipient of the greatest amount of investments. In the second quarter of 1998, Silicon Valley firms garnered $1.25 billion (33 percent of total investments) of the total U.S. venture capital investment of $3.74 billion, which was more than the next four regions combined (Pricewaterhouse 1998). This was not always the case. Until the late 1950s, an entrepreneur in the San Francisco Bay Area depended on informal investors for small-scale funding. For larger sums the entrepreneur had to appeal to East Coast financiers. However, the successes and new opportunities generated by high-technology firms established in the Bay Area offered local financiers the opportunity to become an organized, self-conscious group (Reiner 1989). Through their praxis and success in investing in fledgling firms and in a dialectic with other actors, such as entrepreneurs, lawyers, and investment banks, the institutional mechanisms of venture capital were created.

In contrast to other concentrations of venture capital, such as New York City and Chicago, in Silicon Valley (as in Boston) venture capital evolved in tandem with its technological and entrepreneurial base (Florida and Kenney 1988a, 1988b). Successes spurred the growth of venture capital, and, by the mid-1970s, this crystallized into a virtuous circle with success encouraging greater investment and vice versa. To be sure, while the secular tendency has been growth there have been repeated cyclical downturns always followed by massive growth spurts. Thus for a time the entrepreneurial opportunities appear exhausted, but repeatedly a new technological wave emerges creating even greater wealth than previous waves.

A number of the other chapters have underscored the critical role that venture capitalists play in the portion of Silicon Valley economy dedicated to creating new firms. The contemporary practice of venture investing is the result of an accretion of path-dependent changes that evolved on the basis not only of the activities of the earlier venture capitalists but also in a generative dance with other constituents in the community (see other chapters in this book).[1] Venture capital is now an institutional feature of Silicon Valley and a critical node in a network of institutions that evolved to encourage new firm formation.

Venture Capital

The birth, evolution, and formalization of venture capital is predicated upon one fundamental fact, namely that in aggregate the firms funded have generated sufficient capital gains to support an ongoing specialized institution dedicated to financing them. In most business fields innovations generate new economic opportunities, however generally these opportunities, especially if they are incremental, are exploited within existing firms.[2] In the past, radical innovations opened new economic spaces creating turbulence and opportunities to build firms that exhibited explosive growth. Invariably a dominant design would emerge and the entire sector and even its infrastructure would stabilize. After this stabilization, few firms are established (Anderson and Tushman 1990; Tushman and Anderson 1986). Because of this pattern, any venture capital–like entities whose survival was based on financing new firms had little opportunity to sustain themselves. Organizational survival and growth are predicated upon an ability to garner and utilize resources with some measure of persistence. The institutionalization of an economic function by definition implies the development of a routine. In many cases, the establishment of a dominant design truncates the ability to continue the new firm formation process. The economic opportunities afforded by the innovations no longer offer significant opportunities for capital gains, thus precluding the growth of institutions predicated upon such gains.

In the postwar era, the new electronics industry had a significantly different character from most previous industries. This is because even as one electronics sector stabilized with a dominant design, a stable set of market participants, and a predictable incremental trajectory, new sectors appeared or the dominant design experienced significant disruptions, often due to the invention of new business models.[3] It was these repeated bursts of innovation, which repeatedly lowered entry barriers, made previous products obsolete, and spawned new classes of products, that created an environment conducive to the formation of the institution of venture capital. In contrast to the earlier pattern of one dramatic innovation followed by a set of smaller incremental product or process innovations, there has been an intermittent but regular flow of innovations in electronics and, to a significant but lesser degree, the biomedical research field. Some innovations, such as the semiconductor, the personal computer, and the Internet, were transformative. Others, such as telephone call automation systems, were less pervasively significant. Also, there were derivative innovations, such as semiconductor design software and production equipment, hard disk drive components, and so forth, around which fast-growing businesses also could be built. The ability to capture the value of these innovations offered the potential for enormous capital gains for investors able to discern the right technology, market, or entrepreneur.

In return for their investment, venture capitalists become partial owners. Because of their relatively large ownership positions (ideally, from their perspective, greater than 50 percent), they become partners in the firm. Invariably, venture capitalists demand representation on the firm's board of directors and, in some cases, even become the chairman of the board. Venture capitalists are a special type of partner, because they must dispose of their stake in the firm to distribute to their limited partner investors. So their aim is to dramatically multiply the value of their investment. Because of the equity stake, the venture capitalist is in a different position than is a banker making a loan. The banker has no potential for capital gains but could lose the entire loan. With a limited upside and the same potential downside, a banker is far more risk-averse. The venture capitalists' downside risk is limited to their investment and any follow-on investments, while the potential gains are unlimited (Bygrave and Timmons 1992; Gorman and Sahlman 1989; Zider 1998).

As partners by virtue of their equity, the venture capitalists demand direct input into critical firm decisions, though normal operational decisions are left to the management team. As partners, venture capitalists actively try to affect the outcome of their investments by offering advice, providing contacts ranging from law firms and commercial real estate brokers to potential customers, assisting in corporate recruiting, and various other tasks. Regis McKenna, a high-tech marketing expert and venture investor, described the role of the venture capitalist:

The network of supporting infrastructure in Silicon Valley is the most sophisticated outside Wall Street. The catalyst for that network is the venture capital community, which has evolved to become a strategic planner, management consultant, and corporate watchdog. The network is put to work for new companies and many members of the network have been well honed on dozens of startups. . . . In fact, one of the reasons . . . many companies do succeed is because the network goes to work to help companies survive: they help them find new customers, they help them do refinancing, they help them find new managers if necessary, they help them merge with other companies to be successful. (U.S. Congress 1984)

Veteran venture capitalists have witnessed firsthand the difficulties and transitions that fast-growing firms experience. Often they can provide advice, or even introduce the entrepreneur to other entrepreneurs who experienced similar situations. If the firm faces severe difficulties and they have majority stock ownership, they will replace the firm's executive team. Ultimately, a venture capitalist's loyalty is not to the entrepreneur but rather to their investment.

Venture investing is risky when considered from the perspective of individual investments, but the risk is mitigated by the fact that a venture capital partnership invests in a large number of firms. The venture capitalist's dilemma is to balance between errors of omission, not investing when one should, and errors of commission, investing when one should not. A rule of thumb is that for every ten investments, three are complete losses; another three or four neither succeed nor fail, from which it is difficult to extract the original investment; another two or three return three or more times the initial investment; and one or, perhaps, two investments return more than ten times the initial investment. In effect, the gains from the home runs cover all losses. The larger the number of quality investments, the greater the possibility of funding one of the home runs. Frequently, the greatest successes are those in which the market growth is unforeseen by other investors, because, if success can be foreseen, the true value of the firm can be judged and a correct valuation can be placed upon the opportunity. Of course, it is also true that those "foreseeing" the future have a substantial probability of failure.[4]

The organizational form through which most, but not all, venture capitalists operate is the limited partnership. The limited partners, institutions such as university endowments, pension funds, and wealthy individuals, provide the capital, though the general partners are also expected to invest in their fund so that they have their own money at risk. The general partners—that is, the venture capitalists—receive an annual management fee of between 2 and 3 percent of the total capital and approximately 20 percent of the capital gains after the investors' initial investment has been returned. Thus the emphasis in the partnership is to invest for two or three years and then nurture the investments until liquidation.

Venture capitalists receive an enormous number of business plans and fund only a very few. Usually, those funded arrive through recommendations. After receiving a business plan, the venture capitalists thoroughly investigate the team members' backgrounds, the technology, and the market. Particularly, prior to the megafunds, initial investments were undertaken by a syndicate of venture capitalists. The venture capitalists acquire equity in the firm and in discussion with management establish various intermediate goals, such as the development of a working prototype to be reached prior to receiving further rounds of investment. During the start-up phase, the firm often has no income and is spending money to establish itself. This makes a continuing influx of investment funds necessary for survival. Should the firm's business unfold as planned, it will grow very rapidly, and in less than seven years it should be able to make a public stock offering or be sold to another company. At this point the venture capitalists will distribute either the cash proceeds or the equity in the now public company to the limited partners.

Before Organized Venture Capital

The provision of "risk capital" is not unique to the postwar United States, having been practiced by European and Asian merchants and no-bility for hundreds, if not thousands, of years in long-distance trading ventures. Even before the dawn of capitalistic enterprises, wealthy persons (often merchants) were willing to invest in business start-ups promising significant capital gains.[5] Traditionally, an entrepreneur establishing a firm tapped informal sources, such as family, friends, and wealthy individuals (who are now called "angels"). Financial institutions, such as banks or stockbrokers, generally were not organized to take risks on firms with little or no collateral. Even investment bankers such as the Morgans rarely invested in ideas, preferring to wait until the firm was operating and growing before making a financial commitment. A somewhat more organized effort to find firms emerged in the 1930s as some wealthy families such as the Rockefellers and Whitneys began regularly investing family funds in new firms (Liles 1977; Wilson 1985).

In 1946 a group of Boston civic leaders formed the first nonfamily venture capital organization, American Research and Development (ARD), with the express purpose of funding entrepreneurial firms in the New England area. ARD's first president was a Harvard Business School professor, General Georges Doriot, who taught a widely acclaimed course on entrepreneurship. ARD had a unique ownership structure composed of initial investments by wealthy individuals and then a stock offering on the New York Stock Exchange. ARD's early investments were a combination of debt and equity. In its first two and a half decades, ARD contributed a number of venture capitalists to the Boston area. After funding a wide variety of ventures, ARD achieved great success due to its investments in Digital Equipment Corporation and a number of other high-technology firms, many of which were related to MIT.

Prior to World War II, in the San Francisco Bay Area there was a history of wealthy local individuals financing electronics start-ups (see Sturgeon in this volume). For example, in the mid-1920s, Philo Farnsworth's pioneering attempts to develop a television were funded by a group of wealthy individuals connected with the Crocker National Bank. They provided $25,000 and laboratory space in return for 60 percent of the equity in Farnsworth's venture.[6] In 1931, after Farnsworth finally transmitted a picture, the backers decided to sell Farnsworth's Television Laboratories, Inc., to the Philadelphia Storage Battery Company (which would be renamed Philco), and the entire operation was moved to Philadelphia (Fisher and Fisher 1996). In this case, neither the investors nor Farnsworth experienced significant capital gains.

World War II transformed California from a relatively undeveloped economy into a state boasting a significant number of electronics and aerospace firms (Markusen et al. 1991). In a remarkable similarity to the New England area, during World War II and in the years immediately following, there were concerns in California about a shortage of risk capital for innovative new enterprises. While leading Californians recognized the need to develop mechanisms to fund start-ups, there was less discussion of the civic aspects of venture capital and entrepreneurship that preoccupied East Coast financial elites. In California the main concern was to develop alternatives to what many assumed would be a sharp recession after the end of the war (Reiner 1989).

The California State Reconstruction and Reemployment Commission commissioned a report by a University of California professor, Paul Wendt (1947), on "the availability of capital to small business in California." Wendt's report reflected and reinforced concerns about capital shortages. Wendt described the situation thus:

The market for equity capital for the small enterprise in California is predominantly local and informal in character. Investment bankers, who occupy a key position in furnishing equity and loan capital to large corporations, are an unimportant source of equity capital to the small concern. Consequently, equity funds are obtained through investment of owners' savings and sale of stock privately to friends, relatives, and associates. (Wendt 1947)

His report quotes McMicking, a venture investor in tape recording pioneer Ampex, to the effect that it was difficult to purchase equity in the small electronics companies, such as Varian or Hewlett Packard, because they had little need for outside investors (Reiner 1989). These firms grew by not paying dividends and reinvesting retained earnings. Note the important point, the entrepreneurs were not seeking capital and, conversely, there was only a limited amount of capital.

While the Wendt report highlighted the early venture capital efforts of the Rockefeller Brothers, J. H. Whitney and Co., and ARD, it also described two privately held venture investment companies in California: Industrial Capital Corporation and Pacific Coast Enterprises Corporation. The Industrial Capital Corporation was formed in 1946 with $2 million in capital by five businessmen who had been involved in privately financing small businesses in California. One of these businessmen, Edward Heller, who would become something of a grandfather of California venture capital, had worked with Boston's Ralph Flanders, an early advocate of venture capital and an important principal in the founding of ARD. Pacific Coast Enterprises Corporation was founded in 1946 with $1 million in capital, made loans of between $5,000 and $100,000, and provided managerial assistance to the enterprises it financed. According to one of its directors, Pacific Coast generated better results "with established concerns than with new enterprises," and with loans that carried the privilege of stock purchase rather than by purchasing equity directly (Wendt 1947). These two small firms should be seen as West Coast precursors to venture capital.

In summary, in the aftermath of World War II the San Francisco Bay Area was the home to a number of promising young electronics companies, and there were individuals willing to invest in new ventures. And yet, these relatively scattered and disconnected activities were limited and unorganized. There is reason to believe that similar combinations of entrepreneurs and informal investors existed in other regions. From these beginnings it would have been difficult to envision the Bay Area becoming the innovative locus of the global electronics industry and a hotbed of electronics start-ups and venture capital funds. There was little reason to suppose that an institution, venture capital, entirely based on private funds and dedicated to funding high-technology start-ups, would form. And, if it did form, few would have believed the Bay Area would become the largest concentration.

The Pioneers

Before World War II, and even more so after the war, on the peninsula south of San Francisco, engineers began establishing small companies. Contemporaneously, individuals such as Frank Chambers, a graduate of the Harvard Business School in 1939 and a student of General Doriot's, began investing family funds in Bay Area start-ups. Using personal and borrowed money, Chambers started a company, Magna Power Tools, which made Shopsmith power-woodworking tools, which he later sold to Sears Roebuck. In 1950, he successfully invested in Signboard Trim, and in 1956 he invested in Guardian Packaging (Chambers 1986). Another young investor, Reid Dennis, worked at Fireman's Fund Insurance Company and was able to invest in an early syndicate backing Ampex. These investors and others experienced success and in the process discovered that technology-related firms could pay particularly handsome returns.

In the mid-1950s, some young investors coalesced into an informal network that would later self-consciously call itself "The Group." These young, relatively wealthy individuals began investing collectively in small technology-intensive start-ups in the Palo Alto area. Later, they became key actors in the Silicon Valley venture capital community. The most prominent of these would be Reid Dennis (using the gains from his Ampex investment), William Bryan, William Edwards, William K. Bowes, and Daniel McGanney (Dennis 1986; Edwards 1986).

New firms were being formed and there were a number of informal investors, but there was little organized venture capital in the Bay Area. The exception was the first privately funded California venture capital limited partnership, Draper, Gaither, and Anderson (DGA), which was somewhat successful but closed after one of its major investors, Laurence Rockefeller, withdrew his capital (Wilson 1985). At the national level, some important events would have an impact on the environment for venture investing. First, in 1956 Varian went public and was followed in 1957 by Hewlett Packard. These successful initial public offerings on the New York Stock Exchange demonstrated that there was a market for equity in fast-growing high-technology companies. It also indicated that there were alternatives for small start-ups beyond being purchased by an established East Coast firm. A second and even more significant development was the dramatic increase in federal spending devoted to purchasing high-technology weaponry and gadgets in the wake of Sputnik. This gusher of spending created significant opportunities for small firms to secure lucrative Department of Defense and NASA contracts (for more detail, see Leslie in this volume). These federal agencies had an enormous appetite for the most sophisticated technology, and price was not a barrier. This national environment was highly conducive to the formation and rapid growth of high-technology electronics firms, but start-up growth is often constrained by a need for more capital than entrepreneurs can provide.

In the 1950s the informal venture capitalists had more opportunities than available capital. In 1958 the federal government passed the Small Business Act of 1958, which provided up to $300,000 in government matching money for $150,000 in investments by a person or institution wishing to establish a Small Business Investment Corporation (SBIC). There were also various tax advantages (Soussou 1985). Almost immediately, SBICs were established throughout the country, and Silicon Valley was no exception. The SBIC program allowed investors to mobilize more capital and reduce risks to their personal funds. In return for the capital they had to adopt stricter standards for evaluating risk and making investments. This was an important first step in the institution-alization of venture investing.

In 1959, Frank Chambers established a publicly held SBIC, Conti-nental Capital Corp. Sutter Hill, which was originally formed as a pri-vately held real estate development firm, began venture capital in-vesting in 1961 and received an SBIC license in 1962. The same year an-other SBIC was formed by Bill Draper, the son of William Draper of DGA and an original associate at DGA, and Franklin "Pitch" Johnson, a former Doriot student at Harvard, who would later become a director of National Venture Capital Association (NVCA). While Sutter Hill all but ignored commercial investing for its first two years, in 1964 the firm acquired the assets of Johnson's and Draper's SBIC and hired Paul Wythes, who would become an influential venture capitalist and a di-rector of the NVCA, to manage its venture investments (Johnson 1986; Wythes 1986).

The members of "The Group" also decided that SBICs would be a good vehicle to leverage their investments, and so Bryan, Edwards, and McGanney started family-funded SBICs in 1962. Dennis remained at Fireman's Fund, which had been purchased by American Express Company, managing their venture capital SBIC, AMEXCO Venture Associates. Financial institutions also established SBICs. For example, in 1959, Bank of America created an SBIC, the Small Business Enter-prise Corporation, headed by Thomas Clauson, who later became the bank's president. So, by the early 1960s there were a relatively large number of SBICs dedicated to investing in high-technology start-ups. In 1962, catalyzed by the long-standing relationships among "The Group," the West Coast SBICs formed the Western Association of Small Business Investment Companies (Saxenian 1994). From 1959 to 1968, the SBICs grew rapidly and became the favored organizational form for venture capital investing, controlling roughly twice as much as the total for all other forms of venture capital (*Venture Capital Yearbook* 1983). This SBIC stage is critically important because it enticed these investors to formalize and professionalize their activity.

At this time, there was no consensus on the optimal organizational vehicle for venture capital. One thing was clear: the individuals in-vesting family funds were giving way to the SBICs with their full-time investors that were evolving into professionals. But there were other experiments, such as the DGA limited partnership. Another common early form of venture capital funding for entrepreneurs came from large corporations wishing to invest in new technologies. Fairchild is a quintessential example of this source. When the eight engineers left Shockley Semiconductor, one of them, Eugene Kleiner, used his family connections to contact Hayden Stone, the East Coast investment bank. The business proposal was forwarded to Arthur Rock, at the time a Hayden Stone investment banker in New York. Rock and his immediate superior visited the start-up and agreed to raise $1.5 million. Rock then approached "about 25 industrial corporations with the idea of setting up a separate division or subsidiary," but they all demurred. Rock then approached Sherman Fairchild, the owner of Fairchild Camera, who agreed to invest $1.5 million with the proviso that Fairchild be allowed to purchase the shares of the eight founders for $300,000 apiece should the venture prove successful (Rock 1989: 15). Within three years, Fairchild bought the founders' shares, and the founders no longer had any equity in the firm. As is well known, almost immediately engineers began to leave Fairchild to launch new firms. Often, these early spin-outs were funded by established firms seeking semiconductor technology, but nearly always the founding technologists demanded and received an equity stake.

Securing the funds for Fairchild Semiconductor piqued Rock's interest in high technology, and he began to look for other investment opportunities. Rock's next success occurred in 1960, when he arranged Litton Industries' investment in a new firm, Teledyne, established by Henry Singleton. In 1961, Arthur Rock relocated from New York to the Bay Area and established an important venture capital partnership with Thomas (Tommy) Davis, a Harvard-educated lawyer and then vice president of Kern County Land Company. Davis wanted to leave the Land Company because it had little interest in high-technology investments, though Davis had already made a successful investment in the high-technology firm, Watkins-Johnson (Davis 1986).[7] Rock and Davis formed a limited partnership, with $3.5 million invested by individuals including Henry Singleton and several of the Fairchild founders (Davis 1986; Edwards 1986; Rock 1988). The Rock and Davis limited partnership was very significant, because a number of successful entrepreneurs, such as Robert Noyce and Gordon Moore, invested, thereby giving them a stake in the success of still more new firms (which Fairchild would deliver in spades). Also, the limited partnership organizational format they adopted would become a model for other venture capitalists. In 1965, Franklin Johnson of the Draper and Johnson Investment Company used his gains to form Asset Management Company, a hugely successful venture fund that invested in Coherent, California Microwave, Cromatronix, Boole and Babbage, Accurex (a spin-out from a company he and Draper initially invested in), and SBE. Many of the other early partnerships were very successful. For example, $10 million in investments by Sutter Hill returned $100 million (Wythes 1986). According to one source, nearly all of the venture capitalists that invested and survived this period generated enormous returns by the early 1970s.

The process of division continued throughout the 1960s. In 1968, Rock and Davis did not renew their partnership. Rock brought in C. Richard Kramlich, who was working at an East Coast investment firm as a partner (Kramlich 1995). Tommy Davis formed the very important partnership, the Mayfield Fund, with Wally Davis (no relation), an aeronautical engineer who had started his own firm only to be acquired by the Rockefeller-funded Itek Corporation. The two Davises were introduced by John Wilson, a prominent Palo Alto lawyer who would be the senior partner in the Wilson, Sonsini, Goodrich, and Rosati law firm (WSGR) (Davis 1986). Similarly, Burton McMurtry joined Jack Melchor, who was already investing independently, to form the Palo Alto Investment Company. In 1968, George Quist left the Bank of America's SBIC to join William Hambrecht in establishing Hambrecht and Quist, which would become one of the premier high-technology brokerage firms, and served as the lead agent in many Silicon Valley IPOs (initial public stock offerings). In the late 1960s, William Bryan and William Edwards merged their two family SBICs into the limited partnership, Bryan and Edwards.

In the late 1960s, the SBIC as an organizational vehicle for venture investing fell into disfavor. The reasons for this were multiple. The limited partnership format offered the venture capitalists far greater upside potential. Another important advantage enjoyed by the limited partnership was the ability to mobilize capital from institutional investors. And finally, the rules, regulations, and public disclosure requirements imposed on the SBICs were experienced as a constraint. The SBICs as an organizational form proved to be a critical stage in the creation of a free-standing formal venture capital. After performing this service, the SBICs disappeared as important funders of high-technology firms.

In 1969, Western Association of Small Business Investment Corporations was reorganized into the Western Association of Venture Capitalists (WAVC), with thirty-one voting members. The WAVC list of
voting members compiled in 1970 and 1971 included thirty-nine corporate members and a further sixteen individual members, including important venture capitalists such as Eugene Kleiner and Franklin Johnson. The WAVC (1971) was not confined to local investors: Heizer Corporation, Continental Illinois Venture Corporation (both from Chicago), and Northrup Technology (Los Angeles) were also members, but
the preponderance were from the Bay Area. As was the case with the
WASBIC, the WAVC was formed before there was even a national
venture capital organization (Reiner 1989).

The high rates of returns achieved by Bay Area venture capitalists
attracted still more investors. Many start-ups went public or were acquired, providing the venture capitalists very substantial capital gains.
Also, newly wealthy entrepreneurs and managers were released to become venture capitalists or establish new start-up firms. In other
words, a base of venture capitalists and others sufficiently wealthy and
experienced to nurture spinoffs formed. In addition, East Coast investors, such as the Rockefeller and Whitney family funds, became involved in more Bay Area deals as coinvestors, allowing local venture
capitalists to leverage external funds. These activities also made potential entrepreneurs aware of the fact that investment backing was available.

By the beginning of the 1970s, the limited partnership had become
the standard organizational format for venture capital. Contemporaneously, other legal innovations were developed to facilitate venturing.
An important source of these innovations was the law practice of Wilson, Sonsini, Goodrich, and Rosati, which cultivated a specialty in ca-
tering to start-ups.[8] Working closely with entrepreneurs and venture
capitalists, WSGR developed the legal mechanisms in contracts to protect both the entrepreneurs and the venture capitalists in a new start-
up. One innovation was to provide entrepreneurs with a greater ownership stake. This came from the recognition that the arrangement at
Fairchild Semiconductor did not create an adequate reward structure
for the highly mobile engineers. When Robert Noyce and Gordon
Moore left Fairchild in 1968 to form Intel, they worked with WSGR to
devise a stock ownership plan, and this became the model for later
venture capital–backed start-ups. Eugene Kleiner (1988), explained the

situation this way:

When Fairchild financed us, they gave us one hundred percent ownership of the company. But, they reserved the right to buy the company back at a predetermined price. Once they exercised that option, once they bought back the company, they were slow to give out options. That's one reason people left. That was also about the time, John Wilson [of Wilson Sonsini] began developing plans to give entrepreneurs ownership.

By the end of the 1960s the institutions and incentive systems that created the framework for Silicon Valley's future growth were established. The limited partnership was becoming the dominant investment vehicle, and large financial institutions were willing to invest as limited partners. The principle that the entrepreneurs should retain a significant share of the total equity in their firm was recognized. Finally, in the 1960s many future leaders of the venture capital community learned the discipline.

Expansion and Growth

The number of venture capitalists increased dramatically from 1968 to 1975, as approximately thirty new or reconstituted venture capital operations were established in Silicon Valley. This growth occurred through a complex process of division as existing venture capital funds spawned spinoff funds and entrepreneurial enterprises released managers who became venture capitalists. Through a complex, but cumulative, process this gave rise to more funds.

The process of proliferation is illustrated by the following examples. In 1974, Reid Dennis left AMEXCO and cofounded Institutional Venture Associates with Burton McMurtry of Palo Alto Investment. Two years later, Institutional Venture Associates split into two partnerships: McMurtry's Technology Venture Associates and Dennis's Institutional Venture Partners. In 1977, C. Richard Kramlich's partnership with Arthur Rock ended and Kramlich (1995) formed New Enterprise Associates with two friends from T. Rowe Price. Rock continued as a private investor. Other new funds, such as California Northwest Fund and WestVen Management, also formed during this period.

The Silicon Valley venture capital community also grew by attracting the offices of venture funds headquartered elsewhere. In 1968, Neill Brownstein established the Palo Alto office of the East Coast venture capital firm Bessemer Securities. In 1973, Citicorp, the giant New York bank, opened a venture capital office in Silicon Valley (Wegmann 1986). In 1979, Adler & Company of New York established an office in Silicon Valley. In 1983, two Adler partners, James Swartz (1995) and Arthur Patterson, spun off to create the bicoastal firm Accel Partners, having offices in New Jersey and Silicon Valley. The proximate cause for this was that in the 1960s, East Coast firms such as Venrock and J. H. Whitney were able to join California deals at a relatively early stage and low valuations, because their deep pockets and strong connections to Wall Street were needed by the undercapitalized West Coast venture capitalists. But the growing supply of venture capital in the Bay Area, the rise of boutique investment firms such as Robertson Coleman and Hambrecht and Quist, able to manage an initial public offering, and the increasing pace of investment made it more difficult for East Coast firms to participate in the best deals at good valuations. Since entrepreneurs could easily secure funding from the firms within driving distance, there was less need to travel to New York or Boston, unless Silicon Valley venture capitalists were unwilling to fund the start-up—an event that did occur in the early 1980s.[9] As a result, the establishment of West Coast branches was imperative for investors desiring access to the best opportunities—and this meant still more capital flowing into Silicon Valley.

In the 1970s, some firm managers and executives started joining venture capital partnerships as general partners. Thomas Perkins of Kleiner, Perkins, Caufield, and Byers (KPCB) believes that he and Eugene Kleiner were the "first industry guys to go into venture capital" (*Red Herring* 1994). Moreover, Perkins feels the presence of experienced managers among Silicon Valley venture capitalists is a unique regional strength.[10] KPCB, one of the most successful venture capital partnerships in history, is an example. Eugene Kleiner, one of the Fairchild founding eight, was asked to participate in the Davis and Rock fund as an investor and as a limited partner called upon to help evaluate deals. Later, when Henry Hillman, the Pittsburgh millionaire, asked Tommy Davis to manage his Silicon Valley venture capital investments, Davis declined and recommended Kleiner. Hillman talked with Kleiner and agreed to invest $4 million. Kleiner then called Sanford Robertson, a cofounder of the investment bank Robertson Coleman, to raise another $4 million. Robertson agreed to help and recommended that Kleiner meet Thomas Perkins, who wanted to leave Hewlett Packard and start a venture capital partnership. In 1972, Kleiner and Perkins began operations (Kleiner 1988).

Another very important Fairchild alumni was Donald Valentine, formerly a Fairchild marketing executive, who in 1972 formed the venture capital limited partnership Capital Management Services, which later became Sequoia Capital. The initial capital of $7 million was contributed by a Los Angeles money management firm, Capital Research and Management, now known as the Capital Group (Valentine 1988). Valentine's first investment was Atari, which needed money to enter the home video game market. In 1976, Warner Communications bought Atari for $30 million, and Sequoia quadrupled its original $600,000 investment in less than two years. In 1976, Valentine participated in the financing of Apple Computer. In this case, Steve Jobs was referred to Valentine by Nolan Bushnell, the founder of Atari, and Regis McKenna, the high-tech marketer (Butcher 1989: 108–10). This case illustrates very clearly that networks of human relationships and referrals were and continue to be central to the venture capital practice.

The venture capital arms of banks and financial institutions continued to operate in Silicon Valley. But perhaps their most important impact was that they proved to be training grounds for inexperienced venture capitalists. It was almost impossible for a bank to provide a large enough salary to compensate for the large capital gains a venture capitalist could earn in a successful limited partnership. So, after learning the craft, the bank's venture capitalists formed their own limited partnership. For example, seven individuals left Bank of America's SBIC, five of those in 1979–80, to form new partnerships. New York–based Citicorp, already experiencing defections, had to cope with even more after it opened a West Coast office in 1973. The president of Citicorp Venture Capital Ltd. was reported as saying that twenty-three Citicorp alumni had become independent venture capitalists in Silicon Valley (Dougery 1986; Swartz 1995; Wegmann 1986). Although banks continued venture capital investing, they became increasingly marginal to the overall industry.

The health of the venture capital industry is dependent upon exogenous forces, including the stock market, government regulations, and the perceptions among institutional investors. These factors contribute to the cyclical nature of the venture capital business. For example, 1968 was an excellent IPO market, but the early and mid-1970s were a difficult period. One factor was an effort to curb abuse of employee pension funds by tightening the rules for pension fund investments in the Employee Retirement Income Security Act (ERISA), passed in 1974. The tightened rules made pension fund managers wary of high-risk investments. The difficulties in fundraising were evident in 1975, when only $10 million was raised for new investment (Galante 1996). Because of this, even successful companies such as KLA Instruments, the semiconductor equipment manufacturer, had difficulty securing financing (Levy 1988).

Two major changes in public policy had a significant positive impact on the environment for venture investing during the late 1970s. The first was congressional action to reduce the capital gains tax rate from 49.5 to 28 percent, a change that was strongly supported by venture capitalists and by the American Electronics Association (Siegel and Borock 1982). As a consequence of this change, entrepreneurs and investors could retain more of their capital gains, making equity investing more attractive. Second, the Department of Labor eased the ERISA fiduciary responsibility guidelines for pension funds, alleviating fund managers' concerns about investing in venture capital partnerships (McMurtry 1986). These changes made venture investing more attractive and increased the pool of funds from which venture capitalists could draw. Pension funds, once again, invested and quickly replaced banks, corporations, and wealthy individuals as the leading source for venture capital. This meant that Silicon Valley venture capitalists could attract far larger sums of capital, and the size of partnerships grew, culminating in the formation of the venture capital megafunds.

The huge inflow of resources had important impacts on Silicon Valley venture capitalists. The new sources of capital allowed Silicon Valley venture capitalists more leverage in their relationships with East Coast investors. In return for their capital, the pension funds demanded greater accountability and more formal interactions than did wealthy individuals. Personal contacts with wealthy individuals and trust among investors diminished in importance, and fundraising evolved into a process of making formal presentations to major financial institutions and pension funds. Successful fundraising became more dependent upon benchmarking the performance of previous funds, as pension funds needed justifications for their investments. In other words, the investment track record became far more important. As Eugene Kleiner explained it:

The late 1970s opened up the pension funds, and we got a lot of money. All of a sudden we were very pushed into attempting large amounts of money. In my first fund, for instance, we did not have any pension funds. We only had insurance money and university endowment money, but now it's all pension money. They like to amass confidence in a prudent track record. So the track record became very significant. (Kleiner 1988)

Changes in federal law on taxes and pension fund regulations were not the entire story. The returns on investments made in the 1970s were astonishing, and some of the public stock offerings of venture capital–financed firms attracted widespread public interest. For example, Apple Computer was one of the most successful venture capital investments of the era. The initial round of Apple investments in January 1978 included Venrock, $288,000 (or 9.6 percent); Sequoia Capital, $150,000 (5 percent); and Arthur Rock, $57,600 (1.92 percent), giving Apple a total valuation of $3 million. After subsequent investment rounds, Venrock's stake of less than $1 million was worth $129.3 million when Apple went public in December 1980. Rock's investment had increased to $21.8 million (Moritz 1984: 277–78). What such success could mean for a fund was equally impressive. As an example, take the case of Kleiner Perkins. The original Kleiner Perkins fund, started in 1972, had annualized returns of nearly 40 percent per annum through 1977; the next two Kleiner Perkins funds were similarly successful.

In the 1970s there was a geographic shift in the location of the venture capitalists' offices. Originally, many offices were in the San Francisco financial district, but in the 1970s many moved to Palo Alto to be closer to the entrepreneurs. In 1972 a local developer built three buildings at 3000 Sand Hill Road but was having difficulty securing tenants. Thomas Perkins was looking for office space for his partnership with Eugene Kleiner, and he decided to locate at 3000 Sand Hill Road.[11] After that the developer concentrated on attracting more venture capitalists, and soon members of "The Group"—Reid Dennis, William Bryan, and William Edwards—leased office space. Other important venture capital firms such as New Enterprise Associates and Menlo Ventures relocated, either at 3000 or other addresses on Sand Hill Road. By the late 1980s, Sand Hill Road was home to more than two dozen venture capital firms, making it the largest single enclave of venture capital in the United States (Wilson 1985: 49–50).[12]

The 1970s were eventful years for venture capital in Silicon Valley, which survived an incredible investment drought and a changing investment environment. The limited partnership had become the preferred organizational form, and many of today's largest and most successful partnerships were established. The physical locus of the industry was now concentrated in the vicinity of Stanford University on Sand Hill Road. Most important, what had been an inchoate group of investors, were by 1980 a self-conscious, identifiable group of specialized financial intermediaries.

The 1980s: Continuing Growth and the Megafunds

The 1980s began with major successes for venture capitalists. At the beginning of the 1980s there was an extremely strong IPO market led by Genentech and Apple Computer. The revival of the IPO market and the huge returns generated by funds such as KPCB I and II, Mayfield, IVP, and Technology Venture Associates further heightened interest in venture capital. In response, many new funds were raised. Between 1978 and 1982, more than fifty new or follow-on venture capital funds were established in the Silicon Valley/San Francisco area (*Venture Capital Journal* 1980, 1981, 1982). In July 1980 the *Venture Capital Journal* began publication, indicating that there was sufficient interest to support a dedicated monthly journal. *Forbes* described the environment this way: "[We] are in the midst of the greatest boom in new-stock issues and new-company formations since the late 1960s" (Merwin 1981: 60–68). Pension funds were eager to invest. This resulted in the formation of new partnerships and large numbers of new firm financings.

During the 1980s still more venture capitalists headquartered elsewhere opened Silicon Valley offices. Other East Coast firms inaugurated branches in the Bay Area, including TA Associates (1982), J. H. Whitney (1983), Greylock (1983), L. F. Rothschild (1983), and General Electric Venture Capital (1983). Conversely, it should be noted that most major Silicon Valley venture capital firms did not feel compelled to open branches in other regions.

In keeping with the traditional venture capital cycle, overinvestment in a number of sectors, such as hard disk drives (HDDs) and proprietary computer systems, followed and resulted in the collapse of many start-ups (for HDDs, see Bygrave and Timmons 1992). The list of disastrous deals in the 1980s is long and includes Plexus Computers, Momenta, Dynabook Technologies, MasPar Computer, Go Corporation, ON Technologies, Stellar Computer, Ardent Computer, and a number of other companies. The excess investment was the result of too much capital chasing too few deals; company valuations were too high, making failures even more expensive. So, for example, in the case of Plexus Computer, total losses were approximately $36 million. The result was that many second-tier venture capital firms were unable to float follow-on funds, and the industry experienced a significant shakeout.

During the 1980s the trend that had begun at the end of the 1970s, namely, that successful partnerships were able to attract even larger sums of capital, continued. For example, even before Kleiner Perkins ended in 1983, the partnership added Frank Caufield and Brook Byers. KPCB launched KPCB I in 1978, KPCB II in 1980, and KPCB III in 1983. Mayfield, Sutter Hill, and other partnerships launched new partnerships securing even greater sums. In fact, many of these top-drawer partnerships are perennially oversubscribed and must turn away investors. Thus, the venture capital "megafunds" pyramided one fund upon another. In 1988, Art Rock described this process:

Business is gradually changing because of the amount of money that venture capital funds have raised for the last 7 or 8 years. With the megafunds they have to get that money invested, and as a result I think the venture capitalists are becoming more portfolio managers than actually venture capitalists. . . . There are all these funds, all these monies available in all these funds, it's just literally impossible to spend much time with the companies. . . . If you have 3 or 4 partners you don't have much time to spend with each company. . . . The venture capital companies need to show some results to keep on raising their money, so they keep on pushing the companies. (Personal interview with Rock 1988)

The megafunds had greater funds to invest but added only a few new partners. Therefore they needed larger deals. The earlier pattern of coinvestment became somewhat attenuated because a single partnership could now undertake a deal solo, though coinvestment continued to be the rule. As a result, doing small seed deals of less than $1 million was difficult because of the pressure to invest larger sums.

The difficult environment of the late 1980s took its toll as relatively large partnerships, such as Arscott, Norton and Associates and Dougery, Jones and Wilder, did not raise follow-on funds and were liquidated. Even successful funds such as KPCB experienced depressed returns. For example, KPCB IV had annualized returns of less than 30 percent. When there were downturns in the stock market and it was difficult to do IPOs, the Silicon Valley venture capitalists usually were more severely affected because the East Coast funds were more likely to be involved in financing non–start-up transactions such as leveraged buyouts and mergers.

The higher valuations and pressure to invest made it more difficult to secure good returns. As one venture capitalist said, "Producing a 40% return on investment in a $10 million fund does not require genius. Producing the same return in a $100 million fund needs a superheroic effort" (Gupta 1985: 38). The difficulties were so severe that some portfolio firms were taken public at lower valuations than their last private placement. So, for example, in May 1984, Lam Research, a semiconductor equipment-maker that proved to be very successful, was taken public at $10 per share, which was lower than its private placement in September 1983 (Gupta 1985).

The emergence of the megafunds created the economic space for the establishment of "seed funds" concentrating on seed-stage investments. One of the first venture capitalists to create a fund specifically targeted at seed-stage deals was Wally Davis (1988), who left the very successful Mayfield Fund in 1982 because he believed it had too much money and undertook too many deals, thereby preventing him from nurturing smaller portfolio firms. Davis recruited two partners and raised $17 million for his new fund, Alpha Partners I. As part of its seed strategy, Alpha Partners invested alone and rarely syndicated its deals. The average Alpha investment was $750,000. If the funded firm grew, then other venture capitalists were offered an opportunity to invest at a higher valuation. Alpha II raised $22 million in 1984. In 1988, describing the greater risk experienced in seed-stage investment, Davis (ibid.) said, "[H]alf of the money is lost, so you have to have big winners to make up for the rest." By 1988, Alpha's investment maximum had been increased to $1.5 million because of the high valuations that even seed-stage firms received (ibid.; Wilson 1985). In the mid-1980s other seed-stage funds established in the Bay Area included Crosspoint Ventures and Onset Partners.

In an attempt to deal with the sheer scale of the megafunds, a hierarchy of general partners, partners, and associates was established. Some megafunds actually appointed a partner dedicated to handling personnel recruitment. The creation of functional specialists as opposed to industrial-sector specialists was abandoned by the early 1990s, though recently the role of functional specialists has been revived due to the superheated environment of the late 1990s, when management talent again became a limiting factor for start-ups. In general, it was far more efficient to out-source recruitment to executive search firms than to have a dedicated partner handle this task. It was more effective to draw upon the specialized infrastructure of Silicon Valley than to internalize it inside a partnership. Venture capitalists were more effective at making investments than undertaking other tasks—ultimately capital gains were generated by money invested. At the end of the 1980s, the first-generation venture capitalists were withdrawing from active management to be replaced by more junior partners. For venture capital partnerships there are always more applicants than openings. One difficult issue to resolve concerns the source of venture capitalists; should it be newly minted MBAs or managers from high-technology firms? This debate is unresolved, but a constant criticism of venture capital has been the role of newly minted MBAs. Nonetheless, these transitions have been remarkably successful at the top funds. At some of the other funds, the success of the transitions was less clear.

In the 1980s the sheer mass of venture capital available continued to grow, but, what is more important, the industry continued to mature. The megafunds contributed to a further professionalization of the venture investing. Also, a hierarchy of venture funds had been established. The smaller and less prestigious funds would turn over, but the first-rank funds remained roughly the same. And yet, the hierarchy of Silicon Valley venture capital funds was not static; new funds such as Mohr Davidow Ventures and Accel Ventures entered the first tier. It seems likely that the rise of the Internet will create new entrants to the top tier. Still, by the end of the 1980s the venture capital practice had become a routinized practice for coping with admittedly unpredictable investments.

The 1990s

The difficulties at the end of the 1980s persisted into the early 1990s because the IPO market was moribund, and the unwise investments of the 1980s continued to be liquidated. If the conditions of the early 1990s had persisted, the entire venture capital community might have been in dire straits, but in the mid-1990s the stock market shifted and became more receptive to IPOs. And, most important, the commercialization of the Internet offered enormous new opportunities for firm creation (see Kenney and Curry 1999).

The megafunds continued to grow in importance. Whereas in 1987, the previous peak in fundraising, 105 firms raised $4 billion, in 1994 only 80 funds raised $3.8 billion and only 8 funds captured 25 percent of the total. In the first six months of 1995 approximately half of the $1.5 billion went to six funds, each of which received more than $100 million in capital (Jensen and Fulton 1996). Despite the growth in megafunds, numerous smaller funds continued to operate, thus providing ample alternatives to the megafunds.

The cycle that venture capital experiences once again played itself out, going from feast to famine and back to feast. Each cycle purges less effective venture capital partnerships and their unwise investments while providing openings for new entrants. Often, the short-term and less experienced investors, such as banks and large corporations focused on quarterly results, are the most vulnerable. Not surprisingly, history indicates that the venture capitalists able to invest in the depths of the downturn secure better valuations and are those most able to exploit the next recovery.

The megafunds with large capital bases made it possible for venture capitalists to limit their dependence upon coinvestors, at least in comparison with earlier periods. Large megafunds such as KPCB are capable of providing all of the funding necessary for a start-up. In the eyes of some veteran Silicon Valley venture capitalists, this contributed to a shift toward heightened competition and an erosion of earlier patterns of cooperation and collaboration. Franklin (Pitch) Johnson, cofounder of Asset Management Co., observed: "In the early days, there was not a lot of capital around. We welcomed other investors and you could call around and get into any deal you wanted to. There was competition, but there wasn't enough capital to be really that competitive. The way competition is now, people do create deals; it's not always easy to get in another deal" (Deger 1995: 34).

Despite this erosion, the vast majority of venture capitalists continue to coinvest. These changes are related to the increased institutionalization that has taken place. Also, the relative power balance between venture capitalists and entrepreneurs has shifted to the entrepreneurs. According to Paul Wythes of Sutter Hill:

I think today the industry is much more institutionalized, much more structured than it was in 1964. In 1964, or in that time frame, we could find a wonderful entrepreneur or group of entrepreneurs that were starting a company and husband them or warehouse them with the idea that they would do an investment with you, Sutter Hill, and not talk with any other venture firms, because there were very [few] venture firms.

If you're talking about somebody around here today, [the entrepreneur can] go [to] a lot of places to raise his money; so you don't end up being able to warehouse a deal like you could in 1964. Ergo, it's much more competitive, a very much more competitive business than it used to be. (ibid.)

The late 1990s were a superheated investment environment, especially in the Internet field. The enormous successes in Internet funding prompted the entry of many nontraditional sources of start-up funding. For example, wealthy individuals, or "angels," reappeared as a significant source of funding. One group of informal investors actually has been institutionalized under the moniker "Band of Angels." Also, a few publicly listed firms, such as CMGI, Inc., located in the Boston area, have become major venture capital investors in Internet start-ups. Other organizations, such as Masayoshi Son's Softbank, and Idealab, a privately held idea creation organization and venture fund, have successfully begun investing in Internet start-ups. The point here is not that these institutions are replacing conventional venture capital funds, but rather that they offer competition. The ultimate outcome of these new forms is difficult to predict, but they are an important indication of the continuing innovation in investment models.

Discussion

Silicon Valley played a critical role in the evolution of the modern venture capital system, and, conversely, the local venture capital community contributed to the making of Silicon Valley. Venture capital in Silicon Valley grew by a process of combination, division, and incessant networking. Successful enterprises gave rise to wealthy entrepreneurs who would become venture capitalists, and existing venture capital funds gave rise to new venture funds in a virtuous cycle of investment, growth, and capital accumulation. In this sense, venture capital in Silicon Valley developed far more organically than did a similar community in Boston, where financial institutions and the strategic efforts of key elites played an important formative role.

Silicon Valley venture capitalists adapted and perfected what is arguably the single most important organizational innovation of the modern venture capital system—the limited partnership model. Lacking a substantial base of finance capital like New York, Boston, or Chicago, Silicon Valley venture capitalists use the limited partnership as a vehicle to mobilize funds from institutional investors, while providing the opportunity for the venture capitalists to benefit handsomely from their successes through the carried interest provision.

The limited partnership and increased pension fund investment forced an increasing professionalization of the venture capital industry. This extended throughout the venture capital process as is shown by Suchman's findings (1994) that contract terms between venture capitalists and entrepreneurs stabilized during the 1980s. As pension funds became the dominant investors in venture capital, supplanting wealthy individuals and families, the fundraising process became more formal and turned more on an established track record than personal ties. This institutionalization can be seen in the increased number of rating services, providing information on venture capital success and the establishment of specialized industry trade magazines and databases.

In contrast to venture capital in all other regions, Silicon Valley is unique in the fact that local venture capitalists invest the bulk of their funds locally and have few extraregional offices. In fact, venture capitalists based in other regions felt compelled to open offices in Silicon Valley. According to Donald Valentine, this reflects the fact that Silicon Valley can generate the demand for venture capital:

Generally speaking, whenever our plane leaves the Bay Area, we're flying to some place that has less things to invest in [quantitatively], and qualitatively massively less to invest in. It is not an accident that money migrates from wherever it does to here. It's a qualitative recognition of the alternatives. We [Sequoia Capital] have lost very good opportunities, most of which in our opinion were in the Greater Boston area, [which is] the only consistent other vein of resources that has been productive over a period of 15 to 20 years. . . . Virtually no other part of the country has any history of yield on any kind of a consistent basis. After 150-odd investments we have almost never crossed that frontier. We stay with what Frederick Jackson Turner says to stay [with]. (Valentine 1988)

Venture capital evolved with Silicon Valley's technology base, drawing from it and nurturing it by providing the funds for new initiatives. In this process it became integral to the entire region's dynamism and fueled the creation of an economy based on new firm formation. Effectively, the investment successes created both the wealth and the opportunity for the emergence of technology-oriented investing apart from traditional financial institutions. The current environment is the outcome of a path-dependent evolutionary process in which success drew the entrepreneurs and the financiers along a "generative dance" trajectory, whereby the dancers built the dance floor (Cook and Seely

Brown 1999). Both sides learned the dance and were able to inspire and train others to join the process. In effect, there was a gradual accumulation of the investment and management skills and understanding among all parties of the "dance" rules. This facilitated the development of extended entrepreneurial networks and the broader social and institutional structure that became conduits for sharing information, making deals, and mobilizing resources. Venture capital played a critical role in incubating entrepreneurial activity, attracting entrepreneurs, accelerating rates of new business formation, and stimulating regional growth and development.

The rise of venture capital in Silicon Valley provides a clear and important illustration of the relationship between venture capital and the broader process of technological innovation and regional industrialization. Venture capital in Silicon Valley was not created out of whole cloth; rather it evolved gradually as an element of the endogenous growth of the region. The incessant waves of change in electronics-related and later biotechnology fields opened economic spaces, large and small, which provided entrepreneurs opportunities to build firms. The capital and wealth generated permitted the local informal investors to self-organize into a self-conscious venture capital industry. As they became an institution, they also reorganized their environment. The presence of venture capital meant that new possibilities and enticements were available for entrepreneurs. The possibilities reacted with the technology revolution that was occurring in electronics, generally, and microelectronics, specifically, and ignited a chain reaction that until this day has periodically waned and waxed, but, in secular terms, has only expanded.

CHAPTER SIX

High-Technology Agglomeration and the Labor Market: The Case of Silicon Valley

DAVID P. ANGEL

As Fordist mass production has been displaced from its position as the predominant mode of industrialization within advanced capitalist economies, the interest of many researchers has shifted to alternative manufacturing forms. Of the various new and previously marginalized production systems under study, none have drawn more attention than the dense clusters of entrepreneurial high-technology firms that have arisen in Santa Clara County (Silicon Valley), the suburbs of Boston, and elsewhere within the Sunbelt region of the United States. For many authors, these clusters of innovative high-technology firms represent something of a blueprint for new rounds of urban and industrial growth, a potential solution to the industrialization and manufacturing job loss experienced by older industrial regions (Miller and Côté 1985). More recently, they have been identified as key elements of an emerging post-Fordist landscape of accumulation and as evidence of the growing importance of flexible production systems within the U.S. economy.

Over the past decade, a considerable body of research has emerged in which the structure of these high-technology agglomerations has been examined. Attention has been focused upon tendencies to industrial fragmentation, the formation of new firms, and associated patterns of local and international transactional relations among high-technology firms (Florida and Kenney 1990a; Harrington 1985; Scott 1986; Scott and Angel 1987). Additional research has examined the role of

venture capital finance (Florida and Kenney 1988c) and military procurement programs (Markusen and Bloch 1985) in supporting high-tech-
nology-based industrial growth, and more generally, the political and
cultural conditions under which high-technology agglomerations emerge
and develop (Saxenian 1983b, 1989a; Scott and Paul 1990).

Although these studies have generated considerable insight into
the production systems underlying high-technology industrialization,
there has been little analysis of accompanying patterns of labor-market
activity (Malecki 1989). Access to labor is widely identified as an important determinant of the location and competitiveness of high-technology firms (compare Bollinger et al. 1983; Oakey and Cooper 1989;
Thompson 1989); the detailed structure of labor-market activity (hiring, employment composition, labor mobility, and so on) has, however, yet to be examined. The lack of labor-market analysis is surprising in that changes in employment and labor-market activity are a
central element of contemporary processes of industrial restructuring
and of the search for greater flexibility in production (Morris 1988;
OECD 1986; Piore 1986).

The research presented here examines local labor-market dynamics
and their relation to the organization of production in high-technology
agglomerations. The analysis is based upon a case study of production
and labor-market activity in the semiconductor industry, focusing
upon the dense cluster of specialized semiconductor firms in Silicon
Valley. The technological dynamism and forms of manufacturing flexibility observed in Silicon Valley are predicated upon fluid employment
relations and various efficiencies in job search and interfirm worker
mobility that facilitate the rapid deployment of specialized knowledge,
skills, and experience among firms within the local labor market. These
issues were addressed in a preliminary way in a previous paper (Angel
1989) in which I described patterns of job changing among semiconductor engineers. This chapter is part of a broader analysis of labor-market dynamics that investigates the structure of hiring, labor
turnover, wages, and employment relations for both professional and
low-skilled production workers in the semiconductor industry. The research complements an earlier study of the locational dynamics of the
U.S. semiconductor industry (Scott and Angel 1987). This prior study
was focused upon issues of industrial organization and interfirm linkage, and was largely silent upon the labor-market processes examined
in this chapter.

Background and Literature Review

Previous research has documented the historical emergence and organizational structure of Silicon Valley and other large high-technology agglomerations within the United States and Western Europe (Dorfman 1983; Saxenian 1994; Scott 1986; and the other chapters in this book). Although these production complexes typically differ one from another in terms of their precise history and current industrial composition, they share a common entrepreneurial mode of industrialization involving many small and medium-sized firms focused upon innovation, product design, and the manufacture of advanced high-technology products. This pattern of industrialization differs markedly from the branch-plant orientation observed elsewhere within the United States. Rapid rates of new firm formation and a tendency to the vertical and horizontal disintegration of production create a fragmented local industrial structure in which a multitude of very profitable small producers operate alongside larger established firms. The technological dynamism and commercial success of these clusters of specialized firms have been distinctive features of high-technology industrialization within the United States. For many authors, these production complexes are illustrative of an emerging flexible manufacturing form centered around the innovative capabilities of localized networks of small firms (Scott 1988b).

Despite the large published literature on high-technology industries, there has been little analysis of the contribution of labor-market processes to the growth and development of high-technology agglomerations (Malecki 1989; Malecki and Nijkamp 1988). Geographers have long recognized access to skilled labor as an important determinant of the locational process in high-technology industries. High-technology firms are drawn to locations offering a large supply of engineering and scientific labor (Galbraith 1985; Malecki 1984, 1987; Richie et al. 1983). Attention typically has focused, however, upon the locational decision and upon the possibility of attracting high-technology firms to alternative sites outside of existing production complexes (Barkley 1988; Hekman 1980; Macgregor et al. 1986; Oakey and Cooper 1989; Premus 1982). The broader significance of labor-market processes for the technological and organizational dynamism of high-technology production complexes, and, more generally, for the durability of this manufacturing form, have yet to be examined (for an anecdotal discussion of these issues, see Rogers and Larsen 1984).

We may usefully begin by recognizing that the local labor markets of large industrial complexes are often a source of important economies of agglomeration in production (Hoover and Vernon 1959; Segal 1960). The proximity of many firms possessing complementary labor requirements reduces the costs of job search and interfirm worker mobility, facilitating the free flow of workers and information through the local labor market, the matching of workers with job vacancies, and labor supply with labor demand (Barron and Gilley 1981; Clark 1987; McCall and Pascal 1979; Stuart 1979). At the same time, the large, local labor pool typically allows firms both numerical flexibility in the numbers of workers hired and functional flexibility in the kinds of labor skills employed (Kim 1987; Scott 1988a). Such labor-market efficiencies have been a recurrent feature of specialized industrial agglomerations, and a number of authors have indicated that they are likely to be of significance for high-technology sectors of production (Glasmeier et al. 1983; Hall et al. 1987; Malecki 1984; Scott and Storper 1987), and especially for small start-up firms (Oakey 1984, 1985). These labor-market effects have not, however, been demonstrated for high-technology firms, nor have they ever really been dealt with appropriately—that is, as an endogenous moment of the production system as a whole.

The significance of local labor-market processes goes beyond transactional efficiencies in the matching of labor supply and demand. The movement of workers is a central pathway for the transfer of knowledge and experience among firms and is a key element in the oft-identified, but rarely examined, "innovative milieu" associated with Silicon Valley and other high-technology agglomerations (Aydalot and Keeble 1988; Castells 1988). Ideas and information concerning market opportunities, production processes, and past technological successes and failures diffuse at an accelerated pace through the production complex as workers move from one firm to another, and by means of a variety of informal contacts and collaborations among workers employed by different firms (Ettlie 1980; Rogers and Larsen 1984). On this basis, firms are able to build cumulatively upon a shared set of manufacturing experiences, and this appears to be central to the technological dynamism characteristic of these production complexes and to the ability of firms to identify and respond to market opportunities ahead of their competitors (von Hippel 1988). These links between labor-market structure and processes of innovation and technological change remain unexplored and are the focus of this chapter.

Notwithstanding the contribution of labor-market processes to the success of high-technology agglomerations, this pattern of labor-market activity is not without its costs, including the loss of skilled and experienced workers to competing firms and start-up business ventures. During periods of labor shortage, the proximity of many alternative employment opportunities within a production complex facilitates "job shopping" by workers in search of higher wages, better employment conditions, and the chance to work with new, leading-edge manufacturing technologies. The rapid growth of Silicon Valley and other high-technology agglomerations during the 1970s was apparently accompanied by very high rates of labor turnover among professional and production workers (Parden 1981; Rogers and Larsen 1984). Such intensive interfirm worker mobility may break up existing research teams and lead to the dissipation of resources among many competing firms. It remains unclear, however, whether high rates of labor turnover are simply a reflection of the competition among firms for scarce labor resources or, as Florida and Kenney (1990a) suggest, the result of chronic entrepreneurship and of the fragmented industrial structure of production complexes.

Nowhere are these local labor-market dynamics of greater significance than in high-technology agglomerations such as Silicon Valley. Competitive success in high-technology industries depends, above all, on the ability of firms to apply advanced scientific and engineering knowledge in the development of new product and process technologies. The ease with which firms in Silicon Valley are able to assemble and reassemble teams of highly skilled engineers and technical workers, and the knowledge and experience they embody, are central to the technological dynamism and commercial success of the region. In what follows, I investigate these labor-market dynamics, drawing upon the results of a case study of patterns of employment and labor-market activity in the U.S. semiconductor industry.

Data and Data Collection Procedures

This analysis is based upon employment and labor-market information collected through a mailed questionnaire survey of U.S.

semiconductor firms. Information was obtained on many aspects of the labor-market activity of the sample establishments, including wages, skill and experience requirements, labor turnover, employment tenure, and the organization and geography of employee hiring. In addition to summary employment statistics, detailed information was obtained for three specific occupations—namely, fabrication-line operative, line-maintenance technician, and production engineer. These occupations were selected to represent the broad range of skill levels involved in the production of semiconductor devices.

The survey was administered in 1987. A total of 464 questionnaires were mailed out, of which 67 (14.4 percent) were returned. The low response rate to the survey was anticipated, given the proprietary nature of the labor-market data requested. Additional information was obtained through lengthy in-person interviews with the personnel managers of all the Silicon Valley firms participating in the survey. These interviews confirmed that, notwithstanding the small sample size, the survey results accurately describe general patterns of labor-market activity among semiconductor firms in Silicon Valley. The sample includes a broad array of large and small semiconductor establishments, including specialized "merchant" producers and "captive" facilities of vertically integrated electronics firms. Of the 67 participating establishments, 24 (35.8 percent) are located in Silicon Valley and 43 (64.2 percent) are located elsewhere within the United States.

The Structure of Labor-Market Activity

I begin by examining the overall structure of labor-market activity in the U.S. semiconductor industry. As indicated above, it is anticipated that the proximity of many specialized semiconductor firms in Silicon Valley facilitates the fluid deployment of labor among firms, allowing the firms to meet their employment requirements easily and at low cost from within the local labor market. A full account of semiconductor production and labor-market activity outside of Silicon Valley is beyond the scope of this chapter. For the most part, however, production is dominated by a pattern of industrialization in contrast to that of Silicon Valley, centered on the branch plants of large, high-volume producers.

For the purposes of this analysis, the sample semiconductor establishments were initially classified according to their location relative to

Silicon Valley (Silicon Valley, not Silicon Valley). The latter group of producers (not Silicon Valley) were further classified according to the total number of semiconductor establishments within the county in which they are located (fewer than, or more than, ten establishments). This subclassification serves to distinguish subsidiary concentrations of semiconductor production outside of Silicon Valley (for example, Dallas and Phoenix) from more isolated branch-plant locations elsewhere within the United States. Although the resulting tripartite classification simplifies the overall geography of production, it captures effectively the dominant patterns of industrialization within the U.S. semiconductor industry.

The survey results indicate that Silicon Valley firms meet the majority of their labor demands by hiring workers with considerable occupation-specific experience. This pattern holds for each of the production, technical, and engineering occupations for which detailed employment information was obtained. In each occupation, Silicon Valley firms are distinguished by a tendency to fill a high proportion of job vacancies with experienced workers, and to require more years of experience from the workers hired. Semiconductor producers located elsewhere within the United States tend to recruit a greater percentage of workers at the entry level, generating requisite skills and experience in-house within internal labor markets. In the case of fabrication operatives, for example, Silicon Valley firms fill 78.5 percent of job vacancies with workers possessing prior experience in this occupation. The corresponding percentages for the groups of establishments located outside Silicon Valley are 52.6 percent and 48.7 percent. An F-test confirms that these values are significantly different at the 0.05 level of confidence. Comparisons of individual group means (t-tests) indicate that differences in hiring practices are most marked between Silicon Valley producers and establishments located in isolated branch-plant sites outside of major high-technology agglomerations (with fewer than ten semiconductor establishments in the county). Establishments located in subsidiary concentrations of semiconductor production tend to a pattern of hiring that is intermediate between these two groups of firms.

Silicon Valley firms fill the majority of their job vacancies (at least 85 percent in all occupations) from within the local labor market, drawing upon the large pool of specialized labor skills available within the region. Among semiconductor establishments located elsewhere within the United States, there are significant differences across occupations in the tendency to local hiring. In the case of fabrication operatives, most job vacancies (in excess of 98 percent) are filled from within the local labor market (confirming the well-documented tendency to local hiring of low-wage workers). In technical and engineering occupations, by contrast, a substantial proportion of job vacancies of firms not in Silicon Valley are filled from beyond the local labor market. Silicon Valley firms fill 85.4 percent of engineering job vacancies locally, compared with 54.1 percent and 33.2 percent for firms located elsewhere within the United States. An F-test confirms that these group means are significantly different at the 0.05 level of confidence. In the absence of a developed local supply of specialized engineering labor, semiconductor producers outside of Silicon Valley recruit large numbers of engineers from beyond the local labor market (see also Angel 1989).

These data indicate, in sum, that Silicon Valley firms are distinguished by a tendency to fill most job vacancies by hiring workers with experience from the local labor market. Labor-market activity in Silicon Valley is dominated by a localized dynamic of interfirm worker mobility in which experienced workers move from one firm to another as labor demands change and new employment opportunities arise. The mobility of labor provides start-up firms and existing producers great flexibility in putting together requisite teams of skilled professional and production workers. Rather than hiring workers at the entry level and generating skills in-house, semiconductor firms in Silicon Valley are able to respond swiftly to changing labor demands by hiring experienced workers from the local labor market. Moreover, data drawn from the questionnaire survey indicate that Silicon Valley firms fill a high proportion of job vacancies through referrals from existing employees, thereby obviating the need for more costly and time-consuming search and screening procedures (such as the use of "headhunters" and other recruitment agencies). In the case of production engineers, for example, Silicon Valley firms fill 43.7 percent of job vacancies through employee referrals, compared with 27.8 percent and 8.7 percent among establishments located elsewhere within the United States (in counties with more than, and fewer than, ten semiconductor establishments, respectively). The ability to recruit experienced workers easily from the local labor market is one of the central advantages attracting semiconductor producers to Silicon Valley.

ORGANIZATION OF PRODUCTION

Efficiencies in the recruitment of skilled and experienced workers are likely to be of particular importance to small start-up firms in the semiconductor industry. Start-up firms often have volatile and uncertain labor demands, with employment requirements dependent upon the success or failure of a narrow product base. In the absence of extensive internal labor-market resources, small start-up producers typically depend upon the external labor market to meet their labor demands. Large firms, by contrast, have a greater capacity to develop labor skills in-house (for example, through employee training programs). We may investigate this issue further by comparing the hiring patterns of small and large firms in the semiconductor industry. For this purpose, the sample establishments were classified into two groups based upon the total semiconductor sales of the parent firm (sales of less than, and more than, $100 million, respectively). The latter measure serves effectively to distinguish small start-up producers from large multiplant firms in the semiconductor industry.

We also collected information on the hiring activities (experience requirements) of the sample semiconductor establishments cross-classified by location and size of firm. The intent here is to examine the extent to which the pattern of labor-market activity observed in Silicon Valley is an indirect expression of local industrial structure (that is, of the high concentration of small firms in Silicon Valley). Information is provided on the average amount of experience required of new hires, for production, technical, and engineering workers. These data reveal interesting differences across occupations in the significance of location and scale of production as determinants of hiring practice. In the case of fabrication operatives and technicians (but not engineers), the tendency for Silicon Valley firms to hire workers with experience remains significant, even after controlling for the effect of scale of production. Large and small firms in Silicon Valley both require more experience of workers than do semiconductor producers located elsewhere within the United States.

The hiring pattern for engineers, by contrast, is primarily associated with the size of the firm: small firms are distinguished from large producers by a tendency to hire engineers with experience. There is little difference by location in the pattern of hiring of engineers. Small producers of semiconductors throughout the United States meet their employment requirements by hiring engineers who possess considerable prior experience. In practice, the hiring of experienced engineers reflects the high costs to small firms of developing requisite engineering skills in-house. At the same time, this pattern of hiring has significant locational implications for small firms in the semiconductor industry. The heavy dependence of small firms upon experienced engineering labor increases the importance of access to the large pool of specialized engineering skills in Silicon Valley. The ability to recruit experienced engineering workers easily from the local labor market evidently is one of the central forces attracting start-up firms to the region.

DISCUSSION

The kinds of labor-market economies associated with Silicon Valley are not a new phenomenon. They have been a recurrent feature of the manufacturing flexibility sustained within specialized industrial complexes, from the garment district of New York to the motion picture industry of Los Angeles (Storper and Christopherson 1987). They constitute one element of the "Marshallian economies" that bind specialized producers together within spatially concentrated industrial districts, establishing continuity between contemporary forms of flexible production and their historical precedents. The case of the high-technology industry is of especial interest, however, in that it involves the deployment of advanced scientific and engineering skills and knowledge, and the relatively unexplored relation between the structure of labor-market flows and processes of innovation and technological change.

As Dosi (1988a, 1988b), Freeman (1982), and Rosenberg (1982) among others have indicated, much of the knowledge necessary for innovation in manufacturing is of a tacit kind, embodied in the skills and experience of the worker and not fully appropriable in the form of documents or scientific patents. To a significant degree, the development of new technologies depends upon the ability of firms to assemble appropriate teams of workers and the accumulated ideas and experience they possess. In-depth interviews with the personnel managers of Silicon Valley firms indicate that workers hired away from other firms are an important source of technological knowledge in the semiconductor industry. High levels of interfirm labor mobility allow Silicon Valley firms to go beyond their own manufacturing experience and draw upon the broader stock of knowledge developed within the production complex as a whole. As workers move from one firm to another, they simultaneously help to diffuse knowledge through the Silicon Valley production complex, creating a local manufacturing environment in which firms are able to build *cumulatively* upon a *common* stock of technological successes and failures. These labor-market flows are supported by a broader set of informal contacts and collaborations among workers that, although reaching across the borders of individual firms, are concentrated within the region. The accelerated transfer of technological knowledge among Silicon Valley firms constitutes a key element of the "innovative milieu" of the production complex, enhancing the opportunities for innovation and the capabilities to pursue them.

As we might expect, there are important social and political dimensions to this pattern of labor-market activity. The mobility of workers in Silicon Valley is supported by a local industrial culture in which the allegiance of engineers and scientists is not so much to any individual firm but to the production complex as a whole (Angel 1989). This culture is reinforced by a university-scholarly tradition in which ideas concerning future technologies are considered not the property of individual employers or scientists but of the scientific community at large. Such fluidity in the flow of information does not go uncontested, however, as firms attempt to establish proprietary rights over new technologies and over the manufacturing experience upon which these technologies are based. In this regard, the limits of copyright protection over technological knowledge are currently being tested in the law courts. To the extent that these lawsuits constrain the flow of information among firms, they are likely to undermine the forms of entrepreneurial-based innovation observed in Silicon Valley (see also Jorde and Teece 1989).

Contradictions in Labor-Market Activity

Notwithstanding the contribution of labor-market processes to the success of Silicon Valley, this pattern of labor-market activity is not without its disadvantages, as producers lose key personnel accepting job offers from competing firms. The most visible examples of this "job shopping" and labor-market "piracy" involve the mass exodus of scientists and engineers leaving existing employers for new start-up ventures. The precedent for this process was set early in the 1960s when forty of Fairchild Semiconductor's managerial and engineering staff (including general manager Charles Sporck) left the company for the start-up firm National Semiconductor (Hoefler 1971). Labor turnover is typically highest, however, among production workers. During periods of rapid employment growth and labor shortage in the 1960s and 1970s, turnover among production workers reportedly exceeded 70 percent at many Silicon Valley firms. Labor turnover rates generally were lower elsewhere within the United States, constituting an incentive toward the dispersal of routine production tasks away from Silicon Valley (*Electronics News* 1968).

Data drawn from the questionnaire survey provide considerable insight into the pattern of labor turnover among Silicon Valley firms. The average turnover rates (quits and layoffs) for semiconductor producers located in Silicon Valley and elsewhere within the United States indicate some variability in labor turnover rates by location; analysis of variance (F-test) indicates that the differences are not statistically significant at the 0.05 level of confidence. Two important points need to be made in this regard. First, the rate of labor turnover is relatively low among all categories of semiconductor workers. The quit rate in 1987 for fabrication workers, technicians, and engineers in Silicon Valley was 15.8 percent, 16.8 percent, and 9.6 percent, respectively. Second, the rate of labor turnover in Silicon Valley is not significantly different from that sustained by establishments located elsewhere within the United States. In the case of fabrication workers, the quit rate is actually lower in Silicon Valley (15.8 percent) than in the rest of the United States (20.8 percent). There is, in short, little evidence here of the hypermobility of workers observed in Silicon Valley during periods of labor shortage during the 1970s.

To some degree, the low levels of labor turnover found in our study reflect the depressed state of the semiconductor industry in 1987, when the survey questionnaire was administered. Over the period 1985–87, total employment of semiconductor establishments in Silicon Valley fell by approximately ten thousand workers. Layoffs constituted approximately 20 percent of all job changes in Silicon Valley in 1987. For production workers only, the surveyed semiconductor firms provide comparative information on turnover rates for the period 1984–86. These data are of especial interest in that they extend back beyond the 1985–86 recession to the boom year of 1984. Among the sample Silicon Valley plants, the quit rate for production workers averaged 15.6 percent in 1986 and 21 percent in 1984. Thus, although turnover among production workers in Silicon Valley was higher in 1984, it remained at a relatively low level.

Low turnover rates among production workers also reflect an expanding supply of low-skilled workers in the Silicon Valley labor market, fueled by an influx of Asian and Hispanic immigrants to the region. Silicon Valley producers employ a high percentage of Asian (38.6 percent) and Hispanic (17.0 percent) workers; elsewhere the production workforce is predominantly white (64.5 percent). During the 1960s and 1970s, Asian and Hispanic women replaced white women as the dominant production-line workforce in Silicon Valley (see also Siegel and Borock 1982; Snow 1983). Although the supply of immigrant workers increased in Silicon Valley, however, demand for low-skilled workers grew only slowly as semiconductor firms shifted most routinized production tasks to low-wage locations outside of the United States (Scott and Angel 1988). With fewer job vacancies for low-skilled workers, quit rates tended to fall in this segment of the Silicon Valley labor market, reflecting a well-documented tendency to lower levels of voluntary labor turnover under conditions of labor-market recession (Mackay et al. 1971).

Notwithstanding the overall low rate of labor turnover, the loss of individual highly skilled personnel can have a damaging effect upon the manufacturing and research activities of semiconductor firms. Large firms go to some length to reduce the turnover rate and insulate their workforce from the external labor market at large—for example, by paying premium wages, linking wages to tenure with the firm, and by locating research and design facilities at dispersed sites away from competing firms (Sanger 1987). At the same time, many of these large firms work aggressively to reduce the loss of workers to spin-off ventures established by existing employees. For the majority of small producers in Silicon Valley, however, the loss of personnel to competing firms is apparently counterbalanced by the ability to recruit skilled and experienced workers from the local labor market.

In any event, the costs and benefits of labor mobility and the attendant flow of ideas and information within the local labor market are for present purposes appropriately judged less at the level of the individual firm than at that of the production complex as a whole, and in terms of the relative durability of Silicon Valley in comparison with other forms of high-technology industrialization. In this regard, the decisions of individual workers, whether to stay with an existing employer or to change jobs, would appear to be a highly efficient means through which to deploy labor skills and experience within the local labor market. Florida and Kenney (1990a) and Cohen and Zysman (1987) among others suggest, however, structural limitations to this model of labor-market activity, including a failure to establish a reciprocal flow of workers and ideas between the research and production stages of the manufacturing process. These authors argue that a greater degree of managerial governance over labor and the labor process is required to ensure the effective development of new technologies, and that this governance is most effectively sustained within large integrated firms such as the electronics houses of Japan and South Korea.

Employment Relations in Silicon Valley

The development of Silicon Valley occurred at a time of significant change in employment relations within many sectors of the economy. Thus, for many authors, the central feature of emerging forms of flexible production has been the withdrawal of firms from restrictive union contracts and an associated attempt to shift much of the costs of production instability from the firm to the worker, in the form of reduced job security, lower wages, and increased dependence upon part-time and temporary labor (Amin 1989; Pollert 1988; Shaiken et al. 1986). In the case of the U.S. semiconductor industry, unionization is for the most part limited to the established electronics firms of the Northeastern and North-central United States. None of the specialized semiconductor firms in Silicon Valley are covered by union contracts, and attempts to unionize high-technology firms in the region have been unsuccessful. Scott and Storper (1987) among others have suggested that part of the attraction of Silicon Valley for high-technology producers has been the opportunity to reconstitute employment relations within a local labor market lacking a strong tradition of organized labor.

The questionnaire survey data provide considerable insight into the wages and conditions of work sustained by semiconductor firms in Silicon Valley. In general, semiconductor production jobs in Silicon Valley pay relatively low wages, well below the "family" wage associated with Fordist manufacturing facilities in automobile and other consumer durable industries. The average hourly wage in 1987 of semiconductor fabrication workers employed by the sample Silicon Valley firms was $5.07 at the entry level and $7.82 with two years of experience. The wages of production workers are generally higher among unionized semiconductor establishments in the North-central United States, and lower in the Southern and Mountain states. There is, however, considerable variation across the sample establishments in wages paid, reflecting the influence of such variables as union contracts, skill requirements, and local conditions of labor demand and supply.

We investigate these wage patterns further by using the techniques of regression analysis, where the dependent variable in the regression is the average hourly wage of fabrication workers with two years of experience. It was anticipated that wages would be positively correlated with unionization, captive production, and integrated-circuit production (a measure of the technological complexity of the production process). In addition, it is hypothesized that wages would be positively correlated with high-technology agglomeration, reflecting in part the high cost of living within many major high-technology production complexes within the United States. A variety of other locational variables were considered for use in the analysis, but none significantly improved the explanatory power of the regression equation. We found that the wages of fabrication workers are positively associated with unionization, integrated-circuit production, and with location in a high-technology production complex. As anticipated, the dominant pattern is a tendency to higher wages among union plants, relative to nonunion producers in Silicon Valley and elsewhere within the United States.

In many industries, the attempts of firms to achieve greater flexibility in the labor market have involved an increased dependence upon part-time and temporary workers. This "casualization" of work is much contested in that the switch from full-time to part-time employment often involves a drop in the hourly wage rate and a loss of employment security. In addition, its effects typically fall unevenly upon women and various marginalized segments of the workforce. Over the period 1982–85, the number of workers employed on a temporary basis in Silicon Valley more than doubled to 13,800, whereas total employment in the region increased by only 13 percent (Alvarez-Torrez 1986). This general trend notwithstanding, full-time employment remains the norm among semiconductor establishments in Silicon Valley. Part-time workers constitute on average only 2.7 percent of the production workforce of semiconductor firms in Silicon Valley. The corresponding figure for temporary workers is 4.1 percent. These results reflect the fact that part-time and temporary employment in the semiconductor industry is for the most part limited to low-skilled clerical occupations. Labor-market adjustment in the production occupations considered in this analysis is achieved primarily by expanding and reducing the full-time workforce, and, at a more microlevel, through the use of over-time work. The pattern of layoffs and recalls is a response to strong cyclical fluctuations in labor demand within the semiconductor industry in Silicon Valley.

Employment relations in Silicon Valley are strongly favorable to the interests of high-technology firms and to the continued expansion of semiconductor manufacturing in the region. As indicated, semiconductor firms in Silicon Valley are able to draw upon a large pool of marginalized immigrant workers who lack a strong tradition of organized labor. At the same time, semiconductor firms in Silicon Valley continue to depend upon offshore production facilities as a source of low-cost labor, and there is little prospect of a substantial increase in the number of production jobs within the region. With production jobs in short supply, semiconductor firms currently face little upward pressure on wages, and quit rates among production workers have been suppressed to very low levels. The marked segmentation of professional and production workers remains a striking feature of the Silicon Valley labor market.

Conclusions

This chapter has examined patterns of labor-market activity associated with semiconductor production in Silicon Valley. Silicon Valley firms meet the majority of their labor requirements swiftly and at low cost by hiring skilled and experienced workers from the local labor market. Fluid employment relations and efficiencies in search and mobility within the local labor market provide Silicon Valley firms remarkable flexibility in meeting their labor demands and help to ensure a rapid circulation of knowledge and information within the production complex. The accelerated transfer of technological knowledge allows Silicon Valley firms to build cumulatively upon a common stock of technological successes and failures, contributing significantly to the innovative dynamism of the region.

Recent assessments of U.S. competitiveness in high-technology sectors of production have been critical of the entrepreneurial pattern of industrialization observed in Silicon Valley, depicting the region as a fragmented collection of small producers each pursuing technological and commercial advantage independently, with little coordination or communication among firms (Florida and Kenney 1990a; Johnson et al. 1989). The entrepreneurs of Silicon Valley, these authors argue, are no match for the large integrated electronics houses of Japan and South Korea. These critics, however, fail to recognize the degree to which firms in Silicon Valley are able to go beyond their own manufacturing capabilities and draw upon the broader resources of the production complex. The research presented here draws attention to the local labor market as one arena within which knowledge and experience flow between firms within the Silicon Valley production complex. These labor market transactions are paralleled by a localized network of linkage relations among producers, subcontractors, and suppliers that also serve as conduits for the transfer of ideas and information among firms (see also Saxenian 1994).

In this context, the competitiveness of Silicon Valley is appropriately judged less at the level of the individual firm than at that of the production complex as a whole. Within high-technology industries and other sectors of production, rapid rates of technological change constitute innovation in product and process technologies as an important dimension of competition among firms and across industrial systems (Clark and Staunton 1989). The ability to sustain fundamental transformations in technologies and labor processes is central to the durability of emerging flexible production systems. Nowhere is this more evident than among the many specialized semiconductor producers in Silicon Valley.

CHAPTER SEVEN

The Origins and Dynamics of Production Networks in Silicon Valley

ANNALEE SAXENIAN

This essay analyzes the origins and dynamics of production networks in Silicon Valley from the perspective of the region's computer systems firms. Students of Silicon Valley have focused almost exclusively on the evolution of the semiconductor industry; when that industry fell into crisis in the mid-1980s, most assumed that the region itself would decline. Yet by the end of the decade, the regional economy had rebounded, as hundreds of new computer producers and suppliers of microprocessors, specialty chips, software, disk drives, networking hardware, and other components generated a renewed wave of growth.

These new computer systems firms are at the hub of Silicon Valley's expanding production networks. Well-known companies such as Tandem and Apple Computers, and lesser known ones such as Silicon Graphics and Pyramid Technology, are organized to recombine components and subsystems made by specialist suppliers—both within and outside of the region—into new computer systems. As they collaborate with key suppliers to define and manufacture new systems, they are reducing product development times and institutionalizing their capacity to learn from one another. These production networks help account for the sustained technological dynamism of the Silicon Valley economy.

This chapter is reprinted from AnnaLee Saxenian, "The Origins and Dynamics of Production Networks in Silicon Valley," *Research Policy* 20 (1991), with permission from Elsevier Science.

Geographers and other social scientists have documented the emergence of flexible systems of production in regions such as Silicon Valley (Best 1990; Piore and Sabel 1984; Sabel 1988; Scott and Angel 1987; Storper and Scott 1988). Most of the research on these regions, however, overlooks the changing nature of interfirm and interindustry relationships. In their detailed study of the location of the U.S. semiconductor industry, for example, Scott and Angel document the vertical disaggregation of production and the dense concentration of interfirm transactions in Silicon Valley, but they do not explore the nature of the relations between semiconductor firms and their customers and suppliers.

When Florida and Kenney argue that Silicon Valley's flexibility derives from arms-length exchanges and atomistic fragmentation—and thus provides no match for Japan's highly structured, large-firm-dominated linkages—they, too, overlook growing evidence of the redefinition of supplier relations among U.S. technology firms (Gordon 1987; Larson 1988). Moreover, it is difficult to reconcile their bleak predictions with the continued dynamism of the Silicon Valley economy.

Students of business organization, by contrast, have focused on the emergence of network forms of industrial organization—intermediate forms that fall between Williamson's ideal types of market exchange and corporate hierarchy. Since Richardson (1972) observed the pervasive role of cooperation in economic relations, the literature on interfirm networks and alliances has burgeoned (Hakansson 1987; Jarillo 1988; Johanson and Mattson 1987; Johnston and Lawrence 1988; Miles and Snow 1986; Powell 1990; Sabel et al. 1989). Nonetheless, there has been little attention paid to the emergence of interfirm networks in America's high-technology regions.

The case of the computer systems business in Silicon Valley demonstrates how inter-firm networks spread the costs and risks of developing new technologies and foster reciprocal innovation among specialist firms. The region's systems firms are responding to the rising costs of product development, shorter product cycles, and rapid technological change by remaining highly focused and relying on networks of suppliers. In so doing, they are rejecting the vertically integrated model of computer production that dominated in the postwar period, in which a firm manufactured most of its technically sophisticated components and subsystems internally.

This decentralization of production has triggered the redefinition of supplier relations among Silicon Valley computer firms and their vendors. The creation of long-term, trust-based partnerships is blurring the boundaries between interdependent but autonomous firms in the region. While this formalization of inter-firm collaboration is recent, it builds on the long-standing traditions of informal information exchange, inter-firm mobility, and networking that distinguish Silicon Valley (Angel 1989; Delbecq and Weiss 1988; Rogers 1982). This paper presents three cases to illustrate how inter-firm collaboration fosters joint problem-solving between Silicon Valley systems firms and their specialist suppliers. These cases—of a contract manufacturer, a silicon foundry, and the joint development of a microprocessor—demonstrate how the process of complementary innovation helps to account for Silicon Valley's technological dynamism.[1]

Creating Production Networks

Competitive conditions in the computer systems business changed dramatically during the 1970s and 1980s. The cost of bringing new products to market increased at the same time that the pace of new product introductions and technological change accelerated. Hewlett Packard's vice president of corporate manufacturing, Harold Edmondson (1988), claims that half of the firm's orders in any year come from products introduced in the preceding three years, and he notes that "in the past, we had a ten-year lead in technology. We could put out a product that was not perfectly worked out, but by the time the competition had caught up, we'd have our product in shape. Today we still have competitive technology, but the margin for catch up is much shorter—often under a year." Computer makers like Hewlett Packard (HP) must now bring products to market faster than ever before, often in a matter of months.

The cost of developing new products has in turn increased, along with growing technological complexity. A computer system today consists of the central processing unit (CPU), which includes a microprocessor and logic chips, the operating system and applications software, information storage products (disk drives and memory chips), ways of putting in and getting out information (input-output devices), power supplies, and communications devices or networks to link computers together. Although customers seek to increase performance along each of these dimensions, it is virtually impossible for one firm to produce all of these components, let alone stay at the forefront of each of these diverse and fast-changing technologies.

Systems firms in Silicon Valley are thus focusing on what they do best, and acquiring the rest of their inputs from the dense infrastructure of suppliers in the region as well as outside. This represents a fundamental shift from the vertically integrated approach to computer production characterized by IBM, DEC, and other established U.S. computer firms.[2] In this model, which survived in an era of more slowly changing products and technologies, the firm designed and produced virtually all of the technologically sophisticated components and subsystems of the computer in-house. Subcontractors were used as surge capacity in times of boom demand, and suppliers were treated as subordinate producers of standard inputs.

When Sun Microsystems was established in 1982, by contrast, its founders chose to focus on designing hardware and software for workstations and to limit manufacturing to prototypes, final assembly, and testing. Sun purchases application-specific integrated circuits (ASICs), disk drives, and power supplies as well as standard memory chips, boxes, keyboards, mice, cables, printers, and monitors from suppliers. Even the printed-circuit board (PCB) at the heart of its workstations is assembled by contract manufacturers. Why, asks Sun's vice president of manufacturing, Jim Bean, should Sun vertically integrate when hundreds of specialty shops in Silicon Valley invest heavily in staying at the leading edge in the design and manufacture of microprocessors, disk drives, printed-circuit boards, and most other computer components and subsystems? Relying on outside suppliers reduces Sun's overhead and ensures that the firm's workstations use state-of-the art technology.

This unbundling also provides the flexibility to introduce new products and rapidly alter the product mix. According to Sun's Bean: "If we were making a stable set of products, I could make a solid case for vertical integration" (*Electronic Business* 1987).[3] He argues, however, that product cycles are too short and technology is changing too fast to move more manufacturing in-house. Relying on external suppliers allowed Sun to introduce four major new product generations in its first five years of operation, doubling the price-performance ratio each successive year. Sun eludes clone-makers by the sheer pace of new product introduction.

The guiding principle for Sun, like most new Silicon Valley systems firms, is to concentrate its expertise and resources on coordinating the design and assembly of a final system, to advance critical technologies that represent the firm's core capabilities (Prahalad and Hamel 1990), and to spread the costs and risks of new product development through partnerships with suppliers. Tandem Computers manufactures its own PCBs but purchases all other components externally. Mips Computer Systems set out to manufacture the microprocessors and PCBs for its workstations, but it quickly sold its chip-making and board assembly operations in order to focus on system design and development.

Some of the region's firms explicitly recognize their reliance on supplier networks and foster their development. Apple Computers' venture capital arm makes minority investments in promising firms that offer complementary technology. In 1984, for example, Apple invested $2.5 million in Adobe Systems, which produces the laser printer software critical to desktop publishing applications. Tandem Computers similarly invested in a small, local telecommunications company, Integrated Technology, Inc., and the two firms have jointly developed networking products to link together Tandem nonstop systems.

Companies like Sun, Tandem, and Mips recognize that the design and production of computers can no longer be accomplished by a single firm: it requires the collaboration of a variety of specialist firms, none of which could complete the task on its own. This reliance on out-sourcing is reflected in the high level of sales per employee of Silicon Valley firms: compare Apple's $369,593 and Silicon Graphics' $230,000 per employee to IBM's $139,250 and DEC's $84,972 (Quinn et al. 1990).

These highly focused producers depend on the unparalleled agglomeration of engineers and specialist suppliers of materials, equipment, and services in Silicon Valley, and on the region's culture of open information exchange and interfirm mobility, which foster continual recombination and new firm formation (Angel 1989; Delbecq and Weiss 1988; Rogers 1982). This infrastructure supports the continued emergence of new producers, while allowing them to remain specialized, and it helps explain the proliferation of new computer systems producers in the region during the 1980s—even as the costs of developing and producing systems skyrocketed.

The decentralization of production and reliance on networks is not limited to small or new firms seeking to avoid fixed investments. Even Hewlett Packard, which designs and manufactures chips, printed-circuit boards, disk drives, printers, tape drives, and many other peripherals and components for its computer systems, has restructured internally to gain flexibility and technical advantage.

In recent years, HP has consolidated the management of over fifty disparate circuit technology units into two autonomous divisions, Integrated Circuit Fabrication and Printed Circuit Board Fabrication. These cross-cutting divisions now function as internal subcontractors to the company's computer systems and instrument products groups. They have gained focus and autonomy that they lacked as separate units tied directly to product lines. Moreover, they must now compete with external subcontractors for firm business, which has forced them to improve service, technology, and quality. These units are even being encouraged to sell to outside customers in some instances. In short, HP appears to be creating a network within the framework of a large firm.

The networks extend beyond the system firms and their immediate suppliers. Silicon Valley's suppliers of electronic components and subsystems are themselves vertically disaggregated—for the same reasons as their systems customers. Producers of specialty and semicustom integrated circuits, for example, have focused production to spread the costs and risks of chip-making. Some specialize in design, others in process technology, and still others provide fabrication capacity for both chip and systems firms (Saxenian 1990).

The same is true in disk drives. Innovative producers like Conner Peripherals and Quantum have explicitly avoided vertical integration, relying on outside suppliers not only for semiconductors but also for the thin-film disks, heads, and motors that go into hard drives. Facing the pressures of rapidly changing product designs and technologies, they rely heavily on third-party sources for most components and perform only the initial design, the final assembly, and testing themselves.

The costs and risks of developing new computer systems products are thus spread across networks of autonomous but interdependent firms in Silicon Valley. In an environment that demands rapid new product introductions and continual technological change, no one firm can complete the design and production of an entire computer system on its own. By relying on networks of suppliers—both within and without the region—Silicon Valley systems firms gain the flexibility to introduce increasingly sophisticated products faster than ever before.

The New Supplier Relations

Silicon Valley's systems makers are increasingly dependent upon their suppliers for the success of their own products. Sun founder Scott McNealy acknowledges that "the quality of our products is embedded in the quality of the products we purchase"—which is no understatement, since much of a Sun workstation is designed by its suppliers (Bluestein 1988). The highly focused systems producer relies on suppliers not only to deliver reliable products on time but also to continue designing and producing high-quality, state-of-the-art products.

While many systems firms begin as Sun did, integrating standard components from different suppliers and distinguishing their products with proprietary software, virtually all now seek specialized inputs to differentiate their products further. These computer makers are replacing commodity semiconductors with ASICs and designing customized disk drives, power supplies, keyboards, and communication devices into their systems.[4] As specialist suppliers continue to advance technologies critical to their own products, they reproduce the technological instabilities that allow this decentralized system to flourish. And there is little evidence that the pace of innovation in computers will stabilize in the near future.

Competition in computers is thus increasingly based on the identification of new applications and improvements in performance rather than simply lower cost. Silicon Valley firms are well known for creating new product niches such as Tandem's fail-safe computers for on-line transaction processing, Silicon Graphics' high-performance super workstations with 3-D graphics capabilities, and Pyramid Technology's mini-mainframe computer systems. Nonetheless, even the producers of general-purpose commodity products such as IBM-compatible personal computers ("clones") are being driven to source-differentiated components in order to reduce costs or improve the performance of their systems. Everex Systems, for example, designs custom chip sets to improve the performance of its PC clones.

The more specialized these computers and their components become, the more the systems firms are drawn into partnerships with their suppliers. And as they are increasingly treated as equals in a joint process of designing, developing, and manufacturing innovative systems, the suppliers themselves become innovative and capital-intensive producers of differentiated products.

This marks a radical break with the arms-length relations of a mass-production system, in which suppliers manufactured parts according to standard specifications and competed against one another to lower price, and in which portions of production were subcontracted as a buffer against fluctuations in market demand, output, and labor supply (Holmes 1986). In that model, suppliers remained subordinate and often dependent on a single big customer. IBM was notorious for managing its suppliers in this fashion during the early 1980s, and Silicon Valley systems firms today explicitly contrast their supplier relations with those of IBM (Granovetter 1985).[5]

Silicon Valley systems firms now view relationships with suppliers more as long-term investments than short-term procurement relationships (Davis 1989).[6] They recognize collaboration with suppliers as a way to speed the pace of new product introductions and improve product quality and performance. Most firms designate a group of "privileged" suppliers with whom to build these close relationships. This group normally includes the 20 percent of a firm's suppliers that account for 75–80 percent of the value of its components: typically between fifteen and thirty producers of integrated circuits, printed-circuit boards, disk drives, power supplies, and other components that are critical to product quality and performance.

These relationships are based on shared recognition of the need to ensure the success of a final product. Traditional supplier relations are typically transformed by a decision to exchange long-term business plans and share confidential sales forecasts and cost information. Sales forecasts allow suppliers to plan investment levels, while cost information encourages negotiation of prices that guarantee a fair return to the supplier while keeping the systems firm competitive. In some cases these relationships originate with adoption of Japanese just-in-time (JIT) inventory control systems, as JIT focuses joint attention on improving product delivery times and quality. It often requires a reduction in the number of suppliers and the creation of long-term supplier relations as well as the sharing of business plans and technical information.[7]

Reciprocity guides relations between Silicon Valley's systems firms and their suppliers. Most of these relationships have moved beyond the inventory control objectives of JIT to encompass a mutual commitment to sustaining a long-term relationship. This requires a commitment not to take advantage of one another when market conditions change, and can entail supporting suppliers through tough times—by extending credit, providing technical assistance or manpower, or helping them find new customers.

Businesses commonly acknowledge this mutual dependence. Statements like "Our success is their success" or "We want them to feel like part of an extended family" are repeated regularly by purchasing managers in Silicon Valley systems firms, whose roles have changed in recent years from short-term market intermediaries to long-term relationship-builders. Managers describe their relationships with suppliers as involving personal and moral commitments that transcend the expectations of simple business relationships. In the words of one CEO:

In these partnerships, the relationship transcends handling an order. There is more than a business relationship involved. In addition to the company's commitment, there are personal commitments by people to make sure things happen. Furthermore, there are moral commitments: not to mislead the other party, to do everything possible to support the other party, and to be understanding. (Cohodas 1987)

Suppliers are being drawn into the design and development of new systems and components at a very early stage, and they are typically more closely integrated into the customer's organization in this process. A key supplier is often consulted during the initial phases of a new computer system's conception—between two and five years prior to actual production—and involved throughout the design and development process. Some Silicon Valley firms even include suppliers in their design-review meetings.

This early cooperation allows a supplier to adapt its products to anticipated market changes and exposes the systems engineers to changing component technologies. In the words of HP Manufacturing's vice president, Harold Edmondson: "We share our new product aspirations with them and they tell us the technological direction in which they are heading. . . . We would never have done it this way 10 years ago" (Tierston 1989).

Tandem's materials director, John Sims (1988), similarly describes how information is shared early in the firm's product development process: "There is a lot of give and take in all aspects of these relationships. . . . We have a mutual interest in each other's survival. We share proprietary product information, and we work jointly to improve designs and develop the latest technologies. We continually push each other to do better."

According to an executive at Flextronics, a Silicon Valley contract manufacturer, "In the early stages of any project, we live with our customers and they live with us. Excellent communication is needed between design engineers, marketing people, and the production people, which is Flextronics" (*San Jose Mercury News* 1988).

Once production begins, the relationship between the two firms continues at many different levels. Not only does the customer firm's purchasing staff work with the supplier, but managers, engineers, and production staff at all levels of both firms meet to redefine specifications or to solve technical or manufacturing problems. In many cases, the flow of information between the two firms is continuous.

These relationships represent a major departure from the old practice of sending out precise design specifications to multiple sources for competitive bids. In fact, price is rarely considered as important as product quality and reliability in selecting a key supplier. Most firms choose a reliable, high-quality supplier for a long-term relationship, recognizing that the price will be lower over the long term because unpredictable cost fluctuations will be reduced.

As these relationships mature, it is increasingly difficult to speak of these firms as bounded by their immediate employees and facilities. This blurring of firm boundaries is well illustrated by the case of Adaptec, Inc., a Silicon Valley–based maker of input-output controller devices. When it was formed in 1981, Adaptec management chose to focus on product design and development and to rely on subcontractors for both semiconductor fabrication and board assembly. The key to this strategy is the investment Adaptec has made in building long-term partnerships with its key suppliers: Silicon Valley start-up International Microelectronic Products (IMP); Texas Instruments (TI); and the local division of the large contract manufacturer SCI. Adaptec's vice president of manufacturing, Jeffrey Miller, describes the high degree of trust that has evolved through continuing interaction between engineers in both organizations:

Our relations with our vendors is not much different than my relationship was at Intel with our corporate foundry—except now I get treated as a customer, not as corporate overhead. . . . It really is very hard to define where we end and where our subcontractors begin: Adaptec includes a portion of IMP, of TI, and of SCI. (Miller 1988)

In the words of HP's Edmondson, the partners in these relationships cooperate in order to "pull one another up relative to the rest of the industry" (Edmondson 1988). This blurring of the boundaries of the firm transcends distinctions of corporate size or age. While many Silicon Valley start-ups have allied with one another and "grown up" together, others have benefited from relationships with large established firms, both in and outside of the region.

Moreover, while nondisclosure agreements and contracts are normally signed in these alliances, few believe that they really matter (especially in an environment of high employee turnover like Silicon Valley). Rather, the firms accept that they share a mutual interest in one another's success and that their relationship defies legal enforcement. According to Apple Computers' manager of purchasing, Tom McGeorge:

We have found you don't always need a formal contract. . . . If you develop trust with your suppliers, you don't need armies of attorneys. . . . In order for us to be successful in the future, we have to develop better working relationships, better trusting relationships, than just hounding vendors for price decreases on an annual basis. (Cohodas 1986)

Of course, truly collaborative relationships do not emerge overnight or function flawlessly. There is a constant tension between cooperation and control. It may take years before trust develops or a supplier is given more responsibility. As with any close relationship, misunderstandings arise. Some relationships are terminated—in industry lingo, they result in "divorce"—while others languish temporarily and are revitalized with joint work. What is striking is how many of these relationships appear to not only survive but to flourish.

Although these relationships are often remarkably close, both parties are careful to preserve their own autonomy. Most Silicon Valley firms will not allow their business to account for more than 20 percent of a supplier's product and prefer that no customer occupy such a position. Suppliers are thus forced to find outside customers, which ensures that the loss of a single account will not put them out of business. This avoidance of dependence protects both supplier and customer, and it promotes the diffusion of technology across firms and industries. One local executive suggests that the ideal situation is to hold a preferred position with suppliers but not an exclusive relationship. "Dependence," he notes, "makes both firms vulnerable" (Jarrat 1988).

Regional proximity facilitates collaborative supplier relations. The materials director at Apple Computers, Jim Bilodeau, describes the firm's preference for local suppliers: "Our purchasing strategy is that our vendor base is close to where we're doing business. . . . We like them to be next door. If they can't, they need to be able to project an image like they are next door" (Cohodas 1986). Sun's materials director, Scott Metcalf (1988), similarly claims: "In the ideal world, we'd draw a 100 mile radius and have all our suppliers locate plants, or at least supply depots, into the area."

These managers agree that long-distance communications is often inadequate for the continuous and detailed engineering adjustments required in making technically complex electronics products. Face-to-face interaction allows firms to address the unexpected complications in a supplier relationship that could never be covered by a contract. The president of a firm that manufactures power supplies for computers and peripherals explains: "I don't care how well the specifications are written on paper, they are always subject to misinterpretation. The only way to solve this is to have a customer's engineers right here. There is no good way to do it if you are more than fifty miles away" (Smith 1988).[8] Nor is this desire for geographic proximity reducible to cost considerations alone. The trust, information exchange, and teamwork that are the basis of collaborative supplier relations require continued interaction, which is difficult to achieve over long distances.

This is not to suggest that all Silicon Valley systems firms are tightly integrated into cooperative relationships with all of their suppliers. Traditional arms-length relations persist, for example, with suppliers of such commodities as raw materials, process materials, sheet metal, and cables. Nor is it to imply that all of a firm's key suppliers are located in the same region. Many Silicon Valley firms purchase components such as commodity chips or disk drives from Japanese vendors.

Systems firms in Silicon Valley are, however, redefining their relationships with their most important suppliers. A network of long-term, trust-based alliances with innovative suppliers represents a source of advantage for a systems producer that is very difficult for a competitor to replicate. Such a network provides both flexibility and a framework for joint learning and technological exchange.

Production Networks and Innovation

Silicon Valley today is far more than an agglomeration of individual technology firms. Its networks of interdependent yet autonomous producers are increasingly organized to grow and innovate reciprocally. These networks promote new product development by encouraging specialization and allowing firms to spread the costs and risks associated with developing technology-intensive products. They spur the diffusion of new technologies by facilitating information exchange and joint problem-solving between firms and even industries. Finally, the networks foster the application of new technologies because they encourage the entry of new firms and product experimentation.

Three cases demonstrate how these production networks promote technological advance in Silicon Valley. The first is the relationship of systems firms to their contract manufacturers, which are changing from sweatshops into technologically sophisticated, capital-intensive businesses as they assume more responsibility for product design and process innovation. The second case involves a foundry relationship between a large systems firm and a small design specialist in which each contributes distinctive, state-of-the-art expertise to a process of complementary innovation. In the third case, a systems firm spreads the costs of perfecting a state-of-the-art microprocessor through joint product development with a semiconductor producer. Taken together, these cases demonstrate how collaboration fosters joint problem-solving and how Silicon Valley's firms are learning to respond collectively to fast-changing markets and technology.

CONTRACT MANUFACTURERS

Printed circuit board assembly has historically been among the most labor-intensive and least technically sophisticated phases of electronics manufacturing. Contract assembly was traditionally used by systems firms in Silicon Valley to augment in-house manufacturing capacity during periods of peak demand. Commonly referred to as "board stuffing," it was the province of small, undercapitalized, and marginal firms that paid unskilled workers low wages to work at home or in sweatshops. Many of these assemblers moved to low-wage regions of Asia and Latin America during the 1960s and early 1970s.

This profile changed fundamentally during the 1980s. Systems firms like IBM, HP, and Apple expanded their business with local contract manufacturers in order to lower their fixed costs and respond to shorter product cycles. This enabled the region's PCB assemblers to expand and upgrade their technology. As small shops received contracts and assistance from larger systems firms, they invested in state-of-the-art manufacturing automation and assumed more and more responsibility for the design and development of new products.

Flextronics, Inc., was one of Silicon Valley's earliest board-stuffing firms. During the 1970s it was a small, low-value-added "rent-a-body" operation that provided quick turnaround board assembly for local merchant semiconductor firms. By the late 1980s it was the largest contract manufacturer in the region and offered state-of-the-art engineering services and automated manufacturing.

This transformation began in 1980 when Flextronics was purchased by new management. The company expanded rapidly in the subsequent years, shifting the bulk of its services from consignment manufacturing, in which the customer provides components that the contract manufacturer assembles according to the customer's designs, to "turnkey" manufacturing, in which the contract manufacturer selects and procures electronic components as well as assembling and testing the boards.

The shift from consignment to turnkey manufacturing is a shift from a low-risk, low-value-added, low-loyalty subcontracting strategy to a high-risk, high-value-added, high-trust approach because the contract manufacturer takes responsibility for the quality and functioning of a complete subassembly. This shift greatly increases the systems firm's dependence on its contract manufacturer's process and components. Flextronics' CEO Robert Todd (1988) describes the change: "With turnkey they're putting their product on the line, and it requires a great deal of trust. This kind of relationship takes years to develop and a major investment of people time." Todd claims that whereas a consignment relationship can be replicated in weeks, it can take years to build the trust required for a mature turnkey relationship in which the design details of a new product are shared. These relationships demand extensive organizational interaction and a surprising amount of integration.[9] As a result, firms that consign their manufacturing typically have six or seven suppliers that compete on the basis of cost, while those relying on turnkey contractors build close relations with only one or two firms, selected primarily for quality and responsiveness.

The shift to turnkey manufacturing has clear implications for a firm's location. Flextronics' CEO Robert Todd (1988) claims: "We've never been successful for any length of time outside of a local area. We might get a contract initially, but the relationship erodes without constant interaction. Sophisticated customers know that you must be close because these relationships can't be built over long distances." This explains why the U.S. contract manufacturing business is highly regionalized. During the 1980s, Flextronics established production facilities in Massachusetts, South Carolina, Southern California, Hong Kong, Taiwan, Singapore, and the People's Republic of China.[10] SCI Systems, the largest U.S. contract manufacturer, is based in Alabama where costs are very low, but the firm has a major facility in high-cost Silicon Valley in order to build the relationships needed to serve the local market.

By 1988 over 85 percent of Flextronics' business was turnkey; in 1980 it had been entirely consignment. This growth was initially due to a close relationship with rapidly expanding Sun Microsystems, which by 1988 accounted for 24 percent of Flextronics' business. The two firms have explicitly sought to limit this share in order to avoid dependency. Flextronics has diversified its customer base by developing customers in a wide range of industries. The firm now also serves businesses in the disk drive, tape drive, printer, and medical instruments industries.

Two recent trends in contract manufacturing illustrate how specialization breeds technological advance and increasing interdependence. On the one hand, Silicon Valley systems companies are relying on contract manufacturers for the earliest phases of board design. Flextronics now offers engineering services and takes responsibility for the initial design and layout of Sun's circuit boards as well as the prescreening of electronic components. The use of contract manufacturers for board design implies a radical extension of interfirm collaboration because systems firms must trust subcontractors with the proprietary designs that are the essence of their products. When successful, such a relationship increases the agility of the systems firm while enhancing the capabilities of the contract manufacturers. In fact, Flextronics is now capable of manufacturing complete systems, although this accounts for only 5 percent of their business.

The second trend, the increasing use of surface mount technology (SMT), is transforming printed-circuit board assembly into a capital-intensive business. While the traditional through-hole assembly technique involves soldering individual leads from an integrated circuit through the holes in circuit boards, SMT uses epoxy to glue electronic components onto the board. The new process is attractive because it produces smaller boards (components can be mounted on both sides) and because it is less expensive in volume than through-hole.

SMT is, however, initially far more complex and expensive than through-hole assembly. It requires tight design rules, high densities, and a soldering process that demands expertise in applied physics and chemistry and takes years of experience to perfect. Industry analysts describe SMT as five to ten times more difficult a process than through-hole. Moreover, a single high-speed SMT production line costs more than $1 million.

Contract manufacturer Solectron Corporation has led Silicon Valley in the adoption of SMT, investing more than $18 million in SMT equipment since 1984 (Lasnier 1988). It has captured the business of IBM, Apple, and HP (as well as many smaller Silicon Valley firms) by automating and emphasizing customer service, high quality, and fast turnaround. According to one venture capitalist and industry veteran, Solectron's manufacturing quality is superior to that found in any systems firm in Silicon Valley (Davidow 1988).

This manufacturing excellence is due in part to Solectron's investment in state-of-the-art equipment. It is also the result of the expertise accumulated by applying the lessons learned from one customer to the next. All of Solectron's customers thus benefit from learning that would formerly have been captured by individual firms. Moreover, lessons learned in manufacturing for firms in one sector are spread to customers in other sectors, stimulating the interindustry diffusion of innovations.

The use of contract manufacturers, initially an attempt to spread risks, focus resources, and reduce fixed costs in an era of accelerating new product introductions, is thus producing mutually beneficial technological advance. While many of Silicon Valley's contract assemblers remain small and labor intensive, some, such as Flextronics and Solectron, are no longer subordinate or peripheral units in a hierarchical production system. Rather, they have transformed themselves into sophisticated specialists that contribute as equals to the vitality of the region's production networks.

SILICON FOUNDRIES

Silicon foundries are the manufacturing facilities used for the fabrication of silicon chips or semiconductors. The use of external foundries grew rapidly in the 1980s as semiconductor and systems firms began designing integrated circuits themselves but sought to avoid the cost of the capital-intensive fabrication process (Saxenian 1990). Like contract manufacturers, foundries offer their customers the cumulative experience and expertise of specialists. Unlike contract assemblers, however, silicon foundries have always been technologically sophisticated and highly capital intensive—and they have thus interacted with customers as relative equals offering complementary strengths. This relationship can be an exchange of services with limited technical interchange, or it can offer significant opportunities for reciprocal innovation.

The collaboration between Hewlett Packard and semiconductor design specialist Weitek illustrates the potential for complementary innovation in a foundry relationship. Weitek, which has no manufacturing capacity of its own, is the leading designer of ultra high speed "number crunching" chips for complex engineering problems. In order to improve the performance of the Weitek chips, HP opened up its state-of-the-art 1.2-micron wafer fabrication facility, historically closed to outside firms, to Weitek for use as a foundry.

This alliance grew out of a problem that HP engineers were having with the development of a new model workstation. They wanted to use Weitek designs for this new product, but Weitek (which had supplied chip-sets to HP for several years) could not produce chips that were fast enough to meet HP's needs. Realizing that the manufacturing process at the foundry that Weitek used slowed the chips down, the HP engineers suggested fully optimizing the Weitek designs by manufacturing them with HP's more advanced fabrication process.

This culminated in a three-year agreement that allows the two firms to benefit directly from each other's technical expertise. The agreement guarantees that HP will manufacture and purchase at least $10 million worth of the Weitek chip-sets in its foundry, and it provides Weitek the option to purchase an additional $20 million of the chip-sets from the foundry to sell to outside customers.

This arrangement ensures HP a steady supply of Weitek's sophisticated chips and allows them to introduce their new workstation faster than if they had designed a chip in-house, and it provides Weitek with a market and the legitimacy of a close association with HP, as well as guaranteed space in a state-of-the-art foundry. Moreover, the final product itself represents a significant advance over what either firm could have produced independently.

Both firms see the real payoff from this alliance in expected future technology exchanges. According to an HP program manager who helped negotiate the deal: "We wanted to form a long-term contact with Weitek—to set a framework in place for a succession of business opportunities" (Jones 1987). By building a long-term relationship, the firms are creating an alliance that allows each to draw on the other's distinctive and complementary expertise to devise novel solutions to common problems. HP now has greater access to Weitek's design talent and can influence the direction of these designs. Weitek has firsthand access to the needs and future plans of a key customer as well as ensured access to HP's manufacturing capabilities. Both are now better positioned to respond to an unpredictable and fast-changing market.

In spite of this increased interdependence, HP and Weitek have preserved their autonomy. Weitek sells the chip-sets they produce in HP's fab to third parties, including many HP competitors, and continues to build partnerships and collect input from its many other customers (in fact, Weitek deliberately limits each of its customers to less than 10 percent of its business). Meanwhile, HP is considering opening its foundry to other outside chip design firms, and it still maintains its own in-house design team. The openness of such a partnership ensures that design and manufacturing innovations that grow out of collaboration diffuse rapidly.

Both firms see this relationship as a model for the future. While HP does not intend to become a dedicated foundry, it is looking for other partnerships that allow it to leverage its manufacturing technology using external design expertise. Weitek, in turn, depends upon a strategy of alliances with firms that can provide manufacturing capacity as well as insights into fast-evolving systems markets.

Collaborative Product Development

Joint product development represents the ultimate extension of interdependence in a networked system. The collaboration between Sun Microsystems and Cypress Semiconductor to develop a sophisticated version of Sun's reduced instruction set computing (RISC) microprocessor is a classic example. A RISC chip uses a simplified circuit design that increases the computing speed and performance of a microprocessor.

Sun's first workstations were based entirely on standard parts and components. The firm's advantage lay in proprietary software and its ability to introduce new products quickly. Over time, the firm began to distinguish its products by adding new capabilities, enhancing its software, and purchasing semicustom components. Sun's most significant innovation was to design its own microprocessor to replace the standard Motorola microprocessors used in its early workstations. This RISC-based microprocessor, called Sparc, radically improved the speed and performance of Sun's products—and simultaneously destabilized the microprocessor market.

Sun further broke with industry tradition by freely licensing the Sparc design, in contrast with Intel's and Motorola's proprietary approach to their microprocessors. The firm established partnerships with five semiconductor manufacturers, each of which uses its own process technology to produce specialized versions of Sparc.[11] The resulting chips share a common design and software but differ in speed and price. After supplying Sun, these suppliers are free to manufacture and market their versions of Sparc to other systems producers. As a result, Sun has extended acceptance of its architecture while recovering some of its development costs and avoiding the expense of producing and marketing the new chip. Its suppliers, in turn, gain a guaranteed customer in Sun and a new and promising product—which they are jointly promoting. Collaboration allowed Sun to reduce significantly the cost of producing a new microprocessor. The firm spent only $25 million developing the Sparc chip, compared with Intel's $100 million investment in its 80386 microprocessor. In the words of one computer executive: "The real significance of Sparc and of RISC technology is that you no longer have to be a huge semiconductor company, with $100 million to spare for research and development, to come up with a state-of-the-art microprocessor" (Schlender 1988). Mips Computer Systems has similarly designed its own RISC chip and licensed it to three Silicon Valley semiconductor vendors.

Sun's partnership with Cypress Semiconductor extends such collaboration the furthest. In 1986, the two firms agreed to develop jointly a high-speed, high-performance version of Sparc. A team of approximately thirty engineers from both companies worked at a common site for a year—thus combining Sun's Sparc architecture and knowledge of systems design and software with Cypress's expertise in integrated circuit design and advanced CMOS fabrication processes. This core team was supported through constant feedback from the product development, marketing, and testing specialists in each firm. Cypress's vice president of marketing, Lowell Turriff, describes the collaboration as an "ideal marriage" characterized by "an amazing environment of cooperation" (Turriff 1988).

The two firms benefit from complementary expertise: Sun gained access to Cypress's advanced design capabilities and its state-of-the-art CMOS manufacturing facility to produce a very high speed microprocessor; Cypress gained an alliance with a rapidly growing systems firm, insights into the direction of workstation technology, and a new, high-performance product. Cypress executives envision similar partnerships with customers in other industrial markets, including telecommunications and automobiles.

By building a network of collaborative relationships with suppliers like Cypress, Sun has not only reduced the cost and spread the risks of developing its workstations but has also been able to bring new products with innovative features and architectures to market rapidly. These relationships prevent competitors from simply imitating Sun's products, and represent a formidable competitive barrier.

This explains Sun's championing of systems that rely on readily available components and industry-standard technologies (or "open systems"). Under this approach, computers made by different firms adhere to standards that allow them to use the same software and exchange information with one another. This marks a radical break from the proprietary systems approach of industry leaders IBM, DEC, and Apple. Open standards encourage the entry of new firms and promote experimentation because they force firms to differentiate their products while remaining within a common industry standard. Proprietary systems, by contrast, exclude new entrants and promote closed networks and stable competitive arrangements.

As Silicon Valley producers introduce specialized systems for a growing diversity of applications and users, they are fragmenting computer markets. The market no longer consists simply of mainframes, minicomputers, and personal computers: it is segmented into distinct markets for supercomputers, super minicomputers, engineering workstations, networked minicomputers, personal computers, parallel and multiprocessor computers, and specialized educational computers (McKenna 1989). As long as this process of product differentiation continues to undermine homogeneous mass markets for computers, Silicon Valley's specialist systems producers and their networks of suppliers will flourish.

Conclusions

Technical expertise in Silicon Valley today is spread across hundreds of specialist enterprises, enterprises that continue to develop independent capabilities while simultaneously learning from one another. As computer systems firms and their suppliers build collaborative relationships, they spread the costs and risks of developing new products while enhancing their ability to adapt rapidly to changing markets and technologies.

This is not to suggest that interfirm networks are universally diffused or understood in Silicon Valley. The crisis of the region's commodity semiconductor producers in the mid-1980s is attributable in part to distant, even antagonistic, relations between the chip-makers and their equipment suppliers (Saxenian 1990; Stowsky 1988). Other examples of arms-length relationships and distrust among local producers can no doubt be identified (Florida and Kenney 1990b). However, these failures of coordination do not signal inherent weaknesses in network forms of organization, but rather the need for the institutionalization of interfirm collaboration in the United States.

Proposals to replace Silicon Valley's decentralized system of production with an "American keiretsu"—by constructing tight alliances among the nation's largest electronics producers and suppliers (Ferguson 1990)—would sacrifice the flexibility that is critical in the current competitive environment. Such proposals also misread the changing organization of production in Japan, where large firms increasingly collaborate with small and medium-sized suppliers and encourage them to expand their technological capabilities and organizational autonomy (Imai 1988; Fruin 1988; Nishiguchi 1989). In Japan, as in Silicon Valley, a loosely integrated network form of organization has emerged in response to the market volatility of the 1970s and 1980s.

The proliferation of interfirm networks helps to account for the continued dynamism of Silicon Valley. While the region's firms rely heavily on global markets and distant suppliers, there is a clear trend for computer systems producers to prefer local suppliers and to build the sort of trust-based relationships that flourish with proximity. The region's vitality is thus enhanced as interfirm collaboration breeds complementary innovation and cross-fertilization among networks of autonomous but interdependent producers.

PART III

GENERAL EXPLANATIONS

CHAPTER EIGHT

Flexible Recycling and High-Technology Entrepreneurship

HOMA BAHRAMI AND
STUART EVANS

High-technology firms in Silicon Valley prosper in a constantly changing environment of incessant novelty and innovation, which fuels their volatile and occasionally spectacular growth trajectories. This unique domain is characterized by fleeting opportunities, shifting customer preferences, cascades of technological innovations, brutally short product life cycles, and furious global competition. These forces collectively precipitate a never-ending stream of kaleidoscopic changes that can stimulate the rapid growth of an enterprise and also instigate its sudden demise.

A firm's chances of success may be small in this highly combative arena, yet this unique ecosystem has spawned several of the fastest growing firms in the recent history of U.S. business while maintaining a maverick, entrepreneurial spirit. Silicon Valley is unique in having created a successful high-technology cluster of such a scale in an environment that only three decades ago was resplendent with orchards. The entrepreneurial spirit and commitment to innovation have so far proven effective in producing pioneering products and high-value-added jobs. Furthermore, Silicon Valley firms are pioneering a flexible form of enterprise conceived for the fast-moving, global information age (Bahrami 1992).

Silicon Valley's managerial recipes deviate from conventional business practices, and its business and organizational systems implicitly question several of the core assumptions embedded within the traditional body of management theory and organizational practice. One central assumption, embedded within the conventional model of the business enterprise, is that of "permanence." This deeply rooted ontological assumption pervades economic theory in the search for equilibrium, resonates in the quest for sustainable competitive advantage or enduring strategies, and is viewed as a critical ingredient of organizational effectiveness (see, for example, Williams 1992). Many studies use the notion of organizational death as an indicator of "fit or misfit" within a particular domain (Hannan and Freeman 1977), with important consequences for the analysis of business firms, industrial arenas, and national economies.

The broadly held view that the ultimate goal of any enterprise— and, by implication, its key measure of success—is to exist in perpetuity, is partly at odds with Silicon Valley's experience.[1] Paradoxically, while high-technology firms experience a high failure rate, Silicon Valley continues to thrive and prosper. In this domain, the demise of one firm invariably leads to the formation of others, directly and indirectly.[2] This process of "flexible recycling" can result in novel reconfigurations of knowledge and human capabilities, allowing new firms to rise from the ashes of failed enterprises.

Questioning the universal validity of the "permanence" assumption for all high-technology entities does not preclude many firms from enduring over time. It does, however, raise the specter of alternative models of success and business effectiveness—especially for clusters of knowledge-based high technology and other highly dynamic sectors. Ephemeral firms are an integral part of renewal in Silicon Valley, contributing through a flexible recycling process to the continued success of the ecosystem, so that indeed there is life after death in this knowledge-based arena. Silicon Valley is more than a random cluster of technology firms located in a well-defined geographic context. In much the same vein as a natural ecosystem, Silicon Valley's growth and success can be attributed to the incessant formation of a multitude of specialized, diverse entities that feed off, support, and interact with one another. The constituents of this ecosystem include venture capitalists, a global talent pool of knowledge professionals, universities and research institutes, a sophisticated service infrastructure, as well as many customers, lead-users, and early adopters of new technologies.

While several studies have examined specific industries or sectors (Freeman 1990; Carroll and Delacroix 1982), few have considered this unique "ecosystem" (Rogers and Chen 1990; Saxenian 1994). This paper draws on several field studies of the high-technology arena, conducted in Silicon Valley from 1982 to 1993 (Bahrami and Evans 1987, 1989a, 1989b). It explores the Silicon Valley ecosystem and describes some of its major components. We conclude that while many firms in the dynamic high-technology arena may be ephemeral, the Silicon Valley ecosystem is renewed and nurtured by the continuous recycling process. This ecosystem provides an anchor of stability within which incumbent firms and new start-ups can flourish and become a source of innovation and employment, and yet remain sufficiently flexible to accommodate the constant stream of kaleidoscopic changes.

Historical Antecedents of Silicon Valley

Clusters of firms in related industries have historically coalesced around a critical mass of business activity. During the nineteenth century, many firms in Birmingham, England, clustered around the critical mass of expertise in what is known in the vernacular as "metal bashing." During this century, the automobile sector amassed around Birmingham, Detroit, and Stuttgart. In London, financial industries have evolved around the famous "square mile." Similarly, Italy's textile industry has coalesced around the city of Prato (Porter 1990). High-technology industries of the information era also appear to conform to this tendency.

Several regional technology clusters have sprouted around the United States in recent years—including Austin's "Silicon Hills," Seattle's "Technology Corridor," Illinois's "Silicon Prairie," New Jersey's "Princeton Corridor," San Diego's "Golden Triangle," and Utah's "Software Valley" (Business Week 1992). Scotland's "Silicon Glen" has attracted several technology-based companies, and Singapore has become a center for disk drive and computer subsystems. Additionally, a number of government-sponsored science park initiatives, such as France's Sofia Antipolis, Taiwan's Hisinchu, and England's at Cambridge, have also attempted to induce a critical mass of high-technology firms. Still, the best-known and the largest cluster of high-technology firms in the electronics industry is located in California's Silicon Valley.

Silicon Valley sprouted spontaneously when several complementary forces gelled in the late sixties, producing a mutually supportive spiral of entrepreneurship and innovation, and in the process resulted in the formation of a critical mass of high-technology firms.[3] There was no single event or grand plan that in and of itself led to the meteoric rise of Silicon Valley.[4] Instead, a series of independent events, coupled with fortuitous timing, transformed a regional agricultural community into a global engine of technological innovation and high-technology entrepreneurship. This versatile ecosystem enables fledgling firms to draw on specialized support services and a diverse pool of talent, so they can concentrate on their unique steeple of expertise. Successful firms in Silicon Valley have grown at a phenomenal pace.

From a technological perspective, the parallel development of two major innovations forged the critical building blocks that underpinned the rapid growth of Silicon Valley in the 1960s and 1970s. The first and the most well known of these was the commercial development of the transistor at AT&T's Bell Labs in 1948. The second, which is often overlooked, was the development of disk drives or information storage technology using magnetic recording techniques. Using tape in 1953 and magnetic disks by 1957, the technology was developed by IBM scientists under the guidance of R. B. Johnson and L. D. Stevens at its Los Gatos Laboratory (Harker et al. 1981). Later the development of computer networking technologies would power yet another wave of growth.

One of the early start-ups seeking to commercialize the transistor was established by Shockley—one of the Bell Lab scientists—who set up Shockley Semiconductor Laboratories in Palo Alto during the mid-1950s. His working team of eight scientists became the founding nucleus for the growing West Coast semiconductor industry. This team left Shockley Lab in 1957 and founded Fairchild Semiconductor. Further advances in semiconductor technology and the emergence of a major market in the defense industry helped launch many spinoffs—largely out of Fairchild—during the 1960s; among them were National Semiconductor, AMI, Advanced Micro Devices, and Intel.

During the same period, IBM set up its "skunk works" in Los Gatos with the aim of producing technical breakthroughs and innovative products. The later development of the Winchester disk drive led to the formation of a multibillion-dollar industry in Silicon Valley (Mulvany et al. 1975; Stevens 1981).[5] Several members of the IBM team were later responsible for the founding of Memorex and other well-known disk drive and peripherals firms such as Shugart, Seagate, Conner Peripherals, Adaptec, Auspex, Maxtor, and Quantum. Much overlooked by commentators, the disk drive industry has been a constant source of innovation and international dominance for U.S. companies.

Stanford University's dean of engineering, Frederick Terman, played a crucial role during the early years by forging a close working relationship between the engineering school and technical firms in the area. The formation of the Stanford Industrial Park in 1951 was an additional boost, by providing a mechanism for transferring technology from university laboratories to the nearby commercial firms.[6] During the 1960s the park became an attractive location for growing electronics companies—expanding steadily from thirty-two firms in 1960 to almost seventy by 1970 (Johnston 1982; Rogers and Larsen 1984).

Boosted by California's unique pioneering spirit, these critical building blocks formed the foundation of Silicon Valley's entrepreneurial setting. Since the days of the Gold Rush, California, the frontier land, had attracted the innovative and the ambitious (Kotkin and Grabowicz 1982). It is hardly surprising that many entrepreneurs who felt the need to challenge the status quo and to break with tradition found a conducive home in California. By the mid-1960s a critical mass of technology companies had been established in the South San Francisco Bay Area, and Santa Clara Valley had been transformed from prune yards and orchards into a large petri dish whose nutrient base was an active experimentation and information exchange system for technological know-how.

Constituents of the Silicon Valley Ecosystem

Several components—each playing different and mutually supportive roles—have turned Silicon Valley into a versatile ecosystem. There are five main components, although this grouping is somewhat arbitrary and is not intended to form the basis of a scientific taxonomy of the various "species."

Corporate and government research institutes and universities are the most readily identifiable and perhaps the most publicized component. With a strong technological orientation, these institutions train young engineers who make up the pool of entrepreneurs and professionals in Silicon Valley. Acting as a source of precommercialization stage technologies, it may be argued that these institutions are the nutrient base of the ecosystem.

Universities are also a catalyst for informal networking among future entrepreneurs. The bonds that are forged between the students play a crucial role in the process of firm formation. For example, Sun Microsystems was formed by two Stanford MBA students, a graduate student from the Stanford Engineering School, and a doctoral candidate from Berkeley's Computer Science Department. The name of the company is an acronym for the Stanford University Network, around which the company coalesced. All four founders of ROLM were graduate students at the Stanford Engineering School and had previously attended Rice University.

Once in a while, faculty members also start companies. For example, a professor at Stanford Medical School cofounded Nellcor, a medical electronics company that developed the oxymeter, an indispensable aid for anesthesiologists. Silicon Graphics was founded by Jim Clark from Stanford's Computer Science Department. Cromemco, the pioneering computer company in the 1970s, was founded by two professors from the Engineering School. The nascent biotechnology industry is populated by a number of firms founded by eminent scientists. Many faculty members are also advisors, consultants, and board members of the growing companies.

Corporate research institutes have played a crucial role in this process of generating critical technological know-how and scientific progress. Xerox's Palo Alto Research Center (PARC) was responsible for the development of local area networks. Robert Metcalfe, the inventor of Ethernet at PARC, left Xerox to form 3Com in order to commercialize the technology. Charles Greschke and John Warnock invented Postscript at PARC and then spun off to form Adobe.

Many innovations have emanated from these research institutes without their direct involvement in commercializing the technology. For example, the optical disk drive, the mouse pointing device, and the magnetic ink character system for bank checks were all initially developed at the Stanford Research Institute. The interchange of faculty between the universities and research institutes has also played an important role in the process of innovation and information exchange. For example, Professor Stig Hagstrom, a scientist in charge of one of the laboratories at PARC, later became the department chair of the Department of Materials Science at Stanford. William Miller, former president of SRI, was also a professor at the Stanford Graduate School of Business.

The venture capital community is a crucial second component, which provides financial resources to start and grow new entities. Although it is easy to overstate the role of venture capital in creating new companies, the community is responsible for more than simply investing in fledgling companies. Venture capitalists provide valuable management know-how, particularly in the embryonic stages of a firm's development. Furthermore, armed with a network of contacts, they often recommend individuals who can augment the management team of a start-up.

Many venture capitalists are, in the main, responsible for funding companies beyond the initial "seed" stage. Private individuals often provide seed funding for entrepreneurs before venture capital is obtained.[7] Typically, after seed funding, a firm will require four or five rounds of financing to build manufacturing capacity, forge distribution channels, develop follow-on products, and engage in global expansion. The principal role of the venture capitalists is to provide the funds necessary to grow the enterprise into a sizable business, in a position to undertake an initial public offering, or be acquired by another company.[8]

Start-ups require several rounds of financing before generating sufficient revenue and earnings growth to undertake an initial public offering (IPO). The initial group of venture capitalists, particularly the lead investor in the consortium, typically assist with follow-on financing and the IPO process.[9] Moreover, the relationships forged between entrepreneurs and venture capitalists typically endure over and above any one start-up. To sum up, the roles played by venture capitalists include:

- Several rounds of funding
- Management know-how
- Network of contacts to augment the team
- Follow-on financing
- In certain cases, funding the entrepreneurs' next start-up .

The third crucial component is a sophisticated service infrastructure that allows start-up firms to focus on their chosen steeple of expertise, rather than dissipate their energies across a broad range of peripheral or supporting activities. Contract manufacturing services are available to develop prototypes, or engage in high-volume or "peak-load" manufacturing of subsystems and finished goods. Specialized public relations firms provide assistance with strategic marketing, product packaging, trade shows, company logos, and other collateral services. Accounting firms have specialized high-technology practices and services designed for start-up and high-technology companies.

Executive search firms are used extensively by start-up and maturing firms in order to augment management teams, and to recruit new talent. Real estate firms have expertise in providing facilities especially designed for high-technology firms. For example, some firms may require "clean rooms" or highly purified water supplies; others set out to create a campuslike environment for their professional employees.

As Suchman showed, law firms also play a crucial role in the creation of new ventures. A handful of prominent law partnerships have grown in Silicon Valley by specializing in high-technology services. In addition to litigation, they perform several major functions, including initial incorporation, company name search, stock allocation issues, patent filings, alliance agreements, public offering prospecti, SEC filings, and preparation of acquisition agreements.

At the outset, a new start-up is typically offered favorable fee structures, in the anticipation that substantial legal assistance will be required as it undertakes additional rounds of financing; eventually, four or five years downstream, the start-up may be acquired or embark on an initial public stock offering. Senior partners typically forge longstanding relationships with the venture capital community and often refer entrepreneurs to venture capitalists who have expertise or prior experience with a specific type of venture or industry. This further underscores the role of personal relationships in the dynamics of the ecosystem.

The function of this supporting infrastructure is the timely provision of a wide range of specialized expertise so that things can get done quickly and effectively. If a firm needs to prototype an integrated circuit to test a new design, it can be fabricated in a matter of days; if it needs a booth for a trade show, it can be put together over a weekend; if it requires specialized advice, it can be provided by a phone call.

Another crucial component is the diverse talent pool of professionals that has gravitated to Silicon Valley from all over the globe.[10] Many come to attend the universities and remain in the area; others are recruited overseas to work for Valley-based companies and transfer back to the home base. Since many high-technology firms are global from their inception, this diversity is particularly helpful in developing global operations quickly and efficiently.

Finally, an intangible but nonetheless critical ingredient of the Silicon Valley ecosystem is the pioneering spirit and relentless work ethic. The entrepreneurial culture was initially born out of a Californian history of pioneers making the perilous journey over the Rocky Mountains, coupled with the legacy of the Gold Rush.[11] The culture, developed over time, is characterized by hard work, inspiration, and by doing one thing very well.

Entrepreneurs exhibit many of the qualities of the early pioneers. They are prepared to take enormous risks, innovate in areas where most say it cannot be done, work incredibly long hours over extended periods of time, and even suffer personal problems, all to develop a product or build an enterprise. They have passion and bring a singular focus to their projects. As Schumpeter (1947) said: "The inventor produces ideas, the entrepreneur gets things done."

The "Modus Operandi" of Silicon Valley

In order to grasp the modus operandi of Silicon Valley, it is instrumental to adopt a bifocal perspective: first, at the level of the ecosystem as a whole, and second, at the level of the individual firm. Once the broader context is set, it is possible to better understand how the individual firms function in a symbiotic relationship to this unique ecosystem.

THE ECOSYSTEM: FLEXIBLE RECYCLING

Incessant Creation of New Ventures, Rapid Recycling of Failures

Each year, approximately three hundred new firms are funded by venture capital in Silicon Valley (*San Jose Mercury News* 1993). Notably, more firms are self-funded by founding teams or with investment assistance from private individuals colloquially known as "angels." New firms are founded in several different ways.

The notion of spinoffs is well documented in the management literature and plays a significant role in the creation of new high-technology firms. Indeed, spinoffs, in the traditional sense of the term, do represent a significant source of new firm formation in Silicon Valley. Nevertheless, the commonly accepted definition of a spinoff—individuals from one company forming a new entity—is not representative of the majority of Silicon Valley firms. Instead, founding teams typically get together from different firms and backgrounds to form new enterprises. The founding teams of these hybrid spinoffs may initially get together at networking forums, such as special-interest group meetings, and universities, or through previous relationships as customers, vendors, or working associates.

New start-ups are also founded by technology hobbyists and enthusiasts who may develop a product, initially for their own use. The most famous of garage start-ups, Apple Computer, came into being in this manner (Swanger 1985). A similar process was responsible for the creation of MacroMind (now MacroMedia), the multimedia software firm. There are a handful of "repeat" entrepreneurs. In the disk drive industry, Alan Shugart parted company with Shugart Associates early on, and, although excluded from competing in the disk drive industry for a number of years, he cofounded Seagate Technology with another Shugart cofounder, Finis Conner, in 1979. Following a downturn in the disk drive industry in 1985, Finis Conner left Seagate to form his own company, Conner Peripherals, which became one of the fastest growing companies in U.S. business history. Interestingly, Don Massaro, who replaced Alan Shugart as president of Shugart, recently became vice president of marketing at Conner Peripherals, after cofounding the now-defunct Metaphor Computers with Dave Liddell, a coinventor of Ethernet at Xerox PARC. Similarly, Larry Boucher left his first entrepreneurial venture, Adaptec, to found Auspex Systems in 1988 (Kretchmar 1989).

Yet another type of new high-tech firm can be best described as a "restart." These are typically ventures that are either acquired by larger firms (and may later flounder) or are venture-backed start-ups whose business models need recalibration under new management teams. Some may be able to rise out of the ashes of the failing parent or be bought out to achieve independent viability. SuperMac Technology is a good example. Scientific Microsystems, the now-defunct input/output controller firm, acquired SuperMac in an attempt to diversify. When the parent began to flounder, the founding entrepreneur reversed the process. Some years later SuperMac orchestrated its own public offering, prior to merging with Radius in 1994.

A further source of new enterprises, one that is often discussed in the literature, is that of researchers/scientists wishing to commercialize their ideas. The biotechnology industry is populated by many entrepreneurs who fall into this category, with Herbert Boyer of the University of California, San Francisco, as one of the most famous examples. In the electronics industry, Carver Mead, a professor at Cal Tech, and Frederico Fagin, founder of Zilog, cofounded Synaptics to develop neural processors. Syntex commercialized Carl Djerassi's Nobel Prize–winning discovery of the contraceptive pill. Regardless of their origin, the most striking feature of new enterprises in Silicon Valley is the preponderance of entrepreneurial teams with complementary perspectives and diverse capabilities who band together to found high-tech start-ups.

Continuous Interfirm Mobility

Significant fluidity exists between the various components of the Silicon Valley ecosystem. Executives move from high-tech companies into venture capital, investment banking, and consulting, among others. The movement may be in the other direction as well. Engineers change jobs with much frequency and may move from one firm to another just "down the road" without having to move homes or change their children's schools. Consultants move on to become managers and executives. Many executives leave the relative security of an established firm to join a smaller firm or even to start their own companies.

There are many examples of this mobility in Silicon Valley. For example, Eugene Kleiner, founding partner of Kleiner, Perkins, Caufield, and Byers, one of the Valley's leading venture capital firms with $673 million under management in 1992, was previously at Fairchild Semiconductor. Robert Maxfield and Regis McKenna also joined a venture firm after founding ROLM and Regis McKenna, Inc., the marketing consulting firm, respectively. David Crockett, the founder of Pyramid Technology, also moved into the venture capital arena. Conversely, George Sollman moved from Shugart, the disk drive company, to the venture capital community and later became the CEO of a voice-messaging firm, Centigram.

Executives also frequently move from large firms to start-ups: Cyril

Yansouni moved from Hewlett Packard (HP) to Convergent Technology (and to Unisys when the latter was acquired in 1986), and later to Read-Rite (a manufacturer of thin-film heads for disk drives) as its chief executive. Similarly, his former boss, Paul Ely, moved from HP to Convergent, and subsequently into the venture community. Other examples include Edward McCracken from HP to Silicon Graphics, William Krause from HP to 3Com, Trip Hawkins from Apple to Electronic Arts and subsequently on to found 3DO, Wilfred Corrigan from Fairchild to LSI Logic, and Noyce and Moore from Fairchild to found Intel.

This high degree of mobility across various parts of the ecosystem is not restricted only to the business community. For example, Stig Hagstrom, who was responsible for one of the labs at Xerox PARC, moved to Stanford University's Material Science Department. Moreover, within constraints concerning intellectual property and other legal issues, this mobility is just as frequent among firms that may have been competitors. For example, after stepping down as the chief operating officer of Seagate Technology, Tom Mitchell moved to a similar position at Seagate's rival, Conner Peripherals.

At its core, the Silicon Valley ecosystem functions through an interconnected network of personal relationships. Universities as well as the more established firms such as HP may be the initial context that brings people together and facilitates the formation and nurturing of personal relationships. Since relationships typically endure longer than an individual's tenure at any given company, they provide the fulcrum around which the ecosystem can flexibly operate. Both ROLM and Shugart (and many of their spinoffs) were forged by individuals who had known one another for some time. In the semiconductor industry, Shockley Laboratories was the initial setting that brought together the key group of people who later founded Fairchild, and then spun off to form Intel, National Semiconductor, and LSI Logic, among others. Informal networks thus form the hub of activity in Silicon Valley. These noninstitutionalized relationships are difficult to conceptualize yet are crucial in providing anchors of stability in the dynamic context of the ecosystem.

Rapid Transmission and Widespread Diffusion of Information:
Emphasis on "Doing" Rather than Just "Knowing"

It is exceedingly difficult to keep secrets in Silicon Valley concerning future products and competitive intentions. This is due, in part, to the proximity of companies, the fast-moving nature of high-technology industries, the high mobility of engineers and other professionals, and the frequent formation of partnerships and alliances that cross-pollinate knowledge and ideas. These, together with short product cycles and market windows, imply that the fulcrum of the competitive battle is not just knowing what to do (in terms of next generation products) but building new products that can find a receptive market.

In high-technology industries, information has a limited time value, regardless of the level of secrecy a firm may be able to keep concerning its future intentions. New products are alpha- and beta-tested by potential customers, who may also conduct business with a firm's competitors. In addition, pioneering firms typically have to release technical information in order to ensure compatibility of the various technical subsystems so that related products can interface effectively. Moreover, due to the rapid pace of change, information about products, markets, and competitors is quickly obsolete.

Formal and informal exchanges among "techno-evangelists," on electronic bulletin boards and at user-group meetings, is another source of information diffusion. These individuals have a passion for their technical interests and often interact at user-group meetings or trade shows with others of similar disposition. The ecosystem provides a broad framework within which people can interact and exchange information, ideas, and know-how.

Learning by Doing and by Failing

In Silicon Valley there is no stigma attached to honest failure, although there is for resting on one's laurels or not playing the game. Entrepreneurs are measured by what they are currently doing, not by what they did in the past, whether their previous venture was a success or a failure. Since the stigma associated with failure is depersonalized, both start-ups and incumbents can engage in novel experiments in the belief that it is immeasurably better to try something risky and to fail rather than to wonder about what might have been. Even if a venture fails, entrepreneurs can learn from the experiment and move on to start a successful entity. The inverse of this proposition also applies, in that previously successful entrepreneurs may not be able to repeat their success in a new incarnation.

Attitudes toward failure are critical to the ultimate success of pioneering high-technology companies. As several studies have shown, new products in technology-based industries are successively refined as the result of a learning process, in which innovators not only learn by "doing" but also by "failing" (Maidique and Zirger 1985). Such "failures" in turn may result in a reassessment of the original concepts and the development of new alternatives. The case is illustrated by Apple III and Lisa, two unsuccessful computer systems introduced by Apple during the early 1980s that gave birth to the highly successful Macintosh.

This empiricist approach of trial and error captures the essence of "learning-by-doing" in high-technology companies (Bahrami and Evans 1989a). The emphasis on continuous recalibration is especially critical when there are no historical precedents or recipes for success for a given product or market arena. Even with the most elaborate planning and focus-group meetings, it is not clear, ahead of time, how customers are likely to react to a new class of product.

Interlinked Specialization and Complementary Alliances: Focus on Creating "Steeples" of Expertise

The Silicon Valley ecosystem achieves flexibility through "diverse specialization," with each firm focusing on what it does best and taking advantage of the capabilities of other entities for complementary activities (Piore and Sabel 1984). For example, a start-up can focus on its technical design capability, while utilizing other entities for prototype development, manufacturing, market research, public relations, advertising, and staffing. Such an infrastructure is robust. Each component is semiautonomous, enabling the ecosystem as a whole to withstand shocks and perturbations. It is also versatile in that new competencies can be quickly added, enhancing and upgrading its capabilities.

In this context, the ecosystem may be viewed as a constellation of specialized enterprises and complementary alliances. Alliances are forged between individuals when they coalesce into an entrepreneurial team to form a start-up. Similarly, venture capitalists forge alliances in the form of a syndicate to coinvest in a firm. In addition, a recent trend, which takes the notion of interlinked specialization and complementary alliances one step further, is for large firms to ally themselves with start-ups at the early stages, not just as investors but also as potential manufacturing, development, or distribution partners.

The now-defunct personal communications start-up EO had a number of global partners, including AT&T, Matsushita, and Marubeni, among others, only eighteen months into the venture's life cycle, before being acquired by AT&T. 3DO, a multimedia firm founded by Trip Hawkins of Electronic Arts, was initially a joint venture between Time Warner, Matsushita, and Electronic Arts, before embarking on a public offering in May 1993. Similarly, General Magic, the personal communications software company and an Apple spinoff, was initially forged through an alliance between Apple, AT&T, Philips, and Sony. This partnering trend may be a harbinger of the next evolutionary phase of Silicon Valley, as global and overseas companies have shown a great deal of interest in investing and forging alliances in Silicon Valley companies (Besher 1989; Teece 1992).

Several high-technology firms have long participated in global alliances. For example, Quantum Corporation, the disk drive firm, has, for some time, allied itself with Matsushita as its manufacturing partner, so that it can focus on new product development and distribution. Auspex Systems, the innovative network file server company, forged an alliance with Fuji-Xerox in its formative years, involving both investments and distribution agreements. These arrangements are particularly helpful for small start-ups wishing to penetrate challenging overseas markets or for larger firms intending to build innovative products at the lowest possible cost.

Alliances are forged at many different levels and for different reasons. The much publicized IBM-Apple alliances exemplify concerted attempts to create new industry standards from which both firms may potentially benefit. The relationship that Apple has forged with third-party suppliers is aimed at developing a wide range of products to fit several specialized market niches. Sun Microsystems benefited from early investments by Kodak and AT&T, which among other things legitimized it in the eyes of wary customers, unused to purchasing equipment from new firms.

MODUS OPERANDI OF SILICON VALLEY

The Firm: Barriers to Permanence

Swift action, mobility, and ephemerality are critical features of Silicon Valley business dynamics. Organizational structures and business models undergo frequent strategic recalibrations and constant realignments. The ability of a firm to endure is thus contingent on the continued viability of its business model and its organizational capabilities.

Today's successful models may endure for only a limited time. A firm must either recalibrate its approach or find a new business proposition, before it is made obsolete. Under these conditions, it is often easier to form a new entity in order to capitalize on a technological breakthrough or an unfolding market niche, since rapid concentration of effort is critical for success. A start-up firm has a singular focus and minimal inertia, whereas established companies, despite financial resources and market presence, can take longer to maneuver and recalibrate their business trajectories. There are several underlying forces that drive change and ephemerality in high-technology companies.

Organizational Alignment and Speed of Maneuver

The founders and the senior management team of a start-up are typically the product's developers, manufacturers, and marketers, fusing together thinking and doing, and aligning the organization behind its strategic objectives. As a firm grows, sometimes by as many as hundreds of people per month, its organizational structure can become quickly fragmented. Turf battles invariably arise that can fracture the cohesion of an organization, resulting in a distancing of the generals from the troops. Functional segmentation and compartmentalization, coupled with organizational inertia, can hinder the recalibration of business models, resources, and capabilities. The resulting "loosely coupled" organization may be too cumbersome for rapid maneuvering. The point to note is that inertial forces restrict a firm's flexibility—that is, its ability to change course and maneuver quickly as technological and market conditions change (for a discussion of this, see Bower and Christensen 1995).

Employee Commitment and Motivation

Typically, the enthusiasm and motivation of employees in a start-up are somewhat different from what is found among workers who value security and are attracted to a firm once it becomes an established public company. Although this may be an oversimplification, the former enjoy the challenge of survival and personal growth, while the latter may value security and a relatively stable work environment. Motivated by the opportunities for personal growth, and the potential for significant financial gain (when a start-up becomes a public company or is acquired by another entity), many technical professionals forgo the relative security of a large entity for the turmoil and sense of adventure associated with a start-up.

Incentive and compensation structures and the "political" climate of established firms can also create a chasm between individual motivations and organizational goals. In a start-up, much of an individual's substantive compensation is in the form of stock options, which align individual and organizational goals and generate intense commitment. Since technology industries are knowledge-intensive and knowledge resides in people, individual attitudes and motivation levels can make or break a firm and impact its position in an industry.

Maturing firms may have difficulty matching the cultural intensity of a start-up, which is critical for building a team spirit and focusing emotional and creative energy on achieving the desired goal. Cultural intensity dissipates as a firm grows and becomes functionally segmented, potentially leading to a lost sense of purpose and confusion about the desired cultural values. These can have a disquieting impact on many professional employees and lead to a sense of apathy and loss of a community spirit.

Oftentimes, that initial cultural intensity fades when the founders leave and the original mission has been accomplished (O'Reilly 1989). Large technology firms that have managed to retain their entrepreneurial atmosphere and creative spirit often have founders who stay with the firm for a long time, thereby maintaining the connection with and motivating the troops. Well-known examples of long-term involvement in a firm by its founders include Intel, Hewlett Packard, Tandem, AMD, Sun Microsystems, Seagate, Conner Peripherals, and Oracle. In these situations, the founders can inspire the employees over time, evolving a shared set of strategic and cultural beliefs that bind the different parts of the organization, and focus their collective energies on a common sense of purpose. Alternatively, the founders may actually stay beyond their useful tenure, with an adverse impact on the firm's ability to recalibrate its business model as new realities unfold.

The Credibility of Newness

Another barrier to permanence in certain segments of high-technology industries such as software is the relative ease with which new firms can enter an arena. This process is facilitated by the fact that start-up firms in knowledge-based industries are less susceptible to problems associated with "liabilities of newness" (Aldrich and Fiol 1994; Singh et al. 1986). Many start-ups can circumvent potential "legitimacy problems" by developing a revolutionary product or a service that fulfills a market need in a timely manner. This is often the case when a new product becomes a de facto standard because of its market impact and the speed with which it is adopted. Recent examples include Intuit's Quicken software for home banking, Auspex's network file server, and Verifone's transaction automation systems.

Indeed, in some cases it may be argued that early legitimacy can be a liability because it may set unrealistically high expectations. Silicon Valley has had its share of technology start-ups that had a great deal of initial legitimacy (in terms of the founding team's background, venture capital funding, and favorable press reviews) but failed to deliver successful products and subsequently went out of business or were prematurely acquired.[12]

In conclusion, there are many barriers to permanence in the fast-moving environment of Silicon Valley. First, the scientific know-how and technical expertise on which products are based are rendered obsolete by the constant creation of new knowledge. Markets and distribution channels for technology products and services are fluid as customers become familiar with the capabilities of products. Competitive pressures induced by both the "renegade intent" of start-ups—namely, to transform and disturb the existing status quo—and the entry of large global corporations invariably catch incumbents in a pincer movement. Most firms are founded by entrepreneurial teams that, like a football team or a rock-band, where the "chemistry" between the players is critical, are seldom enduring phenomena.

The following cases illustrate many of these forces in the context of two companies, which we studied in some detail. These pioneering firms were well-known innovators in their respective industries and have ceased to exist in their original form. Their evolution demonstrates the modus operandi of Silicon Valley firms and the dynamic changes that drive the process of flexible recycling in the context of the ecosystem.

Case Histories

SHUGART ASSOCIATES

Shugart was incorporated in February 1973 by a team of eleven engineers, many of whom had previously left IBM to form Memorex (Stanford University 1983, 1985). Funded with venture capital backing from Hambrecht & Quist, the firm was initially engaged in the parallel development of a printer and a central processing unit. When a request for further development funds was put to the board by its founding CEO, the board asked him to leave and appointed another cofounder as president.

The company's first product, an eight-inch floppy disk drive, was introduced in May 1973 with volume shipments beginning in July 1973. Abandoning the earlier "grand" strategy, the firm concentrated all of its resources on disk drives, resulting in the introduction of double-density eight-inch floppy disk drives in April 1975. This was followed by another innovation that has subsequently become part of Silicon Valley folklore, the SA400 5.25-inch floppy disk drive that was introduced in September 1976 (Evans 1991). This product was a major success, propelling the company's growth, with revenues rising to $18.14 million by 1977. Shugart subsequently augmented its product line by developing an eight-inch Winchester disk drive, a process which, like that of the SA-400, was funded by two of its customers.

In 1978, Shugart postponed its initial public stock offering due to inauspicious trading conditions on Wall Street. It was subsequently acquired by Xerox Corporation as part of its office automation strategy. Fueled by increasing demand for the 5.25-inch floppy and other product lines, Shugart's revenues continued to grow rapidly. Following the acquisition, however, several members of its management team and engineering staff left the company, some to form "niche" disk drive start-ups, others to join competing firms. Over time, these spinoff firms were to play an almost patricidal role in the demise of Shugart.

Until 1981, not yet weakened by these spinoffs and by Japanese competition, Shugart continued to innovate and prosper. It pioneered, among others, the Shugart Associates Standard Interface (SASI), so that systems integrators could quickly develop the microcode to allow Winchester disk drives to meet the unique operating systems requirements of different computer system manufacturers. Eventually, this product became an industry standard, enabling the interchangeability of disk drives between different and previously incompatible computer systems. SASI was the forerunner of the now widely accepted SCSI standard,[13] which "controls" both IBM PC (along with PC-compatibles) and Apple Macintosh computers. During this period, Shugart was also engaged in other innovative product development activities, such as optical disk drive technology. In this case, a subsidiary unit, Optimem, was established as an international strategic alliance between Xerox and SGS Thomson of France.

Between 1981 and 1984, Shugart's revenues grew considerably, although during this period the industry and competitive dynamics were also transformed. Several niche spinoffs, together with other start-ups, began to compete with selected parts of its business. Furthermore, Japanese manufacturers had made aggressive inroads into the low-end floppy disk drive segment by competing on the basis of low price and high quality. Yet Shugart Corporation (as it was subsequently renamed) was still, at this stage, the leading "across-the-board" supplier of rotating memory products.

Following an abrupt industry downturn that resulted in two years of consecutive losses, Shugart was spun off by Xerox in 1985 and 1986. The floppy disk business, which at the time constituted about one-third of Shugart's revenues, was sold off to its Japanese joint venture partner, Matsushita. Its Winchester disk drive division was dissolved, and its optical disk drive unit, Optimem, was sold to Cipher Data, which itself was subsequently acquired by Archive. The much pared-down Shugart, stripped of its 5.25-inch and pioneering 3.5-inch floppy and Winchester lines, was sold off to a group of investors and continues to operate as a service and distribution center in Los Angeles. Today it concentrates on drive-refurbishing and end-of-life products.

ROLM CORPORATION

ROLM was founded in 1969 by four former student colleagues, Richeson, Oshman, Loewenstern, and Maxfield, who had known one another first at Rice University and later at the Stanford Engineering School. The founding team's first business venture was to pioneer a unique commercial approach in selling minicomputers to the tradition-bound military establishment. Although the team established a viable business base in this niche market, their overriding objective was to build a sizable "commercial" concern. Minicomputers had been a time-ly opportunity to get the business off the ground. After three years, the founders became concerned about the limited size of that market and its potential for building a sizable commercial enterprise.

In the early 1970s, the founding team embarked on a preemptive search for a new business opportunity and decided to enter the tele-communications business. The 1968 "Carterfone" decision of the Fed-eral Communications Commission had partially deregulated the in-dustry, thereby opening up the vast telephone equipment market to a host of new companies. The intention was to leverage ROLM's core technological skills by developing a computer-controlled telephone switching system, with enhanced capabilities in comparison with the traditional electromechanical units.

During the 1970s, ROLM had to be steered through the uncertain and stormy seas that characterized the industry. Computers were changing the nature of telephones and telecommunications. There was considerable debate and uncertainty about the eventual deregulation of the industry, due to AT&T's concerted efforts to retain its long-standing position as a regulated monopoly. The interconnect distribu-tion channel was just beginning to get off the ground, and competition had intensified with the entry of Japanese and European giants into the field. In short, the industry was in a state of chaos and confusion.

At the time, many expert observers questioned the ability of a young, unknown player like ROLM to survive, let alone prosper, in the face of such uncertainty. Despite these initial grave misgivings, ROLM managed to become a leading telecommunications firm during the next five years. By the late 1970s, telecommunications products accounted for almost 70 percent of its total revenues.

ROLM consolidated its strategic position during the late 1970s by setting up a direct sales and service organization. It recalibrated its business trajectory during the early 1980s by making selected forays into the "office of the future," focusing on integrated voice/data termi-nals and voice messaging systems. It was later acquired by IBM in the aftermath of AT&T's divestiture in 1984, and it was partly sold to Sie-mens, the German giant, during the late 1980s.

At the time of the IBM acquisition, ROLM was called "the ship that is creating the wave of innovation in the field" and a "forerunner in the fast-paced (telecommunications) market" (*San Francisco Chronicle* 1984).

These tributes were clearly reflected in its impressive market performance. After only ten years in the telecommunications business, ROLM had managed to capture 15 percent of the market for office telephone switches, only 9 percent behind AT&T. Another measure of its remarkable success was the dramatic increase in its stock price. Compared with the other 1,920 companies that had gone public since 1975, ROLM's stock had produced the largest long-term relative gain over its initial offering price.

Case Discussion and Observation

As these two cases illustrate, a high-technology firm's strategic trajectory is not sustainable in its original form. Shugart's initial mission, for example, was to develop a complete desktop computer system including a printer, CPU, and disk drives. ROLM's business model evolved through several stages during its fifteen years of life as an independent company. Its original business plan included four different product ideas, none of which was the digital PBX that later fueled its growth.

In order to survive, business models and product offerings must be perpetually recalibrated. This ability to maneuver once a strategy has been recalibrated is the hallmark of success and almost a necessary condition for survival. In many situations, the original intent seldom turns out to be the winning business proposition. For example, Shugart began by developing a complete desktop computer including a printer, before it concentrated on disk drives; ROLM's first business plan included four different business ideas, none of which included the digital PBX that later fueled its rapid growth.

Operating in conditions of kaleidoscopic change, a firm's technical demise, we suggest, is not necessarily detrimental as long as the ecosystem can flexibly recycle its critical know-how and human assets. The ephemeral nature of ROLM and Shugart clearly resulted in a reconfiguration and recycling of their assets and capabilities. Many of Shugart's employees joined its spinoffs, started new companies, and in some cases revitalized other entities. Similarly, many of ROLM's original employees, including their founding team, have since moved on to other entities, started a number of new concerns, and turned around a number of languishing companies. Ken Oshman, its founding CEO, moved on to lead Echelon, a pioneer in the networking field. A number of former employees of ROLM's Mil-Spec Division founded Ultra, a firm working on high-speed local area networks. Richard Moley, ROLM's former vice president of marketing and its first PBX product manager, became CEO of Stratacom, a manufacturer of multiplexers and network management systems.

Conclusion

The constellation including high-technology firms, venture capitalists, support infrastructure, a globally diverse talent pool, and academic and research institutions that has coalesced into Silicon Valley characterizes a dynamic ecosystem of semiautonomous yet mutually supportive entities, communities, and cultures. It has generated a critical mass of global, knowledge-intensive enterprises, whose innovative products and technologies are transforming the global economy. Once the ecosystem in which these firms operate reached a critical mass, the evolution of existing firms and the creation of new entities produced a dynamic domain in which the processes of firm formation, demise, and recycling occur on a continuous basis.

Paradoxically, this ecosystem enables continuity and change to coexist. It thrives on processes of flexible recycling, as start-ups and spinoffs are formed, and on continuous recalibration, as incumbent firms reassess their business models. Flexibility, "the ability to do something differently or do something other than that originally intended" (Hart 1937), is a sine qua non for high-technology firms, since conditions are rarely stable enough to enable what economists term "perfect adaptation" (Stigler 1939).

This process of "flexible recycling" is enhanced in the absence of the typical stigma associated with organizational failure. Indeed the high failure rate may be more of an asset, in that it increases the rates of experimentation and speed of recycling, and, in a Popperian sense (1972), entrepreneurs learn, just as scientists do, much from failed experiments. Since organizational death, in and of itself, is not perceived as a finite expression of failure, entrepreneurs are able to entertain what would normally be considered "outlandish" risks. Moreover, prospects of failure and ephemerality can also reduce feelings of overconfidence and invulnerability among successful incumbents and keep them on their toes. In such a setting, large incumbent firms strive to become "agile giants" capable of rapid maneuvering and recalibrating.

The short life cycle of many high-technology firms may be helpful for sustaining the long-term innovative capability of an ecosystem such as Silicon Valley. In addition to maintaining the stream of new firms, which in turn provide employment opportunities and create new products and services, ephemeral firms increase the variety of experiments, and, when acquired, can help rejuvenate other entities or become reconfigured in the form of new entities. For example, several firms may merge in order to gain a critical mass. This variety can also facilitate the development of the next generation of firms and products. This is crucial, given that it is difficult, if not impossible, to know the "winning formula" a priori.

The notion of an ecosystem that thrives on flexible recycling may provide an alternative vehicle for policy-makers to examine issues related to global competitiveness and the growth of high-technology industries. National and regional governments and local communities may become as concerned with the long-term success of their ecosystems as they are with the survival of larger firms that provide substantial employment opportunities in their communities. In thinking about these considerations, however, the appropriate balance needs to be struck between anchors of employment stability and growth, and the flexibility needed to accommodate kaleidoscopic changes.

It is clear that the managerial recipes and organizational regimes of many Silicon Valley companies are worthy of further study and discussion. In addition to the nimble start-ups, mid-sized "adolescents" and large enduring firms must also be capable of continuously recalibrating their trajectories and reconstituting their business models. They must become "agile giants" to survive in this dynamic ecosystem. However, such firms demonstrate that it is indeed possible for large, mid-sized, and small firms to be flexible as long as their organizational systems are aligned and their strategies are recalibrated as the conditions that they confront inevitably change, thereby rendering them capable of rapid maneuvering.

Permanence or sustainability may not be the most critical measure of success in this fast-moving and knowledge-intensive domain. Other considerations include the extent to which a firm can pioneer new products and services, generate wealth for its shareholders, and foster enduring relationships among its employees. However, most of our

managerial tools, conceptual frameworks, and research studies, reflected in managerial expectations and business theories, are framed in
the context of sustainability and the rhetoric of permanence. As Carol
Bartz (1993), the CEO of Autodesk, observed: "We need to constantly
reevaluate our business models and our industry forces, and take cor-
rective measures along the way. Yes, it's part of natural business evolution, but it also signals the end of an era."

CHAPTER NINE

Social Capital and Capital Gains: An Examination of Social Capital in Silicon Valley

STEPHEN S. COHEN
AND GARY FIELDS

It is difficult to imagine an example of regional economic development that is more successful, or more famous, than California's Silicon Valley. Investors from all over the world arrive with suitcases of money to place in what they hope will be the Valley's next success story. Ambitious, educated people—mostly young—from dozens of nations come to the Valley to take their chances in start-ups fueled by stock options. Regional development theorists study Silicon Valley to identify the underlying characteristics that have enabled this area to become one of the most innovative and prosperous regional economies in the world. Policy-makers visit, seeking to determine whether the characteristics identified by the theorists and journalists—and the stories they are told during their visit—can somehow be transferred to develop innovation-based economic development in their own regions.

Riding the newest wave of regional development theory is the notion of "social capital" popularized by Robert Putnam in his influential book *Making Democracy Work* (1993). Putnam's idea refers to the complex of local institutions and relationships of trust among economic actors that evolve from unique, historically conditioned local cultures. Such institutions and social relationships, built upon the experiences of a shared deep history, become embedded within a localized economy and form what Putnam describes as "networks of civic engagement" that facilitate the activities of politics, production, and exchange. In these locales of tight civic engagement people know one another and one another's families; they meet frequently in non–work related organizations and activities. They constitute a dense and rich social community. Business relationships are embedded in community and family structures. Those structures not only generate contact and information transmission; they also reinforce trust by sanctioning, in powerful and multidimensional ways, the breaking of trust. In Putnam's model, cooperation based on trust, which in turn is rooted in complex and deep social ties, propels development. It is an inherited historical characteristic.

Does the wave of regional development theory represented by Putnam's model of social capital apply to Silicon Valley? No. To use a Valley metaphor, the wave breaks at the shores of Silicon Valley in a way that precludes successful surfing. Put more formally, the thesis of this chapter is that Putnam's concept of social capital, whatever its power as an explanation of local prosperity elsewhere, does not fit the experience of Silicon Valley. Worse yet, it obscures the specific nature of the social capital on which Silicon Valley was built and through which it continues to construct itself.

The sources of technological dynamism in Silicon Valley can be described in many ways, but there is little truth in the idea of Silicon Valley as a community of dense civic engagement. Silicon Valley is notoriously a world of strangers; nobody knows anybody else's mother there. There is no deep history, little in the way of complex familial ties, and little structured community. It is a world of independent—even isolated—newcomers. With its spatially isolated and spread-out residential patterns, its shopping strips and malls, its auto gridlock, its rapid demographic turnover, and the rampant individualism among its most talented workers, Silicon Valley would be hard pressed to present the image of a close-knit civil society that, according to the social capital theorists, is the precondition for economic prosperity.

Silicon Valley is, however, an economic space built on social capital, but it is a vastly different kind of social capital than that popularized by the civic engagement theorists. In Silicon Valley, social capital can be understood in terms of the collaborative partnerships that emerged in the region owing to the pursuit by economic and institutional actors of objectives related specifically to innovation and competitiveness. It is the networks resulting from these collaborations that form the threads of social capital as it exists in Silicon Valley. What these networks of innovation in Silicon Valley share with the networks of civic engagement is simply and only a common networklike structure. There is virtually nothing in the history of Silicon Valley to connect its networks of innovation to a dense civil society.

The network environment in Silicon Valley is the outcome of historically conditioned, specifically chosen collaborations between individual entrepreneurs, firms, and institutions focused on the pursuit of innovation and its commercialization. Its foundations can be traced in part to ideas proposed by Alfred Marshall and Thorstein Veblen that have influenced social capital theory. These collaborations also result from what some theorists refer to as "historical accident," as well as broader, nationally based, institutionally driven trajectories of development and competitive choice (Arthur 1989; David 1993). They are buttressed by the nature of the Silicon Valley markets for labor and capital, by the internal dynamic of successive innovation, and by the simple momentum of economic success. From the convergence of local historical chance, national historical currents, and choice emerged the collaborations at the foundation of Silicon Valley's technological dynamism. This paper seeks to describe the social capital networks in Silicon Valley by reviewing how these historical choices were made, examining the relationships resulting from these choices, and inquiring how policy can help to create functionally comparable relationships in other economic regions.

Social Capital Networks in Silicon Valley

Silicon Valley is traditionally defined as an area beginning about thirty-five miles south of San Francisco and extending through San Jose. It encompasses some fifteen hundred square miles, with a population of 2.3 million and 1.2 million jobs (although the Valley has been rapidly growing). About one-fourth of the residents are foreign born. The area has added about two hundred thousand jobs since 1992, with about fifty-three thousand being added in 1997. Average annual wages are $46,000; the U.S. average is $29,000 (Joint Venture: Silicon Valley 1998). In the fourth quarter of 1998, the venture capital invested into Silicon Valley amounted to $1.7 billion, constituting about 41 percent of the national total (Pricewaterhouse Coopers 1998). Some 3,575 new firms were incorporated in the Valley in 1997 (Joint Venture: Silicon Valley 1998).

The Silicon Valley economy is dominated by rapid innovation and commercialization in an expanding set of new technologies. Micro-electronics (that is, semiconductors—e.g., Intel, AMD, National Semi-conductor) and later computers (Apple, Sun Microsystems, Hewlett Packard) put the Valley on the world map, and they continue to be major activities. Computer networking, both hardware and software (e.g., 3Com, Cisco, Netscape, Yahoo, Broadvision), has recently ex-ploded as a central activity. Biotechnology along with medical devices and drug delivery systems constitutes the third major new technology in which the Valley is a world center, perhaps the world center. Along with these core industries, venture finance and intellectual property law have become significant activities in their own right (see Kenney and Florida; and Suchman in this volume). The Valley is an enormously prosperous region. Standard income data, which rely on wages and salaries (which were more than 150% of the national average) miss the critical turbo charger: capital gains from stock options, which add hugely to the Valley's wealth accumulation, not just at the very peak of the income distribution but also quite a way down into the engineering, professional, and managerial ranks, and occasionally even lower. The constraint on this growth, Ricardo's law of rent, is classic: real estate prices, rising wages (average wages in software, semiconductor, and semiequipment firms hit $85,500 in 1996!), and congestion (average delays in auto traffic keep rising) create a constant spinoff of new plants and facilities into other, lower-cost regions. Silicon Valley firms no longer manufacture many semiconductors in the Valley.

The main networks of social capital in Silicon Valley are not dense networks of civic engagement but focused, productive interactions among the following social institutions, instruments, and entities:

1. *The great research universities:* Stanford; the University of Califor-nia, Berkeley; and the University of California, San Francisco (which is a medical school) provide personnel and ideas. These universities have tight relationships to outside actors who commercialize applications of their research and researchers. Also, they recruit faculty and graduate students from all over the world, not just locally or nationally. For a nontrivial example, about one-third of the graduate students at Ber-keley in electrical engineering and computer science are foreign nation-

als; a similar proportion of the faculty is foreign-born (University of California, Berkeley 1997).

2. *U.S. government policy:* In the early phases of microelectronics and computer networking, government policy served both as sponsor of university research and, critically, as lead-user (see Leslie, this volume, for further discussion).

3. *Venture capital firms:* The venture capitalists serve not only as a home-grown source of early-stage capital but also as loci of high-tech investment expertise and "godfather" services to start-up companies, including the provision of experienced executives at critical moments in a firm's development, strategic and operational advice, and links and leads to potential customers and partners (see also Kenney and Florida in this volume).

4. *Law firms:* Law firms provide another source for locating key personnel, finance contacts, as well as corporate and intellectual property legal services; they often take payment in stock rather than cash (see Suchman in this volume).

5. *Business networks:* The leading figures in university engineering departments, venture firms, law firms, and operating firms in the Valley know one another through frequent business and professional contact. The density of lawyers in this community (about one lawyer per ten engineers) (Employment Development Department 1997) provides an operational definition of the limited role of informal, familial, and communitarian trust. The opposite of trust is "accountability," and the arbiters of accountability are accountants and auditors; in Silicon Valley they outnumber the lawyers (ibid.). In sum, there is one lawyer or accountant per five engineers.

6. *Stock options:* Employees (not counting a firm's founders and CEO) often hold options and shares amounting easily to 10 or 15 percent (or more at the early stages) of a firm's capital value.[1] This practice rewards success with giant payoffs (as well as serving to extend loyalty and the employment tenure of key employees for the several years of the option holding period). The amounts are substantial. For example, a currently super-successful Valley firm, Cisco Systems, now has a capital value that exceeds that of the Ford Motor Company.

7. *Labor market:* The Valley labor market has several important characteristics that define the Valley's particular brand of social capital. First, as Angel has shown (this volume), there is no stigma in leaving a large and very successful company such as Hewlett Packard or Sun Mi-

crosystems to launch a start-up. A few years ago, that was not the case in many leading companies in Europe—not to mention Japan. What also continues to differentiate the Valley is that even if the start-up fails, there are numerous jobs awaiting a seasoned engineer or manager at other Valley firms—as well as through venture capitalists and head-hunters looking for executive leadership for other new companies. Second, there is rapid turnover. People (at all levels) shift from company to company. This has many consequences, one of which is technology diffusion. In Silicon Valley technology and know-how have legs. Third, there is recruitment of talent, especially scarce technical and entrepreneurial talent, from literally the entire world. To meet the needs of their clients, Silicon Valley law firms have developed a substantial capability—sometimes in-house, sometimes networked—in immigration law.

8. *The nature of the industry:* Industries differ. The industry that defines a region's specialization also defines its social structure and institutions more than any other single factor: coal and steel districts in Wales, Wallonia, Asturias, and Pennsylvania had similar social structures. Industries define their regions in two ways: first, by the speed of their growth and transformation. The semiconductor industry, the initial shaper of Silicon Valley, has grown by about 3,000 percent over the past twenty years.[2] Such growth makes small companies into big companies at amazing speed. Second, locally dominant industries shape their societies by valuing some kinds of social structures over others (e.g., unions and friendly societies in coal and steel communities, intellectual property and employment contract law in Silicon Valley). Automobile districts, wherever they are, differ more from footwear districts or software districts than from one another. In much of the recent literature that focuses on the social characteristics of specialized industrial districts, and how those social structures propel or retard growth and transformation, too little attention has been paid to how substantively different kinds of industrial activities favor different industrial and social structures. This is true even when the industries are quite close in kind. For example, comparisons between Boston's high-tech industrial district and Silicon Valley vastly neglect the important differentiating characteristics between electronic defense systems and then minicomputers—the defining activities on the Boston side—and microelectronics and computer networking, the defining activities in Silicon Valley (Kenney and von Burg 1999). Similarly, research universities, abundant engineering talent, and venture capital play only a

limited role, if that, in Milan's dynamic high-fashion district, or in the Italian tile-making district, or in Detroit's (and now Kentucky's) auto districts, or in Georgia's carpet and towel belt. Ultimately, what you do shapes how you do it—all the way back up the value chain, and all the way out into forms of social organization. It would be ill-advised policy that strives to make electronics innovation into the new industrial standard bearer in the same social milieu as footwear, underwear, axles, or carpeting.

It is the cooperative—and competitive—interaction of these critical elements that defines Silicon Valley as a system of social capital. All the rest, such as informal conversations in bars or bowling teams, is, relative to other places, somewhat underdeveloped and ancillary. Unlike Putnam's vague but radically deterministic concept of the historic formation of civic culture and social capital—which fixes the future development paths of the Italian regions he studies back in the late Middle Ages—these key elements of social capital both accurately define the reality of Silicon Valley's experience and are far more amenable to shaping by well-informed policy.[3]

The Lineage of Social Capital and Its Critique

In his engaging account of the divergent economic fortunes manifested by different Italian regions, Robert Putnam insists that there is a connection between the degree of social capital accumulated within a region and its economic performance. The vexing question for Putnam, along with others sympathetic to his approach, is what constitutes this elusive concept, social capital.

According to Putnam (1993b: 37), social capital is akin to a "moral resource." It refers to the features of social organization that facilitate coordination and cooperation for mutual benefit (ibid.: 35–36; id.: 1993a: 167). Social capital is embodied in what Putnam calls "networks of civic engagement" that evolve over time owing to historical traditions of citizen involvement in a broad range of social, economic, and political activities. Where there is a vibrant civil society, there are bonds of trust and reciprocity. These bonds facilitate the networks of civic life at the core of social capital. The relative strength or weakness of these networks within a region will have a paramount impact on the character of the region's economic life.

Despite the somewhat mysterious nature of how these networks actually get created, Putnam is very clear on the link between social capital and economic development, and the policy implications of this link. Communities, he argues, did not forge networks of civic engagement because of their prosperity. On the contrary, communities in Putnam's view (1993a: 152–62) become prosperous because they are civic. "The social capital embodied in networks of civic engagement seems to be a precondition for economic development" (Putnam 1993b: 37). According to Putnam, there is an obvious policy lesson to be learned from the connection between social capital and economic prosperity, and he implores policy-makers to take note of the way that "civics matters." The policy lesson to be drawn from Putnam's thesis is that if communities create networks of social capital, prosperity is likely to follow.

Two distinct theoretical lineages converge in Putnam's work on the relationship between social capital and localized economic performance. One tradition derives from Alfred Marshall and his notion of economic vibrancy within localized industrial districts. The other tradition, perhaps less commonly associated with social capital, is traceable to the writings of Thorstein Veblen on how institutions create competitive trajectories of growth and technological innovation.

While the emphasis of Marshall's monumental work (1890: 267–77, 314–20) is on the power of supply and demand to generate equilibrium prices in markets, he nevertheless established a unique framework for understanding the dynamism within certain localized regions through his concept of external scale economies. According to Marshall, economies of scale are not restricted to the internal operations of the individual firm. The concentration of firms in an industry in one location can also provide benefits to individual firms owing to the effects of proximity. Such firms that are clustered together can take advantage of access to specialized suppliers, skilled labor, and an environment that makes possible the spillover of technological knowledge from one firm to another. For Marshall, these external economies operate much like internal economies by lowering costs and helping to explain the phenomenon behind the agglomerations of firms from the same industry that Marshall termed "industrial districts."

In his celebrated metaphor describing the concentration of the cutlery industry in the area of Sheffield, England, Marshall writes that in such a district where firms from the same industry are concentrated, "The mysteries of the trade become no mysteries, but are as it were in the air" (ibid.: 271). Thus, from Marshall and his notion of external scale economies emerges a picture of localized economic vibrancy, nurtured by the cost savings of resource-sharing and information exchange that occurs within a localized industrial environment. But Marshall's magisterial work provides more of an understanding of an industrial district—that is, a successful specialized local economy—than any special insight into the nature of social capital.

In contrast to Marshall, Thorstein Veblen (1898, 1899) rejected the neoclassical notion of equilibrium in markets and embraced metaphors from evolutionary biology in arguing that the key to economic development resides in the capacity of institutions to adapt to ever-changing market conditions. Veblen (1899: 188) likened the economy to an evolutionary phenomenon of disequilibrium in which competition and natural selection prevail. In this evolutionary process, industrial structures, spawned from market competition, and institutions develop in an interlocking embrace. Once established, however, within the context of this interactive evolution, institutions play a fundamental role in shaping the market process by assuming one of two basic tendencies. Institutions either remain static and rigid, thereby giving rise to a type of "friction" between an existing industrial structure and the institutional arrangements that have emerged around it (Hodgson 1994: 25; Veblen 1915), or institutions may adapt to changing market forces, enabling industrial structures and economic development to assume a dynamic and more technologically advanced character. What Veblen was intent upon uncovering were those factors promoting or precluding institutional adaptation that enabled the process of technological innovation to occur for economic advance.

What eventually led the insights of Marshall and Veblen to resurface in the social capital literature were the debates initiated in the late 1970s on the differences distinguishing regional economies. These debates rekindled interest in the phenomenon of industrial districts. Providing the catalyst for these debates was a dramatic reversal in economic development trends beginning in the 1970s. These trends included (1) the tendency of certain regional economies with heavy concentrations of small and medium-sized firms to outperform other economies owing to their capacity for innovation (Brusco 1982); (2) the apparently disproportionate contribution to economic growth and development made by smaller firms in the context of this crisis (Birch

1979; Teitz et al. 1981); and (3) the competitive difficulties experienced by large firms beginning in the late 1970s and their seeming inability to evolve and adapt to a transforming world marketplace (Piore and Sabel 1984; Sengenberger et al. 1990).[4]

In our view, the observations about the relative weaknesses of giant firms, especially the assumption about their inability to adapt and evolve, constitute a major weakness at the very heart of this literature. In its emphasis on local culture and regional development, this literature was somewhat blind to sector-specific effects and a bit too quick to generalize from a small set of overlapping case studies. In most sectors, in most of the industrialized world, established industrial giants such as GE, Boeing, Coca-Cola, Hewlett Packard, Nestle, Merck, Monsanto, Unilever, AT&T, Ford, Volkswagon, Merrill Lynch, Citicorp, United Parcel Service, and even IBM have grown, adapted, and evolved quite handsomely. Big firms proved to be quite flexible and adaptable— perhaps more so than most specialized districts!

James Coleman, another social capital theorist, provides a romantic—and telling—analysis of New York's diamond district. There, trust is total. Diamonds worth thousands are taken without signatures or serious control. This highly functioning trust is built on the deepest of civic engagements and secured by the sinews of a totally closed society. But Coleman (1988) never extends his admiring analysis upstream to mention the name De Beers, the giant multinational that completely controls the diamond industry.[5] It is likely that many of the "deep trust" industrial districts exist in relation to major multinational corporations the way the New York diamond district lives in relation to De Beers: total dependency with ties of civic engagement serving to exclude outsiders, thereby both improving efficiency and capturing rents that would ordinarily be competed away. Silicon Valley is the exact opposite. The society is open and so is the market. Silicon Valley is not an ecology of small and dependent companies holding onto a small rent in a larger revenue stream. Valley companies sell to a broad universe of clients and sometimes grow to be very large indeed; the small ones harbor big ambitions and see themselves as young, not permanently small.

Nonetheless, theorists working within this particular approach began to reassess what drives the process of economic development within regions, and to contemplate how the factors driving development could be reproduced, through policy choices, from place to place.

The result was the "rediscovery of the region" by contemporary regional development theorists and a search for the factors underlying the "resurgence of regional economies" (Storper 1995).

Perhaps the defining moment in this reappraisal of the region and search for what made certain regional economies technologically dynamic was the celebrated work by Michael Piore and Charles Sabel, *The Second Industrial Divide* (1984). For Piore and Sabel, the second industrial divide marked a profound historical separation between the formerly dominant system of mass production and a newly emerging paradigm of flexibly specialized production. In the divide was a very real phenomenon—the late-twentieth-century industrial district—which was the economic and geographical manifestation of the future. In the midst of the difficulties experienced by large firms and the districts dependent upon them, certain industrial districts had continued to prosper—most notably in Italy but also in Germany, Japan, and even the United States. Firms within these enclaves had become more innovative, owing to their small size and their resultant capacity to overcome the constraints of mass production. According to Piore and Sabel, such districts, based upon small, flexibly specialized companies, had their origins in the craft production of the late nineteenth century.

This contemplation of the future in terms of the past by Piore and Sabel garnered further support in the research of historians such as Sidney Pollard (1973, 1981), and more recently by Gary Herrigel (1996) and Philip Scranton (1997). Both Pollard and Herrigel supplied potent historical justifications for the phenomenon of industrial districts in Europe, arguing that such regional industrial economies, based upon smaller specialized firms, had far-reaching historical roots in the period of so-called proto-industrialization of the eighteenth century. Scranton depicted a similar regional phenomenon in the historical landscape of the nineteenth century in the United States. These historical accounts provided additional evidence that the (re)discovery of localized industrial systems by Piore and Sabel was not something ephemeral or limited in scope. Economic development within vibrant, regionally based industrial districts had a strong historical basis.

Inspired by the historically based thesis of Piore and Sabel, scholars searched for the secrets of what made these localized regional economies technologically dynamic and successful. In this search, the aim of theorists was not only to link the economic performance of successful regional economies to flexible networks of resource- and information-

sharing among firms and adaptive local institutions. Instead, the research agenda of regional theorists focused on uncovering what was at
the foundation of local networks and adaptive institutions. What was
added to the framework established by Marshall and Veblen by theorists who, in attempting to explain the vibrancy of industrial districts
were inspired by *The Second Industrial Divide*, was a critically important
albeit elusive concept—the concept of trust. It is this notion of trust that
ultimately resurfaces as a key element in Putnam's theory of social
capital and economic prosperity.[6]

Trust lies at the foundation of relationships between firms and individuals whose collective activity in competing and cooperating within
a regional setting is a key aspect of innovative local economies. A broad
literature has emerged dealing with this concept and how the presence
or absence of an environment of trust among economic actors within a
place helps explain regional economic performance and regional differentiation. According to Charles Sabel, trust refers to the mutual confidence that no party involved in an exchange transaction in the market
will exploit the vulnerability of others (Sabel 1993: 104). For Sabel (ibid.:
105), such trust requires time to evolve. Where it does evolve, it makes
possible an environment of cooperation existing alongside competition,
which becomes a source of mutual benefit for firms and individuals
and helps explain how regional economies engendering such trust are
able to prosper. According to Sabel, the creation of trust in certain localities is actually a process of learning—a process of determining how
to create forms of consensus-building among economic actors with
both competing and mutual interests. The associations of mutual confidence that emerge from this learning process result in what Sabel (ibid.:
103) terms "studied trust." For Sabel, the fact that trust is learned provides cautious optimism that policy-makers can actually play a role in
promoting the creation of trust as a strategy for economic revitalization
(ibid.: 131, 141).

Much of the debate about trust and cooperation among economic
actors has focused on whether social networks—social and personal
ties—or more formal, institutional hierarchies are the carriers of this
learning process. In a much-cited contribution to this literature, Mark
Granovetter (1985) accepts the premise (outside the assumptions of
neoclassical economics) that trust is a necessary precondition in successful market relations, but he argues that formal institutions, as en-
forcers of rules and norms, are insufficient to explain why firms and in-

dividuals cooperate in the process of market exchange. He insists instead that trust is "embedded in networks of interpersonal relations which avoids the extremes of both under-socialized [market-oriented, rational choice] and over-socialized [legal institutional] views of human action" (ibid.: 504). For Granovetter, social relations developing in both work and nonwork settings, and the process by which relationships become embedded over time, form the bonds through which human beings learn to cooperate. What results is the reciprocity that facilitates both idea-sharing and market exchange, the keys to growth and prosperity.

Granovetter's view of human action attempts to construct the missing link in Putnam's concept of social capital. Absent trust and the social interactions upon which trust is built, it is difficult to conceive how networks of civic engagement can be created. And without networks of civic engagement—the foundations of social capital—there is, for Putnam, little chance of economic prosperity, since, in Putnam's view, social capital is the precondition for economic prosperity, not the other way around.

There is a problem, however, in assigning a causal link between this particular kind of social capital and economic prosperity, and using such a connection to build a policy program for regional economic development. This problem stems from the way that Putnam specifies how networks of civic engagement, built upon trust, reciprocity, and social interaction are created historically, and how these elements interact to produce the phenomenon of social capital. Putnam insists that those regions in Italy endowed with social capital have been built upon traditions of civic involvement with roots in the Middle Ages. He traces the origins of social capital networks on the Italian peninsula to the medieval communes of the eleventh century! Does this mean that absent such historical experience and the exceedingly long period of gestation seemingly required for networks of civic engagement to flourish, social capital networks cannot take root? If the phenomenon of social capital, as Putnam suggests, is contingent upon a particular historical experience, how then, short of altering history, can social capital networks be created? Such questions raise the disquieting possibility that the connections between social capital and economic outcomes, if such connections even exist, are in some way historically predetermined. Putnam is well aware of this dilemma, but his argument that uncivic regions can "learn by doing" amplifies, rather than resolves, the paradox of his historical approach (Putnam 1993a: 183–84). If, in effect, it is the past that establishes a certain pathway for the creation of social capital networks, and if, by definition, the past is basically fixed, how then can social capital networks be created? The result of this historical puzzle is that, while the concept of social capital provides an imaginative insight for explaining economic outcomes, it is a limited concept for framing policy choices.[7]

One effort to resolve this dilemma appears in the work of AnnaLee Saxenian, who borrows aspects of Putnam's thesis on social capital and economic life but uses Putnam in connection with ideas from Marshall and Veblen to develop a much broader explanation for regional economic competitiveness. In her account of the Silicon Valley economy, Saxenian develops the concept of a localized "industrial system" (adapted from Gary Herrigel's notion of "industrial order") to account for the region's competitive advantages. According to Saxenian, industrial systems vary from one locality to another and consist of three primary characteristics: (1) local institutions; (2) a local industry structure based upon relationships among firms; and (3) a dominant organizational structure within firms. What differentiates regional economies such as Silicon Valley and helps explain why some regions are able to prosper, is the capacity of regional industrial systems for adaptation and change—the capacity to become what Saxenian (1994: 161) calls "Protean Places." Where Saxenian borrows from social capital theorists is in her effort to account for the differences within regional industrial systems. Aspects of social capital such as trust may help explain what makes industrial systems flexible or rigid. Saxenian's work, however, aims not at any definitive link of social capital to economic prosperity. Instead, she is interested in revealing how—but not how much—actual social capital networks, verifiable in an ethnographic sense, contribute to the formation of institutions and industrial structures that are taken to account for competitive performance.

A more comprehensive approach to the issue of what makes regions competitive begins from the premise that comparative advantage is not necessarily a function of natural endowments but is instead something that can be created over time. Underlying this view are three important arguments. One argument insists upon the idea that markets and the market process are products of politics and institutions. At the core of the second argument is the idea that institutions and institutional frameworks play a key role in the performance of economies. In the third argument, institutions can be transformed through policy choices in order to affect market outcomes. These three arguments, embedded in a substantial literature, create the basis for a theory of economic development that more accurately depicts how the networks of innovation in Silicon Valley emerged, and how policy can be used to affect economic outcomes in other regions (BRIE 1999).

In a classic exposition of the first argument, Karl Polanyi shows how political authorities throughout history have shaped the formation of markets by creating the institutions and the rules that govern the process of market accumulation (Polanyi 1944). By comparing the formation of markets during periods of feudalism, mercantilism, and industrial capitalism, and by uncovering a common political and institutional theme in this story, Polanyi's work shows clearly that markets—not the markets of economists but those in the real world—do not exist independently or operate spontaneously as in neoclassical models of rational choice. They are the products of institutional, political, and legal frameworks that structure how buying and selling and the very organization of production takes place.

From this historical observation of the role played by institutions and politics in the creation of markets, it is but a small step to the idea in the second argument, that "institutional frameworks are the key to the relative success of economies" (North 1990: 69). This idea, elaborated by adherents of new institutionalism, actually derives in part from Veblen and his contention that economic development is a function of institutional adaptation. In addition to influencing institutionalist economic history, insights from Veblen have resurfaced as part of a literature known as "late development" to explain how nations in a condition of relative backwardness have successfully industrialized (Gerschenkron 1962). In recent contributions to the literature in this lineage, the ascendancy of postwar Japan as a system with characteristics distinct from both liberal market economies and centrally planned economies, and later Korea, have provided compelling examples of how economic performance (current difficulties notwithstanding) is linked to unique institutional settings (Amsden 1989; Johnson 1982).

When Polanyi's observation of institutional embeddedness in markets is added to Veblen's notion of institutional adaptation and economic development, the result is a powerful policy prescription for creating competitive advantage. In this framework, competitiveness is a function of the way politics and institutions imbue markets with certain attributes. These attributes are the result of the choices made by economic and political actors to shape institutions for the purpose of achieving desired economic outcomes. If one economy is more competitive than another, it is due to the capacity of institutions to shape the market process in a way that generates risk-taking, innovation-creating behavior by economic actors, and the capacity of economic and political actors to frame policies that shape the structure of institutions. From this perspective, competitiveness is a function of policy choices in which institutions can be adapted to achieve economic outcomes.

In this view, Silicon Valley is built of social capital, but it is the interaction of the economic and institutional actors in pursuit of explicitly competitive aims, not dense networks of civic engagement, that structures the region's innovation networks. The choices that configured and continuously reconfigure these networks are shaped by a specific environment of local and national history, in which institutional decisions, policy programs, and industrial trajectories play leading roles. The fact that government policy and decisions by major institutions play such a critical role provides encouragement for efforts to create innovative milieus elsewhere. This is very different from Putnam's vague but radically deterministic concept of historically framed civic cultures, which seems so inaccessible to development policy initiatives.

While the broad outlines of this story are well known, they are worth recounting in order to identify how the region's networks of innovation have emerged from specific historical and institutional settings (Borrus 1988; Malone 1985; Rogers and Larsen 1984; Saxenian 1994; Wilson 1997). It is this history and the culture of innovation stemming from this history to which this essay now turns.

There Is No Gemütlichkeit in Silicon Valley

The story of the Silicon Valley economy is dominated by a single overriding theme: innovation/commercialization. While the folklore of innovation in Silicon Valley tends to elevate the role of the individual inventor or entrepreneur—and there are indeed numerous examples of how such individuals have affected technological outcomes in the region—the history of the region reveals innovation to be the result of a collaborative process. At the center of this process in Silicon Valley is a dense concentration of high-technology companies with individual entrepreneurs and highly skilled workers recruited from all over the world. As mentioned previously, this international community of firms is supported by three of the world's foremost research institutions—Stanford University, the University of California, Berkeley, and the University of California, San Francisco—along with a broad range of service providers unique to the region. These include an indigenously created venture capital industry, a legal community specializing in issues related to high technology, and "headhunter" firms that help find and supply high-technology firms with talent. In its composition and in the way it engenders collaboration, this community is, literally and metaphorically, both local and global.

In the collaborative process leading to innovation in Silicon Valley, these actors generate and refine what is essentially the intangible raw material of technological change—ideas (Mokyr 1990). The pathway from ideas to innovation occurs in Silicon Valley along networks of communication in which the region's economic and institutional actors engage in relationships to solve problems. The solutions become the raw material for technological transformation. Where these networks proliferate, as is the case in Silicon Valley, the capacity for transforming ideas into innovation and innovation into commercial advantage increases. It is these innovation networks that constitute the region's resource base of social capital. Despite the case made by social capital theorists on the link between a vibrant civil society and an innovative local economy, it would be difficult to establish such a connection in Silicon Valley. Instead, the puzzle posed by Silicon Valley is how the networks of innovation that have made the region one of the world's most technologically dynamic economies emerged from a combination of local historical chance; national historical trends; specialized, locally based "borderless" institutions; and competitive choices exercised by economic and institutional actors.

One of the most important historical attributes of Silicon Valley, in comparison with other regional economies in the United States, is its status as a relative industrial latecomer. As an industrial economy, Silicon Valley, after all, has no eighteenth-century or even nineteenth-century beginnings. As Sturgeon shows, it is only in the early twentieth century that an electrical industry began to develop. This characteristic, while posing a challenge for industrial development, actually conferred certain advantages upon the region. In the absence of an existing industrial structure, and unencumbered by an established local business culture tied to a specific set of institutions or industrial practices, economic actors in Silicon Valley were able to create an economic environment conducive to risk-taking, innovation, and growth. From the favorable conditions offered by this economic environment emerged the partnerships between individuals, firms, and institutions that would evolve into the networks of innovation at the foundation of the Silicon Valley.

Notwithstanding the earlier activities, the origins of innovation networks in the Silicon Valley are to be found in the relationships between Stanford University and a small group of entrepreneurs during the late 1930s from which emerged the region's first high-technology companies. The most famous firm spawned from this relationship was the Hewlett Packard Company, founded in 1937. Fredrick Terman, an electrical engineering professor who moved to Stanford from MIT, encouraged and financially supported his two graduate students, William Hewlett and David Packard, to commercialize an invention known as an audio oscillator. After the initial prototype development, Terman helped arrange additional financing with a Palo Alto bank that enabled them to begin commercial production of the invention. During this same period, Stanford also helped support Charles Litton as well as Sigurd and Russell Varian, whose efforts would result in the founding of Litton Industries and Varian Associates.

This activity foreshadowed Stanford's role in what was to become the Silicon Valley, and the role of that economy in making Stanford one of the world's premier universities. Perhaps more important, however, this collaboration signaled how major research institutions, and farsighted individuals within such institutions, could provide the catalyst for entrepreneurship. What resulted from the role played by Stanford in the formation of these firms was the blurring of boundaries between individual entrepreneurialism and large institutions in the pursuit of common technologically oriented objectives. It was this blurring of boundaries between entrepreneurial and institutional actors during the formative years of the region's high-tech development that provided the initial threads of the Silicon Valley's networks of innovation. Forged on the basis of linkages, these networks of innovation lie at the foundation of the region's broader social structure of economic development, the goal of which is seemingly incessant technological change.

An equally important catalyst for the region occurred in the form of military contracts during World War II and the Cold War (see Leslie, this volume). The fortunes of Hewlett Packard, for example, increased roughly twentyfold from 1941 to 1945, with sales expanding from $37,000 to more than $750,000 as a result of military contracts for the company's electronic measuring devices and receivers. The klystron microwave tube, invented by the Varians with the support of Stanford, was also an integral component in radar systems used during the war, resulting in big benefits to both the company and the university. Military funding also helped support other start-ups in the Silicon Valley during their formative years. Nevertheless, it is important to recognize that while the Valley's fledgling companies benefited from the war, East Coast high-technology companies—firms such as RCA, Philco, GE, and Westinghouse, which in size dwarfed the Northern California firms—profited from the wartime situation to a hugely greater extent than their tiny brethren in Northern California. And they have all since failed in advanced electronics! More research and development for the war effort took place in East Coast universities, and even Terman himself left Stanford for the Defense Department's major effort at Harvard during the war years.

Owing to this disparity, it became the goal of the high-technology community in Silicon Valley to strengthen the Valley's attractiveness as a research center and to identify ways that Silicon Valley firms could secure a greater share of government contracts. After the war, Terman returned to Stanford to become the dean of the Engineering School and dedicated himself precisely to these goals, by strengthening Stanford as a center for research that would support a technologically advanced industrial base in the region. His idea was to use the engineering program at Stanford to build a "community of technical scholars." This community would be the foundation for the networks of innovation upon which the regional economy of Silicon Valley would develop and thrive.

Three institutional innovations initiated by Stanford reflect the relationships between research institutions, entrepreneurs, and firms that Terman pioneered in the region. The first innovation was the creation of the Stanford Research Institute (SRI) to conduct government-supported research, and to assist West Coast high-technology firms in securing government contracts. Initially dedicated to military-related research, SRI for a while became an important conduit for solidifying the relationships between private sector high-technology firms, government, and university research establishments.[8] Second, Stanford opened its engineering classrooms to local companies through its Honors Cooperative Program, in which employees could enroll in graduate courses. This program had no parallels elsewhere. Third, Stanford promoted the creation of the Stanford Industrial Park, one of the first in the country, which reinforced the emerging pattern of cooperation between the university and electronics firms in the area to the long-term prosperity of both. In effect, these institutional arrangements encouraged the types of public/private partnerships and collaborations between universities, government, and firms that helped create an environment that made possible the networks of innovation in Silicon Valley.

This model of collaboration between a university research institution and high-technology firms spread beyond Stanford to nearby Berkeley and later to the University of California Medical School in San Francisco. During the 1960s, owing to the example of Stanford, the University of California, Berkeley rapidly expanded its programs in electrical engineering and encouraged the outreach of its university environment to firms in Silicon Valley. By the mid-1970s, Berkeley was training more engineers than Stanford and had become a premier research center in its own right for Silicon Valley firms. Programs for technology transfer and professorships endowed by Silicon Valley firms were the hallmarks of this growing partnership between Berkeley and the Silicon Valley. In addition, the University of California, San Francisco was, and continues to be, one of the nation's preeminent medical research establishments, with vital links to another emerging high-technology industry in which the Bay Area is the world's leading center—the biotechnology industry, with about 168 biotechnology firms (University of California 1998). In effect, the presence of three world-class scientific, medical, and engineering research institutions that were actively involved in Silicon Valley industry created the most formidable university-industry partnership in the world, its only rivals being MIT and Harvard.

Owing to innovations at Stanford that institutionalized and promoted the expansion of links between the world of university research and high-tech entrepreneurialism, the cluster of electronics firms in Silicon Valley grew rapidly during the 1960s and 1970s. This growth involved not only new start-ups but also older established firms interested in taking advantage of the collaboration between Stanford and the high-technology community. Lockheed Aerospace, for example, set up a research lab for its Missiles and Space Division in the Stanford Industrial Park in 1956—one in which Stanford agreed to train Lockheed employees while Lockheed in turn would help rebuild Stanford's aeronautical engineering department. Westinghouse, Ford Aerospace, Sylvania, Raytheon, ITT, and IBM would follow. Perhaps the most celebrated example of an older established firm coming to the Stanford/Silicon Valley research complex is Xerox, which in 1970 set up its storied Palo Alto Research Center. From Xerox PARC emerged such technologies as the computer operating system that was first successfully used by Apple and then even more successfully by Windows, laser printing, the computer mouse, and computer networking. Most of these technologies served to enrich neighboring companies rather than Xerox, headquartered "back East," which was preoccupied by "its core business."

By 1975 the region's high-technology enterprises employed more than 100,000 workers. Fueled by the links between industry and preeminent research and educational establishments, this growth, in turn, compelled similar types of partnerships to develop between Silicon Valley firms and the system of local community colleges, along with institutions such as San Jose State University. By the 1970s San Jose State University was actually training as many undergraduate engineers as either Stanford or Berkeley while the region's six community colleges offered specialized technical programs oriented specifically to the needs of the area's firms. The latter followed a familiar and successful model. Community colleges contracted with local companies to teach their employees while companies provided consultants to the colleges to help develop curricula along with part-time teachers. Firms also donated equipment to area schools and allowed students to use equipment during evening hours. After Tandem Computers donated more than $1 million in computer equipment to Foothill College, for example, the school was able to triple (to over five thousand) the number of students in its computer course.

While firms and supporting institutions in Silicon Valley expanded together, the region also grew as a result of an entirely new industry: the semiconductor industry. This industry fundamentally transformed the economic landscape and provided the region with its identity, so-named after the silicon strata on which both semiconductors and the Valley were built.

The semiconductor industry had taken root in the area with the location of Shockley Transistor in Palo Alto in 1955. Founded by William

Shockley (a Stanford graduate and, at Bell Labs in New Jersey, one of the inventors of the transistor), the firm was the first in a lineage of spinoffs and competing ventures that led first to Fairchild Semiconductor and eventually to the spinoffs of Intel, AMD, and National Semiconductor, among others. These "Fairchildren," as they were called, constituted after the very small generation of Messrs. Hewlett, Packard, and Varian, the senior generation of the Valley. Between 1966 and 1976, a total of thirty-six semiconductor firms were founded in the United States. Of these thirty-six, thirty-one were located in the Silicon Valley (Borrus et al. 1983: 26–27). The semiconductor industry and the Silicon Valley had effectively become synonymous.

The impetus for the early growth of this industry came almost exclusively from the military. Virtually no other customers existed for semiconductors when they were initially developed. In 1962 the government was the sole market for semiconductor devices (ibid.: 18). Gradually however, as the computer industry itself expanded, the government in the form of the military and its prime contractors accounted for a diminishing share of the semiconductor business. By 1978 the government accounted for only a 10 percent market share for semiconductors (ibid.: 18). This diffusion is indeed impressive, but in the early development of the semiconductor, the Department of Defense and NASA played a crucial role as "creative first users" of the new technology (ibid.: 17). What this suggests is that the innovative trajectory of the semiconductor industry in Silicon Valley was forged upon the partnership between government, in the form of the military establishment, firms, and research universities. A key element in the creation of the Valley's industrial structure and business culture was the Defense Department's insistence in the early formative years on "dual sourcing" for its orders of critical electronics from these young, untried firms. It diffused technology and helped to proliferate competing—and cooperating—firms.

By the early 1970s, the military's importance in the development and purchase of semiconductors diminished, and venture capital, specifically venture capital limited partnerships, came to replace the military as the lead source of financing for Silicon Valley start-ups. The explosive growth of venture capitalists in the region paralleled the growth of the local semiconductor industry itself (for further discussion, see Kenney and Florida in this volume). By 1974 more than 150 venture capital firms operated in Silicon Valley, with Stanford University investing a portion of its own endowment in venture activities. By 1988, Silicon Valley was attracting 40 percent of the national total of venture capital investment (Florida and Kenney 1990c: 66).

What distinguished this industry from venture capital in other parts of the country was the fact that many venture capitalists in Silicon Valley had prior careers with technology firms in the region. As a result, Silicon Valley venture capitalists understood the technical dimensions of the business far better than their East Coast counterparts. Perhaps more important, the personal connections of Silicon Valley venture capitalists to colleagues in local firms forged the personal knowledge and shared business and technological outlook, if not deep the trust, upon which relationships between entrepreneurialism, innovation, and financial backing flourished. Venture capitalists in the Valley are "hands-on" investors heavily involved in the strategic and critical managerial decisions of the companies they back (ibid.: 69). As a result of their unique relationship with technology firms, Silicon Valley venture firms are embedded within the broader fabric of high-technology development and are an integral part of the social structures in this region that facilitate the process of innovation. In effect, venture capitalists in Silicon Valley created a new and different kind of financial institution in which technological and business expertise, equity stakes, and direct involvement in the firms being financed became the hallmark. They became central actors in the establishment of networks in the region incorporating finance, entrepreneurship, innovation, customer and partner identification, and trouble-shooting (see Kenney and Florida in this volume for further discussion).

Alongside the venture capitalists, local law firms function as important actors within the region's networks of entrepreneurship and innovation (for a more detailed account, see Suchman in this volume). The Valley's leading law firms have grown to specialize in areas important to high-tech companies, such as intellectual property rights, technology licensing, and now, increasingly, encryption law as well as tax and corporate matters. Immigration is rapidly becoming an in-house specialty or is out-sourced in a tight relationship. The lawyers know the venture capitalists; they both know large numbers of experienced technology executives who can be called in to help deal with an organizational or strategic problem or opportunity facing rapidly growing young firms. They sit on boards of companies that can be key customers or partners for new firms. The networks of overlapping board memberships could be considered another element of social capital but cannot be considered deep civic engagement—except, of course, the boards of nonprofit institutions, where many of the same players are to be found.

An absolutely defining element of the networks of innovation of Silicon Valley is the character of the labor market. One word perhaps best distinguishes how this labor market functions: mobility (for a more detailed discussion, see Angel in this volume). From the early 1970s, Silicon Valley has been differentiated from other regional economies by the unusually high number of employees moving from one job to another, one company to another. The proximity of so many firms within the same industry undoubtedly contributes to this fluidity. Two other explanations, however, quite different in tone, lie at the core of how the extremely mobile job market in Silicon Valley operates.

The first explanation focuses on how Valley employees' loyalty is greater to the craft of innovation than to any particular company (Saxenian 1994: 36). The result of such commitment to the cause of innovation over company loyalty is rapid turnover of employees from one company to the next. As individuals move, however, from one project and one firm to another, their paths overlap and create networks of information-sharing that accelerate the diffusion of technological capabilities and know-how within the region. It is in these pathways of labor mobility that networks of innovation get created.

The second explanation depicts a much darker image of this mobility process. In this picture, employees in Silicon Valley work under exceedingly high levels of pressure to produce the types of technological breakthroughs characteristic of the region. With pay linked to performance and management techniques that push workers to the limit, employees put in superhuman work hours (Florida and Kenney 1990c: 44). Owing to the strain, they eventually "burn out" and consequently move to other firms, enticed by the recruitment efforts of competitors. Nevertheless, while this picture is of a much more Hobbesian world, the end result of labor mobility in this interpretation of Silicon Valley is still the same—networks that support and fuel innovation and its rapid commercialization. Despite the differences in interpretation of what causes the phenomenon of job mobility in Silicon Valley, both explanations admit to a similar innovative environment as the outcome.

Labor turnover and the competition for workers has created a market niche for another entity that participates in the creation of innovation networks—headhunter companies. Like the venture capital firms and the local legal profession, headhunters supply high-technology companies with perhaps their most essential resource. Without their highly skilled "think" workers, high-tech companies would be without the source of ideas lying at the foundation of the innovation process in Silicon Valley.

Perhaps the most striking consequence of the mobile labor market and the efforts of headhunter firms to supply the region with talent is the truly international character of the high-technology community. Aspiring entrepreneurs and ambitious engineers from all over the world come to Silicon Valley to start companies. At the same time, engineering talent in the region reflects an enormous diversity of nationalities. Many of these overseas individuals remain in the area after attending one of the local universities. Others come from abroad, attracted by the open hiring gates of both established firms and start-ups. The openness of the labor market to foreigners is one of the region's most valuable assets. We would go so far as to say that the region's—and the nation's—premier ranking as the world's innovation and commercialization center could not be sustained without the steady influx of educated, motivated high-level technical and entrepreneurial/technical talent. No other place in the world has this critical "labor pool" advantage. Its importance can only increase as the levels of technical education and sophistication increase around the world while America's domestically bred and produced supply does not keep pace. And by labor pool, we do not mean the lower or middle ranks of employees. "Immigrants" are creating a very large percentage of new technologies and new firms. Silicon Valley has, over the years, created a kind of social/economic machine that brings together science-based technologies, vast amounts of capital, and the ability to sift through proposals for technological-based new companies and projects. It has, in the process, created a unique, and vastly valuable, system for bringing together new people, whether from India, Israel, or Iran, with these other resources, in an ongoing process of technological innovation, company creation, and wealth creation. Just as capital is flowing in from all over the world, so is labor—at the highest end. The resources are now global; the ability to combine them, productively and smoothly, is local.

The benefits of the Silicon Valley system for bringing talented "immigrants" from all over the world into creative and vastly profitable contact with technological resources, commercialization systems, and capital are not confined to the Silicon Valley community, or to the United States. Over time it has become a key, enabling asset for other regions with aspirations to high-tech specialization. A network of nationals plugged into the Valley is proving to be one of the most important assets for other regions in other nations in launching their own high-tech industries. There are, for example, perhaps as many as twenty thousand French in the Valley, at least three times as many Taiwanese, growing tens of thousands of Indians, and a few thousand Israelis.[9] The data is inherently imprecise. The categories are difficult to define with great precision or meaning. "Taiwanese" can be vague, when analyzing a life trajectory. Place of Birth? Citizenship? Multiple passports? People come and go. Some pass through quickly, but many work for years and years. Many become U.S. citizens but return "home" much later. But they are the vital transmission belt, diffusing technology and market knowledge, sometimes establishing off-shore facilities that seed new districts, and serving as connectors into the Valley. In our judgment, they have been an absolutely key factor in developing successful—sometimes very successful—high-tech districts "back home." As a development policy, few investments have paid off so well for the "brain drain" nations.

Conclusions

A particular industry defines a region's specialization, and industries differ in growth potential, in their capacity to generate new activities and new industries, and in the kinds of social structures they breed. Ricardo argued most famously for the Iberians to specialize in wine and the British in textiles. That choice decisively shaped the economic and social history of the two regions. The British specialized in the activities that proved generative of growth, entrepreneurship, innovation, and power. High-fashion districts, coal and steel districts, and mass production textile districts typically resemble one another independent of nation or ethnicity. In our view, the recent literature, especially the profuse literature stemming from Sabel's work on Italian districts, pays too much attention to the social characteristics of specialized industrial districts and consequently too little to the relatively more technical issues surrounding the specific nature of the industries.

For example, comparisons between the Boston high-tech industrial district and Silicon Valley overstate the weight of "Boston Brahmin" culture. But Brahmin culture never defined or even penetrated MIT, the fountainhead of Boston high tech. A more useful comparison would focus on the structural differences between Boston's dominant activities—defense electronics systems and then minicomputers, versus Silicon Valley's semiconductors and then microcomputers and computer networking. Similarly, Silicon Valley is not to be distinguished by the mild California climate, or the absence of neckties. Southern California's massive aerospace industry in no way resembles Northern California's electronics cluster: not in industrial structure, not in forms of payment, not in rates of new company formation, not in the proliferation of intermediating métiers, and not, ultimately, in flexibility. Research universities play a limited role, if that, in Milan's dynamic "Marshallian district" of high fashion. Venture firms, law firms, and graduate students occupy little space in the much studied Italian tile district, or in Antwerp's diamond center, or in the Midwestern auto district, or in Georgia's carpet and towel belt. Ultimately what you do shapes how you do it—all the way back up the value chain, all the way out to forms of social organization.

Of course, there is trust in Silicon Valley; there is no such thing as a productive milieu, or even a functioning society, where there is no trust. At issue is the specific nature of that trust. What kind is it? What does it do and not do? From where does it originate—that is, where are its social foundations? Frequent, commercially focused contacts generate judgment: "He's reliable; he's straight; you can count on him to fulfill his end and do it well, reliably, on time." This is the stuff of reputation, of commercially valuable trust. Such specific, performance-generated trust is the building block of Silicon Valley's particular brand of social capital. The sequence runs from performance to trust, not from community. Perhaps policy would be well advised to aim for that trajectory, even if it entails loosening some deep, exclusionary, civic engagements. In Silicon Valley all the rest, such as informal conversations in bars or bowling teams or, more plausibly, children's soccer leagues or gyms, is, relative to many other places, somewhat underdeveloped and ancillary. It exists. It matters. But it is secondary in sequence and importance. It is not the defining or distinguishing element.

The performance-focused trust in Silicon Valley is different in kind from the trust engendered by deep civic engagement that makes for the economic success in some regions. It is more than just a more easily assembled substitute. It might be a superior form. It is open to outsiders. Trust can be extended, rather quickly, to people from other places, other cultures; even to people with different ideas.

CHAPTER TEN

Institutions and Economies: Creating Silicon Valley

MARTIN KENNEY AND

URS VON BURG

Traditional studies of industrial clustering have focused on the specific features of the industries in question to explain the origins and growth of such clustering. There is little doubt that Silicon Valley hosts several such clusters; in fact, many regard Silicon Valley as a quintessential case of industrial clustering. The characteristic that sets Silicon Valley apart from many regions and creates difficulty for most theoretical explanations of industrial clustering is the region's ability to periodically generate new industries and clusters. Well-established industries are renewed at the same time as entrepreneurs leave older firms to exploit new possibilities in the same industry, or perhaps to create entirely new types of firms. Silicon Valley is even more intriguing, because not only is it a productive site for the creation of new firms, technologies, and industries but it also has fostered the development of innovative new business models.

Although Silicon Valley can be usefully conceptualized as an electronics cluster or set of electronics clusters, this common-sense understanding provides only a partial picture of the situation: it does not account for all the important players in the region's dynamics and consequently misses important factors for the area's growth. Silicon Valley became the dominant location for a set of electronics/data communications companies that included semiconductor and hard disk drive manufacturers, local and wide-area networking equipment suppliers, biotechnology and software firms, and Internet companies, not merely because of the "natural" or "logical" evolution of the electronics industries but because of the growth of a set of nontechnical institutions. The area's remarkable ability to spawn new industries is the result of a complex of nontechnical institutions that both support and thrive on entrepreneurial businesses that are capable of growing rapidly.

Silicon Valley hosts a set of interdependent institutions that observers have termed an "ecosystem," a "social structure of innovation," or an "incubator region" (Bahrami and Evans, this volume; Florida and Kenney 1990c; Schoonhoven and Eisenhardt 1989). Silicon Valley can be considered as two intertwined but analytically separable economies. The first set of organizations consists of established firms, corporate research laboratories, and universities that are the constituents of the existing economy—and, in one form or another, are not unusual for any industrial cluster. Silicon Valley, however, has another set of organizations that combine to create an "economy" predicated on facilitating entrepreneurs in the creation of new firms. This other economy is the *differentia specifica* of Silicon Valley, the trait that sets it apart from most other regions of industrial clustering.

Recent theoretical advances in the social sciences provide new insights into the path-dependent evolution of social and economic arrangements (David 1986; Dosi et al. 1994; Nelson and Winter 1982). These arrangements are the environment within which organizations are embedded. The organizations and institutions in Silicon Valley dedicated to nurturing new firm formation have evolved gradually from quite informal or personal business arrangements into institutions that are specialized in the delivery of specific services for new firms. In this article we describe the types of firms that evolved, and how these institutions emerged, proliferated, and became increasingly formalized. We focus on the institutions whose raison d'être was to perform specific functions easing the establishment of new firms. Each successful start-up reinforced the earlier developments, and the economy grew in size. More important, it became ever richer, with an increasing diversity of specialists providing services to new firms. This richness contributed to ever greater success, propelling a positive feedback loop.

Despite our emphasis on the socioeconomic institutions, we recognize that this entire economy of institutions and organizations dedicated to start-ups is possible only because the underlying electronics and biomedical technologies are improving so quickly. The rapidity of the pace of change ceteris paribus provides more business opportunities and points of entry than does a slow-changing industry. In electronics, new products often are either massively superior to previous products (the common metric in Silicon Valley is a 10× improvement) or perform almost completely new functions. This means that older products are constantly becoming obsolete and being replaced by new, improved versions for roughly the same price (Kenney and Curry 1999). These technical parameters do not mandate new firms as necessarily the way to commercialize their possibilities; however they did allow Silicon Valley to create an entire community of organizations and institutions dedicated to allowing new firms to exploit these spaces.

Theory and Previous Research

The agglomeration of related firms in specific locations has attracted great scholarly interest among social scientists since the time of Alfred Marshall (1890). Stylized formal models, such as that of Arthur (1994), have shown that in industries with agglomeration economies, regional clustering will occur. Michael Porter (1998) examines specific clusters and identifies three broad ways in which they effect competition: first, they increase productivity of the firms in the cluster. Second, the cluster helps drive the direction and pace of innovation. Third, clusters stimulate the formation of new businesses. These conclusions are not very different from those of economic geographers (see, for example, Storper and Walker 1989; Walker 1985, 1988). The strength of understanding firm activity in the context of clusters is how it highlights the importance of the local environment for a firm. In other words, these explanations emphasize that the firm or the viable economic unit is imbricated in its context.

Cluster creation is a highly contingent process in which the various actors embedded within previous social relationships and institutions try to manipulate the environment for their benefit (Granovetter 1985; Uzzi 1996). Here, we are drawn to the social constructionist perspective that sees actors and artifacts as creating their world within a malleable, though already given, environment (for a general discussion, see Bijker et al. 1987; Latour and Woolgar 1986). Clusters thus are not simply a bundle of economic benefits; they are regions of constructed benefits. To create a self-reinforcing cycle, it is important to construct a set of institutions and routines that reward particular social actors for systematically beneficial behavior.[1]

A weakness in the classic portrayal of clusters refers specifically to Silicon Valley. The classic cluster is one in which competitors, important suppliers, and other related institutions in a specific industrial field are gathered closely together. The new firms draw upon the core competencies of the region and the existing firms. These critical masses of existing industrial knowledge should guide innovation and spawn new firms—and Silicon Valley clearly has such clusters (e.g., semiconductors, computer networking, and now the Internet). However, we argue that these industrial clusters are not the essence of Silicon Valley. The essence of Silicon Valley is the cluster of institutions dedicated to creating firms. These institutions do not easily fit the criteria of an industry; they are from a variety of industries.[2] Nevertheless, they are central to the dynamism of Silicon Valley.

Observers have credited many variables as critical for the development of Silicon Valley. As Bahrami and Evans, and Cohen and Fields, show (this volume), structural and organizational explanations attribute Silicon Valley's success to one or a combination of the following variables: supplier networks (Saxenian 1994); proximity to research universities (Storper 1993; Storper and Salais 1997); labor mobility (Angel 1991; Saxenian 1994); cutting-edge technology; abundance of venture capital; and entrepreneurship (Gilder 1989). For some, the norms and cultural patterns are held to explain the willingness to create new firms (Weiss and Delbecq 1990). These cultural explanations are not simply scholarly constructions; rather, they draw upon the lived experiences of the actual actors and as such are significant and are data to be explained.

The previous explanations contain powerful insights, but seem also to be wanting—an understandable difficulty when examining a phenomenon as multifaceted as Silicon Valley. For example, the organizational structure might explain difficulties experienced by existing firms, but it cannot explain the operation of the institutions encouraging new firm formation. The critical issue is not the growth of the existing firms; many industrial clusters, such as Detroit (for autos), Pittsburgh (for steel), and Los Angeles (for entertainment), have had strong or growing firm clusters. The interesting aspect of Silicon Valley and the critical issue is the establishment of new industries and clusters.

This new firm formation phenomenon has drawn interest. An empirical study of the creation and the survival of new semiconductor firms from 1978 to 1986 led Schoonhoven and Eisenhardt (1989) to conclude that Silicon Valley is an incubator region consisting of institutions that nurtured and sped the growth of small semiconductor start-ups. They attributed the higher survival rate and faster rate of growth of semiconductor start-ups in Silicon Valley to this incubator effect. Studying venture capital both in Silicon Valley and Route 128, Florida and Kenney (1988a, 1988b) found what they termed a social structure of innovation, by which they meant an interactive set of institutions dedicated to encouraging technological innovation commercialized by new firms.[3] On the basis of the difficulties Silicon Valley experienced in the late 1980s, Florida and Kenney (1990c) argued that this new firm formation process might actually prove harmful to the established firms— and thus Silicon Valley. Whatever the effect on established firms, in retrospect this conclusion was clearly incorrect for Silicon Valley as a whole. More recently, Bahrami and Evans (1995) described Silicon Valley as an "ecosystem" consisting of various institutions, skill sets embodied in individuals, and an entrepreneurial spirit. These studies document an institutional environment that lowers the difficulty of launching a new technology firm and also accelerates early growth.

The importance of networks for business activity prompted Robertson and Langlois (1995) to conceptualize Silicon Valley and Route 128 as regions composed of networks able to mobilize the resources necessary to create a viable firm around a promising business opportunity. For them, the Silicon Valley network structure was an organizational response to the opportunities manifested in the turbulence of "predominant design" stage environments when new technologies emerge (on dominant design, see Henderson and Clark 1990). They conclude that the stage in the product cycle influences the industrial organization. This links the product to the prevailing industrial organization, thereby assisting in explaining the differences between the various industries and, by extension, regions.

Previous research explains Silicon Valley from a variety of perspectives. Some focus on the norms and culture encouraging new firm formation, while others emphasize the institutions that nurture new firm formation. The role of technological trajectories receives limited attention. For us, the critical feature in the dynamism of Silicon Valley is, in a sense, not the existing firms, but rather the institutional complex specialized at creating new firms aimed at exploiting fast-moving technological trajectories.

The Two Economies

To understand Silicon Valley necessarily means to understand the process by which new firms are created to exploit technological innovations. For our purposes, Silicon Valley has two important economic activities: the first includes the conventional activities of existing organizations. These established firms and other organizations, such as universities and corporate research laboratories, are the components of what we term Economy One. The other economic activity can be found in the fabric of institutions aimed at encouraging and nurturing new firm formation. This complex of institutions we term Economy Two. Silicon Valley's Economy One and Two are interlinked by organizational histories, personal relations, and technological trajectories; yet they can also be seen as conceptually distinct.

Economy One consists of the existing organizations whose ultimate goals are, in the case of private firms, profitability and growth. In the case of universities and nonprofit research institutions, success is measured in terms of research and education.[4] The point here is that these organizations did not espouse the economic goal of encouraging and nurturing spinoffs, even though the activities of Frederick Terman did encourage them from Stanford. Still, the organizations of Economy One in Silicon Valley contributed many of the ideas and entrepreneurs. It should be noted, however, that the existence of Economy Two attracts entrepreneurs and even entire start-ups from outside the area to relocate into the region.[5]

Part of Economy One is a dense network of specialized suppliers and often customers supporting the existing firms (Saxenian 1994 and this volume). For a start-up, these companies can very often be early supporters and often important lead customers. This "sophisticated customer" phenomenon has been true for prominent technologies such as semiconductors, computer networking, and HDDs. Economy One thus is a necessary, even vital condition for the dynamism of Silicon Valley, but, by itself, it is not sufficient.

The organizations in Economy One—either because of their charter to do research, as in the case of universities and R&D laboratories, or as a by-product of their normal activities, as in the case of many firms— create inventions, some of which may be capable of being capitalized in an independent firm. This ability to extrude an invention from an existing firm is facilitated by the rapid pace of advance in high-tech industry, which often creates technological discontinuities and accompanying economic opportunities. In the electronics industry there have been recurring discontinuities, and very often the existing firms are unwilling or unable to exploit them—or simply miss them because they are preoccupied with their current businesses and customers (for a more general statement of this, see Christensen 1997).

Economy Two is the institutional infrastructure that has evolved to enable the creation and growth of new firms (Bahrami and Evans 1995; Florida and Kenney 1988a; Schoonhoven and Eisenhardt 1989; Todtling 1994). In Economy Two, new firms are products roughly analogous to the actual products, such as computers and microprocessors, of Economy One. Usually, the start-ups are specialists organized to translate the entrepreneurial team's technology or idea into the basis for an operating company with products and customers.[6] The sources of the ideas and the founders vary greatly, but the most common sources in electronics are engineers and managers within established firms. In biotechnology the most common source has proved to be university faculty and students (Kenney 1986). Many regional industrial clusters provide the resources for new firm formation, but few have an entire infrastructure completely dedicated to it.

In Silicon Valley, the ideal start-up is one capable of growing rapidly while maintaining large profit margins. Investments in firms meeting these criteria are most likely to increase in value sufficiently quickly to support the dedicated institutional infrastructure of Economy Two. The value is realized when the entrepreneurs or investors sell their stake in the start-up. Whether or not the various organizations providing services to the start-up actually receive equity in exchange for their services, the capital gains fuel the entire process.

Economy Two is populated by organizations whose sole purpose, or a significant component of their business, is related to servicing start-ups. These organizations have evolved to provide the inputs necessary to create a firm de novo. Deciding which institution of Economy Two is the most significant is difficult, because they are interdependent. In a capitalist society, however, the two most basic inputs to any firm are labor and capital. The entrepreneurs are the initial labor, and venture capital (and, increasingly, angels) are the source of capital.

The fundamental input to Economy Two is entrepreneurs, their ideas, and their efforts. In this venue it is not necessary to dwell on the various social or psychological dimensions of entrepreneurship; it is sufficient that there be a constant flow of entrepreneurs. Because of the high overhead associated with maintaining the institutions of Economy Two, as we mentioned earlier, not all entrepreneurial ideas are suited for Silicon Valley.

Capital is the second critical input for a firm. Venture capital is, for all intents and purposes, an institution that developed in the United States after World War II (Kenney and Florida, this volume; Wilson 1985). Venture capitalists invest in new firms promising high growth rates and possibly huge capital gains in return for a partial ownership stake. Ideally, venture capitalists hope to sell the start-up within seven years, either through an IPO or to an existing firm for a return of ten times their initial investment. Sufficient capital makes it possible to mobilize the necessary personnel and other resources to create a firm around a potential market opportunity. Speed is a critical variable. If there were little competition many firms could grow by self-financing, but in fast-changing markets market share is critical. Venture capital fuels the ability to secure market share. As Freeman (1999) points out, venture capitalists buy time.

The organizations of Economy Two, with their experience with previous firm establishments and knowledge of the process, can rapidly mobilize the resources necessary to create a new firm. Organizing a firm requires rather routine but necessarily time-consuming tasks, such as legal incorporation, securing personnel experienced in the various corporate functions, leasing facilities, finding furniture and supplies, creating an accounting system, and marshaling a myriad of other goods and services. When entrepreneurs and investors sought assistance for these functions, they turned to local organizations, many of which initially did not have special expertise. After dealing repeatedly with similar issues, the local organizations evolved knowledge and expertise suited to the unique needs of high-tech start-ups. Success, and the concomitant capital gains, led to the building of still greater expertise. This accumulation of experience contributed to the acceleration of the start-up process and the success of the new firms.[7] This created positive feedback loops, lowering start-up barriers, thus further improving the probability of success. Higher success rates encouraged more start-ups, creating more experience and even more specialists in assisting new start-ups. To use Bahrami's and Evans's term (this volume), an even richer ecosystem evolved. In economic terms, these institutions lowered entry barriers, eased the costs of entry, and, most important, sped the process of building a viable firm.

As Suchman (this volume) shows, legal firms are central actors in Economy Two. Their functions are not confined to legal tasks—more important, they are crucial intermediaries alleviating the uncertainty that entrepreneurs often experience in their negotiations with venture capitalists. They also have deep expertise in incorporating a new firm funded by venture capitalists and handling delicate issues such as the intellectual property obligations that an entrepreneur has to a previous employer. Over the years, Silicon Valley law firms have developed enormous expertise in handling the unique issues faced by high-technology start-ups.[8]

Investment banks are another part of Economy Two in the San Francisco Bay Area. Hambrecht and Quist, Robertson Steffens, and Montgomery Securities, for example, specialize in managing initial public stock offerings and analyzing high-technology firms. Recently, these boutique investment banks have merged with much larger financial institutions seeking a foothold in high technology. Their expertise and connections with venture capitalists and entrepreneurs are core assets, from which other specialties have arisen. During the formation of Silicon Valley, the founders of these investment banks built close relationships with entrepreneurs and venture capitalists. For example, Sanford Robertson, one of the founders of Robertson Steffens, introduced the two founders of Kleiner, Perkins, Caufield, and Byers, Eugene Kleiner and Thomas Perkins, to each other. Due to their specialization, proximity, and personal relationships with venture capitalists and entrepreneurs, these boutique banks were able to wrest IPOs from their larger and more experienced New York counterparts. Conversely, the existence of these boutique technology investment banks reinforced Economy Two by providing local expertise on the financial details and protocols necessary to go public. Proximity created relationships and saved time: it was no longer necessary to travel to New York to get advice and assistance. To compete, the New York firms such as Morgan Stanley were forced to open Silicon Valley offices, further reinforcing Economy Two.

A start-up almost immediately needs to recruit managers and executives to complete the management team. At times, the firm's venture capitalists assist in employee recruitment, but there are also local and national executive search firms with offices in Silicon Valley that are contracted to conduct searches. The prime hunting ground for the search firms are the existing firms in Economy One. Without such search firms, the recruitment of the staff necessary for an expanding firm would be slowed, adversely affecting growth and critical momentum. For small firms these hiring decisions are critical and must be made quickly. Thus executive search firms are vital contributors to the start-up process.

Other services are readily available to the start-up. For example, there are marketing organizations specializing in assisting start-ups. The most famous of these is the McKenna Group, formed by Regis McKenna. McKenna was a Fairchild marketing star who left and built his own consulting practice. His most important early success was the famous Intel "Operation Crush" that successfully secured adoption of the early Intel microprocessors. Similarly, he was central to the development of the early Apple marketing strategy and the design of the Apple logo (McKenna 1998). The McKenna Group's signature has been campaigns that project a larger-than-reality image for the start-up. Of course, the McKenna group is not alone; there are a number of other marketing specialists in Silicon Valley.

Although the accounting firms serving Silicon Valley start-ups are the large, general accounting firms, they have special practices located in Silicon Valley dedicated to servicing the unique needs of start-ups and venture capital partnerships. Moreover, the Silicon Valley offices have become the accounting firms' global expertise center for high-technology accounting issues. Often they are willing to bill start-ups at below market rates in hopes of securing future business. Similarly, landlords are often willing to provide relatively low lease rates to start-ups, and office furnishing suppliers will provide preferential rates. In other words, the region has evolved toward a socioeconomic structure that recognizes the unique economics of start-ups. These practices were not preordained; their genesis is rooted in a trial-and-error, learning-by-doing process in which actors tried to improve their position and were able to monitor and communicate the results.

Silicon Valley sustains a division of labor in the new firm creation process that would be inconceivable in other regions. For example, a recent *Wall Street Journal* article featured a Silicon Valley–based consultant whose sole activity is preparing corporate executives for their presentations to stock analysts ("roadshows") before the company undertakes its IPO. The consultant was introduced to this opportunity through a venture capitalist, who believed that there was a need for such a service. His consulting fee for four days of training for the corporate officers was $20,000 plus the right to purchase up to one thousand shares at the preoffering price (Hardy 1998). The important issue here is not the fee, but the existence of a market for such a specialized skill and the consultants' interest in securing equity as partial compensation. This illustrates the richness and symbiosis of Economy Two.

There is a final interesting category of highly specialized intermediaries in Silicon Valley, namely those that liquidate failures (O'Brien 1998). This illustrates the point that these small firms are constructing an entity. The first form of liquidation is to simply sell the firm at near-liquidation prices. If the firm cannot be sold, then traditional liquidation is undertaken. Before the 1990s, most liquidators focused on the physical assets such as office furnishings and computers. Often these could be recycled into new start-ups. In the 1990s a new type of liquidator emerged to sell any intellectual property the firm might have developed. In some cases, even though the firm is unsuccessful, its patents have value.

Capital gains are the fuel for Economy Two. A striking feature of the region is that nearly all of the professional service providers are willing to extend below-market rates to start-ups in exchange for some quantity of equity or the implicit (or explicit) promise that the firm will continue the relationship if it proves successful and grows larger. In other words, they are trading for a piece of an uncertain future. This provides the opportunity to participate in the success of the firm; for the start-up, it has a functional benefit of decreasing the negative cash flow during its most vulnerable period.

There was "space" for Economy Two to evolve because the electronics technological paradigm provided so many recurring opportunities for entrepreneurs to create firms capable of growing very fast and within which innovations could lead to enormous capital gains. The institutions evolved as pioneers adapted to their circumstances by creating mechanisms that satisfied. Put differently, they used the institutional materials at hand and refashioned them for their needs. These mechanisms, when successful, were reused and tweaked. Eventually, the successful experiments mutated into paths making the process clearer and more easily reproduced. In a word, they became "natural." As is often the case in vibrant industrial ecologies, an ever greater division of labor evolved with new and unique specializations. The hot-house atmosphere of Economy Two was fed by the constant new opportunities uncovered by the pace of change. Conversely, the institutions were organized to search for opportunities that could generate enormous capital gains. When opportunities for such capital gains disappeared in a sector, funding waned.

Silicon Valley was not always such a lush ecosystem. In the 1950s there were start-ups, but not a discernible set of institutions to support them. In the next section we examine the development of the semiconductor industry to understand how Economy Two grew and effloresced. The semiconductor industry was, of course, the critical industry for igniting the positive feedback loop that built Silicon Valley. Semiconductors led to the first discernible industry cluster, but many others would also form as Silicon Valley diversified.

Silicon Valley and Semiconductors

In the postwar electronics industry, transistors and then integrated circuits were the enabling technology for nearly every important electronics innovation. For example, the personal computer and workstation were a direct result of the invention of the microprocessor. Computer networking would have been almost impossibly difficult without sophisticated integrated circuitry to transform, process, and direct the data. In other words, the semiconductor became the basic component in all electronics products.

The semiconductor was invented at Bell Laboratories in the late 1940s and was quickly commercialized. Beginning with the transistor and then evolving to the integrated circuit, as a product semiconductors exhibited unusual technoeconomic properties. The most significant property is the constantly increasing processing power available at the same cost. Gordon Moore, one of the founders of Fairchild and later Intel, observed that the number of transistors on an integrated circuit (a rough approximation of the functionality of an integrated circuit) doubled approximately every eighteen months yet remained at the same price point. This came to be called Moore's Law. With these learning curves it was possible to constantly lower the price of a particular chip until it was superseded by a more powerful model at roughly the same cost. Braun and Macdonald (1982) illustrate this with the example of a Fairchild transistor that sold in 1959 for $19.75 and in 1962 cost only

$1.80. Despite the price declines, the transistor was extremely profitable at both prices (Gilder 1989). Since many functions of physical artifacts can be rendered digitally with sufficient calculating power, the result is a constant unfolding of new opportunities to apply integrated circuits to new uses (Schaller 1996).

The Santa Clara Valley and semiconductors were not always synonymous, although even before World War II a number of innovative electrical and electronics firms had been established in the Bay Area (see Sturgeon, this volume). Silicon Valley's capture of the semiconductor industry is the result of a series of small events that would make an enormous difference. In 1955, William Shockley, coinventor of the transistor at Bell Laboratories, decided to establish a firm to exploit his invention. To launch a firm, he needed capital. In an effort to secure funding he approached a number of organizations on the East Coast, in particular negotiating with Raytheon, the important Boston-area high-technology manufacturer founded by MIT professor Vannevar Bush and an early leader in transistor production. He demanded $1 million, but after a month of bargaining Raytheon demurred (Scott 1974: 305). He also negotiated with the Rockefeller venture capital arm, but no agreement could be reached. After these failures he was introduced to Arnold Beckman, the founder of Los Angeles–based Beckman Instruments; Beckman agreed to fund Shockley to start a firm in Palo Alto (Riordan and Hoddeson 1997).

Shockley hired eight brilliant young scientists and engineers and brought them with him to Palo Alto. Shockley proved to be an ineffective manager, and the eight resigned in 1957 to form their own start-up. Not knowing how to find capital in the Bay Area, they went through an East Coast investment bank to get funding from an East Coast firm, Fairchild Camera and Instrument Company, owned by Sherman Fairchild. The firm founded by these eight engineers was named Fairchild Semiconductor. Fairchild quickly became a technological leader in the transistor industry and spearheaded the transition to the integrated circuit. In 1960, Jean Hoerni, one of the Shockley defectors, invented the planar process that made mass production of integrated circuits possible, and a cascade of innovations followed (Rogers and Larsen 1984).

Fairchild Semiconductor had been established at ground zero of the most important technological development of the twentieth century, the integrated circuit. When Fairchild Camera and Instrument Corporation provided capital to Fairchild Semiconductor's founders, one clause in the agreement gave it the option to purchase the founders' shares of Fairchild Semiconductor within three years for $3 million. Quite naturally, as the firm was immediately profitable and the market boomed, Fairchild exercised its option and the founders lost their equity participation in the company.

With the Sputnik-related military buildup throughout the 1960s and the adoption of transistors and integrated circuits by the manufacturers of consumer electronics and computers, sales boomed and profits were exorbitant (Hanson 1982). As a by-product of the exuberant growth of the semiconductor industry in the 1960s, many firm founders and early employees became very wealthy (Tilton 1971: 80). Their success, and willingness to invest in new ventures, put in motion a path-dependent logic, in terms of an example and an incentive for others to follow. Earlier successes justified future ventures. The dimensions of this spinoff process were immense; a genealogy of semiconductor start-ups through 1986 indicated that 124 start-ups could trace their roots to Fairchild. Robert Noyce, a founder of Fairchild and Intel, described the situation of firms on the cutting edge of the semiconductor industry as one in which so many commercial opportunities were created that there was no way for one company to exploit them all. This stimulated the teams of engineers with rejected projects to launch their own firms.

Fairchild and its spinoffs were important in the history of Silicon Valley venture capital. In addition to Arthur Rock, who arranged the Fairchild investment in 1958, organized the funding for Intel, and provided funding to many other start-ups (such as Apple and Scientific Data Systems), other important venture capitalists who began their career at Fairchild are Donald Valentine and Pierre Lamond of Sequoia Partners, and Eugene Kleiner of Kleiner Perkins. Also, Floyd Kvamme of Kleiner Perkins is a former National Semiconductor executive. Most important, the success of Fairchild's spinoffs (such as Intel, Advanced Micro Devices, National Semiconductor, LSI Logic, and their spinoffs) created enormous capital gains for their founders, key employees, and investors in venture capital funds. Some gains were reinvested in venture capital funds and independent start-ups. The final important contribution of Fairchild and its early start-ups was a number of managers and engineers that had become independently wealthy and were able to invest in or join start-ups without risking their financial future—in other words, the labor power was being freed to join new firms.

Fairchild was a critical firm not only because it was the source of so many entrepreneurs but also because it was a monument to how not to manage a firm in the semiconductor industry and, more generally, in Silicon Valley. The lesson to the entrepreneurs and investors was that all key employees must share in the wealth created by their activities. Equity participation and stock options became the vehicles of choice for compensating and retaining key employees. Finally, Fairchild and its spinoffs created an enormous concentration of semiconductor design expertise that could interact with various other electronics firms and provide them with the information-processing power they needed to create their new products.

New Business Models

The previous sections approached the developments of the two regions from the perspective of technical change and the institutions encouraging new firm formation. Over the last four decades, Silicon Valley has repeatedly generated new business models within which to encase technological innovations. The long-term trend has been for the new firms to become what the Silicon Valley venture capitalist William Davidow called "virtual" (Davidow and Malone 1992). In effect, the firms concentrated increasingly upon intellectual property creation and design functions and less on manufacturing activities. It also became easier to out-source many functions, such as accounting, personnel, and, especially, manufacturing that normally had been considered core firm activities. In effect, the nature of the firm was continually redefined.

This continuing creation of new firm models can be seen in the semiconductor industry. The initial wave of firms were integrated producers, which meant that they integrated the entire semiconductor value chain from design through manufacturing. During the early days of the semiconductor industry, this was quite feasible because the costs of manufacturing capability were low. Nearly from the outset manufacturing costs escalated rapidly and by the mid-1980s had become far too high for even venture capital consortia to undertake. Historically, the escalating cost of production facilities has often been a reason for a decreasing number of entrants into an industry and is an important sign that an industry is maturing (Abernathy and Utterback 1978; Tushman and Anderson 1986). Here the reconceptualization was to see that the design was where the most value was created. Of course, if the value realization required building a fabrication factory, then it would be impossible to realize this value separately. However, if manufacturing could be severed from design, the value could be captured in a free-standing firm.[9] Fortuitously, at the time Asian manufacturers were building fabrication facilities that they were willing to "rent" out to other firms. In effect, it became possible to design chips and then pay another firm to actually make them. This made it possible to create the "fabless" semiconductor company, which designed chips and then marketed them (see Saxenian, this volume).

At the time, there were significant doubts about a model that explicitly presumed that the firm would have no dedicated production capacity. It was asserted that they would lack capacity during boom periods and be vulnerable to opportunism by their fabricators. There was also a belief summarized in the aphorism "Real men have fabs"—that is, a semiconductor firm requires fabrication facilities. In hindsight, it is obvious that the fabless firms were successful and formed a new industry segment. Notice, however, that they did not displace the earlier firms that did have fabs such as Intel, AMD, and National Semiconductor—they became a new category—and eventually some of the fabless firms did build or purchase fabs.

Most interesting, in the mid-1990s yet another business model was pioneered, namely what might be termed a design-only semiconductor firm. These firms, best exemplified by Rambus, Inc., are predicated upon licensing their intellectual property to others. They will only design semiconductors and then sell the designs as intellectual property that other firms will incorporate into their products. In this model the firm markets its designs and neither manufactures nor markets finished semiconductors. Their product, the designs, are treated as simply a type of software.

The Silicon Valley semiconductor business model has evolved from one in which start-ups integrated design, manufacture, and sales to one in which only design remains. The other functions are conducted by non–Silicon Valley firms. Seen more comprehensively, the more purely intellectual activities are being divorced from the more physical components of the value chain. This development was pushed by both the rising costs associated with production and marketing and the opportunity to slough off activities that could not generate high returns. For the purposes of this paper it is not necessary to examine all the reasons for this evolution; what is important is that business models capable of circumventing these barriers to entry were developed and entrepreneurs were funded to actualize the possibilities.

If the generation of new business models were confined to the semiconductor industry, it could be dismissed as an interesting but peculiar development. However, a similar evolution, though with different specifics, occurred in the computer networking industry. The initial industrial entrants in the early 1980s built fully integrated firms (von Burg and Kenney 1999). The next generation of firms, such as Cisco, subcontracted most production activities to concentrate upon software, chip design, network design, and marketing. By the late 1980s, the earlier entrants, such as 3Com, Cisco, and Synoptics, occupied the computer networking space to such an extent that new entrants would have a difficult time succeeding. The industry was oligopolized, and few new start-ups could be expected.

Computer networking technology, however, exhibited one other characteristic: namely, it was changing rapidly, and the technology was expanding its reach and becoming more complex. As a result, there were opportunities to establish single-product firms in the myriad emerging niches. For many there was little likelihood that the new firm could grow to be a large firm, but it could become a division or product line for larger firms. The larger firm purchased the start-up in a stock swap and then integrated the product and the firm's technical personnel.[10] In this case the founding team and the venture capitalists would reap capital gains, because the fledgling firm proved a technology and had a head start over the larger firms. From the outset, the start-up was designed to be acquired. This acquisition-as-exit-strategy model uses the independent firm to catalyze the creative team, which generates a quantum of value. The value is realized when the firm is purchased by the larger firm. In effect, Economy Two institutions were able to extract the new-division creation process from existing firms.

The development of new business models has proliferated most dramatically in the current race to create businesses using the Internet. For example, many firms, such as Yahoo! or Excite, are simply giving away their services in the race to capture users (Curry and Kenney 1999). Whether these firms will be able to turn a profit is interesting, but not important for our purposes here. What is important is the decision to fund businesses that have no clear and significant profitability. Of course, for Economy Two it is merely sufficient that the firm be capable of being sold to the public or another firm for the investment to be profitable. However, by accepting these new business models Economy Two has contributed to the creation of an entirely new industry.

Establishing whether it is the actors in Economy Two or the entrepreneurs that develop these new business models is difficult. What is certain is that the constituents of Economy Two have been willing to support these new models. Thus industries that appeared to stabilize, in terms of organizational forms or business models, could be reopened for new rounds of firm formation. With the exception of Saxenian's discussion (1990) of the fabless semiconductor firms, little attention has been given to the ability of entrepreneurs to innovate new business models. And yet, these innovations are almost on a par with the importance of technology itself in the history of Silicon Valley's development.

Sources of Diversification

Semiconductors have been the paradigmatic Silicon Valley industry. But Silicon Valley's Economy Two exploited and seized a leadership role in a significant number of the other electronics technologies introduced in recent decades. Repeatedly, either lead firms, local universities, or private firm research laboratories invented new technologies that diffused into the environment of Economy Two, where they rapidly matured into the core technology for some extremely rapidly growing firms and industrial clusters. These technologies now cover quite a broad spectrum, even including such nonelectronics fields as biotechnology and medical instruments.[11]

One critical institution was the electronics research center that IBM located in San Jose in 1952. IBM's goal was to secure access to talented West Coast engineers unwilling to relocate to its East Coast research laboratories (Mayadas 1998). The San Jose laboratory had IBM's global mandate for magnetic data storage research, and its neighboring factory was responsible for magnetic storage device manufacturing. Many of the innovations in the HDD industry were developed in IBM's research laboratory and commercialized by its employees. Magnetic storage manufacturing and marketing operations were also located on the site and could be raided for the necessary managers to build a complete start-up. Thus, it is no surprise that many of the firms in the Silicon Valley HDD industry, both assemblers and parts suppliers, were established by entrepreneurs from the IBM San Jose operations (Christensen 1992). One figure, Al

Shugart, a former employee of the IBM San Jose Laboratory, was especially important in creating new firms, and his start-ups were also training grounds for a number of the other entrepreneurs that made Silicon Valley the center of the disk drive industry (Bahrami and Evans, this volume; Christensen 1992). Because of IBM's presence, a number of the largest merchant HDD firms in the world—Seagate, Quantum, and Maxtor—are located in Silicon Valley, as are many of the most important suppliers. For example, Komag, a supplier of disks, was started by a former Xerox PARC researcher, two researchers from IBM's laboratory, and a manager from yet another company (Komag, Inc. 1996).

The IBM San Jose Laboratory also developed the technology for relational databases. But, as was typical for IBM in the early 1980s, commercialization was slow. This provided an opportunity for Larry Ellison to establish Oracle, which is now among the largest independent software companies in the world (Wilson 1997). With the other two Silicon Valley relational database start-ups, Sybase and Informix, and IBM, Silicon Valley has the largest concentration of relational database software companies in the world. Drawing upon this strength, a number of data warehousing and database mining software firms have also been created in Silicon Valley. Economy Two converted IBM's seeds into successful and lucrative companies. This was not a normal occurrence, IBM's other major research laboratories, be they in Tokyo, Yorktown Heights, or Zurich, never were hotbeds of new firm spinoffs—but then they were not located in Silicon Valley.

Of all the corporate research laboratories in Silicon Valley, Xerox's Palo Alto Research Center has received the most attention and probably contributed the most to Silicon Valley. Xerox established PARC in 1970 with the express mission of conducting the basic research necessary to develop the "office of the future." Initially there was debate within Xerox about the best site for the laboratory, but proximity to Stanford and the burgeoning Silicon Valley semiconductor and computer industry convinced George Pake, the first director, to locate in the Palo Alto area (Smith and Alexander 1988: 56). In the 1970s, PARC pioneered many of the technologies defining computing in the 1990s, including graphical user interfaces, local area networks (Ethernet), desktop workstations, and a host of others. But, as fate would have it, Xerox proved incapable of commercializing these new technologies; however, Silicon Valley's Economy Two was perfectly capable of funding entrepreneurs to commercialize them.

Not all corporate R&D centers contributed so much to the growth of the Silicon Valley economy. For example, in the 1960s there were a number of laboratories dedicated to military microwave applications. There were also many spinoffs, some of which received venture capital funding; these were not so successful and remained trapped in niche markets supplying the military. If microwaves had had greater civilian use, Silicon Valley might have been called Microwave Valley, because of the large number of small start-ups (see Leslie, this volume).

It is tempting to consider today's Silicon Valley firms and industries as the result of the brilliance or foresight of venture capitalists or some other agent. The reality is more capricious. Venture capitalists have lost huge sums on perfectly reasonable investments in technologies such as pen-based computing, superminicomputers, and artificial intelligence, to name only a few. But the system is self-correcting. After a number of failures, the venture capitalists see no return, the firms fail, and that technological space no longer receives funding. Failures do not destroy Economy Two, as long as Silicon Valley continues to produce successful new firms and industries. Venture capitalists have a diverse portfolio and are connected informationally, but they are financially independent; learning by example occurs. Even after huge overinvestment and a devastating downturn, some venture capitalists survive by adapting to the new conditions. This multiagent environment, which thrives on communication, allows multiple bets to be placed. The failure of individuals is not significant as long as a sufficient number of successes occur to reproduce the ecosystem.

Discussion

This paper began with the premise that Silicon Valley's remarkable success could be best understood by the institutions that have evolved to nurture and encourage the formation of particular types of fast-growing firms. The introduction of a separation between Economy One and Economy Two was heuristic, but it provided significant insight into the dynamics of the growth of the region. There are many industries in Silicon Valley, but the critical feature for Economy Two is the varied players dedicated to creating new firms capable of generating large capital gains for its entrepreneurs and investors.

The distinction between the established institutions of Economy One and institutions dedicated to creating new firms, Economy Two, provided a useful heuristic for orienting our analysis. Here, we drew upon earlier works by Schoonhoven and Eisenhardt (1989), Florida and Kenney (1988a), and Bahrami and Evans (1995) that explicitly focused on the entrepreneurial dimensions of Silicon Valley. These economies are not entirely separate, and there is a path-dependent evolutionary interaction between them. It is also quite clear that over time Economy Two in Silicon Valley became powerful through a dynamic interaction by which the economy became richer in specialists and, conversely, this positively affected the success of Silicon Valley firms.

Silicon Valley firms have been successful in capturing some core industries in what some have called knowledge-based industries. They moved faster than other regions in building these industries and benefited from the economics of clustering. Sometimes, Silicon Valley firms failed later because the product became a commodity, or firms in another region developed competitive advantages. It is difficult to establish causation firmly, however Economy Two lowered the barriers to establishing firms and successfully encouraged future spinoffs. In fact, the dynamics of Economy Two create a self-reinforcing process as the participants "produced" the new firms.

Economy Two has evolved from loosely connected local individuals investing their own funds into a complicated interactive community. In the 1950s there were simply entrepreneurs and informal investors operating in an inchoate economic space. The successes gave impetus to the creation of an economic infrastructure consisting of specialized intermediaries such as venture capitalists, lawyers, accountants, investment bankers, executive search firms, and a plethora of other specialized activities all centered on easing firm creation. Repeated successes encouraged the practitioners of these activities, all of which began informally, and encouraged institutionalization.

Economy One technologies and firms were intimately connected with Economy Two. The rapid pace of change occurring in Economy One provided many new technological opportunities around which new firms could be formed. Of course, many Economy One firms were born in Economy Two, thus they themselves provided the examples for the next generation of entrepreneurs. Many entrepreneurs managing Economy One firms were willing to invest in new start-ups, and their managers were willing and even eager to establish or to join a start-up or small firm with good growth prospects.

By highlighting Economy Two, we provide a socioeconomic explanation for the Silicon Valley start-up culture. The institutions of Economy Two have every interest in encouraging the "garage start-up" myth; it encourages deal flow. Myths are not simply fanciful stories; they are also pedagogical tools to train and inspire the young. The entrepreneur that finds the new killer application or next "best thing" and then executes the business plan can also become a Steve Jobs, Bob Noyce, or Larry Ellison. And, in the background, the institutions of Economy Two will reap capital gains, content to celebrate the entrepreneurial success they facilitated and even made possible.

From the entrepreneur's perspective, Economy Two has attractions. Although entrepreneurs often must surrender control of the firm, the quid pro quo is access to the resources necessary to propel rapid growth. In the early days, the venture capitalists often wished to see the entrepreneurs' entire net worth invested in the firm, on the principle that this would make them more driven to succeed. However, more recently, there has been less emphasis on placing the entrepreneurs' entire financial existence in jeopardy. Many venture capitalists now feel that this unnecessarily burdens the entrepreneur and, as important, raises the entrepreneur's cost of failure, thereby discouraging venturing and not necessarily increasing the probability of success. The participants have a concrete stake in celebrating entrepreneurship. Put simply, they need and feed the entrepreneurs.

There have been many, mostly unsuccessful, attempts to reproduce Silicon Valley in the United States and around the world. Usually, these have been conceived by government officials and local land developers with little understanding of the historical conditions that evolved into Silicon Valley. Not surprisingly, it has been difficult to duplicate the organic, path-dependent evolution replete with learning-by-doing, learning-by-example, and, most especially, learning-by-failure. We are somewhat pessimistic about policies aimed at cloning Silicon Valley. However, the increasing importance of innovation and knowledge in value-creation in capitalist economies might provide more space for the creation of Economy Two–type institutions in other regions. Certainly, the Internet and the increasing centrality of software are creating a proliferation of opportunities. This growth of opportunities and the possibility that new ones will continually emerge not only in Silicon Valley but also elsewhere might provide the constant flow of deals necessary

to create more persistent institutions for supporting new firm formation in other regions. One indicator of this possibility is the increasing
number of venture capital partnerships in other regions of the United
States. If this pattern persists in these places, local institutions might
form and deepen their roots. Then, and only then, will the Silicon Valley model become more generalized.

Notes

1. Kenney: Introduction

1. For further discussion of these problems, see Joint Venture: Silicon Valley (1998).

2. For a comprehensive set of critiques and extensions of the concept of path dependence, see Garud and Karnoe (1999).

3. One of the intellectual progenitors for path dependence is evolutionary economics as propounded by Nelson and Winter (1982).

4. *Innovation* (1969), a magazine covering new technology, was the first journal with national coverage that discussed the spin-out process in the region's industry. Presciently, they wrote: "One of the striking characteristics of this industry is the rate at which it spins off new small companies, and the surprising number of these that survive and grow. Despite predictions that the giants will absorb the little companies and grow more dominant . . . there are signs that the opposite tendency is operative."

5. An important source for the "prehistory" of Silicon Valley is Norberg (1976).

6. For a more general discussion of the development of local institutions specialized in providing needed inputs for local industry, see, for example, Porter (1998).

2. Sturgeon: How Silicon Valley Came to Be

1. The history of science has generated a few more complete accounts of Silicon Valley's history. Arthur L. Norberg (1976), a historian and archivist who was at the University of California, Berkeley from 1973 to 1979, and James C. Williams (1987, 1990), who teaches at De Anza College in Cupertino and is executive director of the California History Center, have both made clear links in their work between the electric power industry, pre–World War II electronics development in the Bay Area, and the subsequent emergence of Silicon Valley. Hugh G. J. Aitken (1985) and David and Marshall Fisher (1996) provide detailed accounts of some of the activities described in this paper, but since these histories focus on the emergence of the radio and television industries, respectively, their focus is on contributions made to technological, not geographic, development. An excellent history of the early electronics industry in the San Francisco

Bay Area does exist (Morgan 1967), but it is a young person's book published through a small press and has thus escaped wide attention. The only widely circulated account of Silicon Valley that draws on this latter source is a journalistic account by Michael Malone (1985) entitled *The Big Score: The Billion Dollar Story of Silicon Valley*. Unfortunately, none of these works have altered widespread misperceptions about the timing and nature of Silicon Valley's genesis.

2. For a discussion of the history of the San Francisco Bay Area, see Walker 1996.

3. The first radio station in the United States with regularly scheduled programming was set up in 1909 in San Jose by Charles Herrold. At first, since commercial radio receivers were not widely available until the 1920s, he gave crystal receivers away to farmers and townspeople within range of his station. "Doc" Herrold had spent three years at Stanford, and soon after he established the Herrold College of Engineering and Wireless in the Wells Fargo building in downtown San Jose, where he also located his radio station. During World War I, more than one thousand wireless operators trained there (Morgan 1967).

4. The idea for using continuous waves to improve radio transmission came from Nikola Tesla, the Serbian physicist.

5. For an excellent history of the development of the radio, see Aitken 1985.

6. Elwell had received a request to evaluate the commercial potential of a wireless telephony system backed by two Oakland bankers, the Henshaw brothers. The brothers had invested a significant sum of money in the development of the system, but the inventor, Ignatus McCarty, was killed when the horse car he was driving overturned (Rosa 1960).

7. When Poulsen offered Elwell the rights for $250,000, Elwell traveled to Copenhagen to inspect the Poulsen system, which could transmit speech messages 10 miles and telegraph signals 180 miles. He purchased the option on the patent rights and went to New York City, where he unsuccessfully courted investors, including a Mr. Lindlay, who had raised the capital to start AT&T. Undaunted, Elwell returned to Copenhagen, where he struck a deal allowing incremental payment terms if the patents purchased included those on the telegraphone. This was a precursor to the tape recorder that allowed telegraph messages to be automatically recorded upon reception, allowing after-the-fact decoding. The price, including this device, was raised to $450,000. Elwell agreed, on the condition that the patent rights cover not only the United States but all U.S. possessions as well (Rosa 1960).

8. Charles Crocker was the son of one of the "Big Four" transcontinental railroad magnates, the others being Colis Huntington, Mark Hopkins, and Leland Stanford.

9. Fuller's family physician in Portland, Oregon, had been solicited to invest in Elwell's company, so Fuller was sent down to inspect the system and give his opinion.

10. True to form, Elwell succeeded in persuading the British Admiralty to build an arc station at Portsmouth. The station was completed one month before the outbreak of World War I. He also installed small arcs on two battleships and two cruisers. During the war, Elwell went all out designing sets for the British

military (Rosa 1960). In 1914, he went to work for the French Signal Corps, installing arc stations in the Eiffel Tower and at Lyons, Nantes, Toulon, and in many French colonies and on ships. In 1916 he built a station in Rome that included a set of antenna towers 714 feet high, then the tallest wooden structures in the world. This station, completed in just five months, was able to communicate directly with the station in Tuckerton, New Jersey, then run by the U.S. Navy. After the war, at the British Admiralty's request, he helped form the Mullard Company to supply vacuum tubes to the British Navy. This company became the largest tube manufacturer in England. In 1947, after nearly thirty years as the company's director, Elwell returned to Palo Alto, where he studied aeronautical engineering at Stanford and worked as a consulting engineer for Hewlett Packard (Rosa 1960).

11. The surplus eighty-ton magnets intended for this system were donated to Ernest Lawrence and Stanley Livingston of U.C. Berkeley for use in the construction of the eleven-inch cyclotron, used for pioneering nuclear physics experiments in 1932. Charles Litton, who consulted on the cyclotron project, brought the existence of the magnet to Lawrence's and Livingston's attention.

12. On his return to the East Coast in 1913, de Forest was to bring Logwood with him as an assistant (Rosa 1960). De Forest's other key assistant, Herbert Van Etten, did have formal training as a telephone engineer (Aitken 1985).

13. Whether and when de Forest realized the three-element vacuum tube's potential as an oscillator is the subject of some controversy, then and now. See Aitken (1985) for a full discussion.

14. Clarence Mackay, the son of a gold miner who had struck it rich, had established Postal early in the century to compete with Western Union. Mackay's original plans were to overtake and eventually absorb Western Union, but in 1927, Postal had only 17 percent of the U.S. telegraph market, in comparison to Western Union's 83 percent (Sobel 1982).

15. Fuller had earned his doctorate from Stanford in 1919 with a dissertation based on the improvements he had made to FTC's arc transmitters.

16. Farnsworth's ideas may have been based on the published work of the Scottish scientist A. A. Campbell-Swinton, who in 1908 proposed a method of electronic scanning by which the cathode ray tube could be used as the camera as well as the picture tube. Campbell-Swinton's theory forms the essential features of today's television system.

17. The increased power from this tube allowed Globe Wireless to get through to Manila during daylight hours. Because regular mail service from Manila took twenty-six days, the company instituted a "radio mail" service at a 25 percent cost reduction over RCA and FTC. San Francisco was the U.S. collection point for the teletype messages from across the Pacific. There they were printed, put in envelopes, and sent on to U.S. destinations through the postal service. Alternatively, the messages were forwarded through wire telegraph systems. Federal Telegraph was linked to Postal Telegraph, while RCA was linked to Western Union (Heintz 1974, 1982).

18. Tape recording was first developed by the Telefunken Company in Germany during the 1930s. During World War II, the German military played

tapes of speeches and music over makeshift radio stations set up in the remains of cities that had been destroyed by Allied bombs. The tapes were too long and of too high a sound quality to have been recorded onto phonograph disks, confusing Allied intelligence about the success of bombing raids and as to the whereabouts of important political figures whose voices could be heard on the tapes.

19. The development team at Ampex for the video tape recorder included Charles Ginsburg and Ray Dolby. A portable version was introduced in 1967. In 1965, Dolby went on to found Dolby Laboratories in London. Dolby Laboratories became a leader in audio noise reduction and "surround sound" technologies and was still producing equipment specifically designed to work with Ampex's professional audio recorders in the mid-1980s.

3. Leslie: The Biggest "Angel" of Them All

1. Saxenian (1994) makes a strong argument for Silicon Valley as an industrial district where cooperation and corporate culture have given it the edge over competitors such as Route 128.

2. For the history of one would-be Silicon Valley, see Dobbs and Wollner, 1990.

3. Luger and Goldstein (1991) survey the promises and perils of this strategy.

4. Osborne (1988) provides a booster's view of state experiments in promoting high-technology industry.

5. Leslie and Kargon (1996) provide some examples of failed imitators.

6. Miller and Côté (1985) attest to the continuing attraction of the Silicon Valley model, while pointing out some of its limitations.

7. Hansen 1982; Malone 1985; and Rogers and Larsen 1982 all argue the heroic model of the All-American entrepreneur.

8. An important exception is Gray et al. (1999), which includes the military as one of the four faces, along with large civilian high-technology firms, foreign branch plants, and networked start-up companies. Curiously enough, Lotchin (1992) pays virtually no attention to the complex of defense electronics firms in the Bay Area that had already gained national prominence by the 1950s.

9. Of course, as Kenney and Florida show in chapter 5 (this volume), there was only limited venture capital available in the early days.

10. Norberg (1976) is the best account of the early West Coast radio industry.

11. The best sketch of Terman's early career is McMahon (1984).

12. David Packard's recollections in *Stanford Engineering News* 17 (July 1965); for Hewlett and Packard's early years, see Packard 1995.

13. Ginzton (1975) and Galison et al. (1991) offer the best account of the klystron's origins.

14. See *Stanford Engineering News* (1950), and Harris and Harris (1986), for more detail on Stanford's TWT research.

15. For the early history of Varian Associates, see Varian (1983).

16. Lowood (1988) provides an excellent sketch of the Industrial Park's origins.

17. For further discussion of the importance of Kern County Land Company in the history of Silicon Valley venture capital, see Kenney and Florida, this volume.

18. Schoenberger (1996) includes a perceptive chapter on Lockheed's move to northern California.

19. On Philco, later Ford Aerospace, see Lindsey (1964), Siekman (1966), and *Time* (1961).

20. See Sturgeon, this volume, for a different perspective on the garage that founded Silicon Valley.

21. Richard Florida and Martin Kenney (1990c) emphasize this missing link as a key element in recent American failures in consumer electronics and other industries.

22. Miller and Côté (1985) underscore this point.

23. Markusen et al. (1991) convincingly argue for the central importance of defense contracting for high-technology regions in postwar America, though with limited attention to Silicon Valley.

4. Suchman: Dealmakers and Counselors

This research was supported in part by the National Science Foundation and by a dissertation fellowship from the American Bar Foundation's program on Law, Professionalism and Economic Change. The author thanks W. Richard Scott, Nancy Tuma, Robert Gordon, Robert Nelson, Lauren Edelman, Teresa Scheid, and Linda Pike for their invaluable advice and assistance during various stages of the project.

1. For alternative approaches to integrating ecological and institutional models, see Baum and Oliver (1991, 1992); Baum and Singh (1994); Fombrun (1988); Hannan and Freeman (1986, 1989); and Singh et al. (1991).

2. Since Palo Alto houses the core of the region's legal sector, the statistics presented here describe that city alone. By and large, the legal communities of other Silicon Valley localities have lagged substantially behind. With the exception of a few San Jose firms, most law offices elsewhere on the peninsula have roughly paralleled the unexceptional growth of Palo Alto's less-successful "second tier" firms.

3. Several other firms, particularly those with litigation expertise, opened branches in San Jose, the site of the state and federal courthouses (Cox 1988b: 48).

4. Because *Martindale-Hubbell* takes a year or more to compile its listings of lawyers (Galanter and Palay 1990), each point in figure 3 actually represents the state of the law firm a year or so earlier. Unfortunately, this reporting delay is not sufficiently systematic to justify simply translating the curves one year to the left.

5. During the 1980s, a similar gap appears in the prestige of law firm personnel, with graduates of elite law schools increasingly favoring the region's most rapidly growing firms. Here, however, differentials emerge less among the

leading three firms than between these firms and the rest of the community (Suchman 1994).

6. Needless to say, not all law firms located within Silicon Valley practice "Silicon Valley law." Many continue to serve individual and small commercial clients, in much the same way as before the region's economic boom—and in much the same way as law firms in other suburban communities throughout the country. Thus, the "Silicon Valley" legal practices described below are, in reality, the practices of only a small segment of the local bar. Nonetheless, it is this segment that most directly interacts with the region's high-technology economy, and it is this set of practices that most directly reveal the legal profession's role in organizational reproduction and community structuration.

7. The following pages draw quotations from a series of roughly twenty-five semistructured interviews, conducted by the author during the summer of 1991, with Silicon Valley lawyers, venture capitalists, and entrepreneurs. These interviews included roughly equal numbers of respondents from each of the three groups—along with several individuals who had played multiple roles during their careers, and a handful of journalists, academics, and other informed community-watchers. The sampling frame was a systematic, multiple-snowball sample of individuals who were active in Silicon Valley during the formative period from 1970 to 1990. In order to capture as full a range of accounts as possible, the sample was informally stratified along such dimensions as industry, seniority, tenure in the community, location, and the like. In two months of interviewing, the response rate (ratio of interviews to initial contacts) was over 85 percent.

The quotations presented here have been edited for confidentiality, brevity, and readability. In order to preserve the flow of the text, most of this material appears without ellipses, brackets, or other diacritical marks. Care has been taken, however, to maintain the substance and tone of respondents' remarks, while eliminating some of the more awkward constructions of impromptu speech.

8. It is perhaps worth noting that the venture-capital community is not without dissenters when it comes to the importance of law-firm dealmaking: "Dealmaking by lawyers is present, but it's not essential. If the profession was barred from referring entrepreneurs to VC firms, the business wouldn't change. The guys would ultimately get to the VC firms anyway. Maybe differently, but they'd still go for the VC" (070802.14).

Significantly, however, even this respondent acknowledged subsequently that lawyer dealmaking is a prominent feature of how Silicon Valley's venture capital sector currently operates. His skepticism revolves, instead, around the counterfactual question of whether, in the absence of lawyer dealmaking, the venture-capital industry would develop functional equivalents. Nothing in the analysis presented here disputes his position on this hypothetical point.

9. A final frequently cited advantage of Silicon Valley attorneys is simple proximity. The spirit of most respondents' comments, however, suggests that the issue is less physical than cultural proximity.

10. Indeed, law firms often encounter new clients even before the actual

founding of a company, while the entrepreneurs are still extricating themselves from a previous employer.

11. Despite the structural advantages described above, law firms are rarely the only entities capable of engaging in these activities. Significantly, however, when other organizations take on this pollinator role, they often do so precisely because of their ability to match attorneys on the key dimensions of exposure, access, and trust. Thus, for example, the counseling behavior of Silicon Valley venture capital funds seems directly attributable to the success of community culture in suppressing perceptions of opportunism in the investor-entrepreneur relationship. Interestingly, as noted above, much of the Silicon Valley lawyer's proselytizing role revolves around mobilizing attorney-client trust to promote this ideology of nonadversarial financing—suggesting that in this regard, at least, lawyers and venture capitalists are more symbiotic than competitive.

5. Kenney and Florida: Venture Capital in Silicon Valley

1. I borrow the term "generative dance" from Cook and Seely Brown (1999).

2. For a categorization of types of innovation, see Henderson and Clark (1990). In their schema, venture capital opportunities would be located as radical or architectural product innovation, although "me-too" and incremental product innovations in rapidly changing technology fields often allow sufficient economic space to start a firm. It is often the case that a number of firms funded by different venture capitalists will be formed to exploit the same market opportunity. If the market grows sufficiently rapidly, there may be space to allow capital gains for more than one entrant.

3. Some have attributed this to the operation of Moore's Law, Metcalfe's Law, and a similar trajectory in the density of data storage in magnetic media. However, these technical attributes do not necessarily call forth specific institutional structures.

4. Many have remarked that in Silicon Valley there is little stigma attached to failure. Most have attributed this to a "cultural" trait; few have considered that it is in the interest of the venture capitalists to lower the cost of failure. It is critical for the entire system that entrepreneurs continue to venture. Discouragement and punishment increases the cost of failure and offers little economic return to the venture capitalists. Also, it should never be forgotten that success is valued far more highly than failure!

5. For example, Febvre and Martin (1976) discuss the role of merchants in funding the establishments of printing presses. Jardine (1996) discusses the rise of the merchant in more general terms.

6. Curiously, 60 percent of the equity is the amount most contemporary venture capitalists aim to control.

7. Davis (1986) knew General Doriot through Davis's brother, who was General Doriot's student assistant at the Harvard Business School.

8. Suchman describes this in greater detail in the previous chapter.

9. For a discussion of the reluctance of Silicon Valley venture capitalists to fund the earliest entrepreneurs in the local area networking business, see von Burg and Kenney, forthcoming.

10. There is no doubt that Boston and especially New York venture capital is largely staffed by individuals with a financial background.

11. KPCB would later move to 2755 Sand Hill Road.

12. To this day there are disparaging assessments of the "Sand Hill Road Crowd" by other successful venture capitalists located elsewhere in the area.

6. Angel: High-Technology Agglomeration

This research was supported by the National Geographic Society under grant number 3528-87 and by the National Science Foundation under grant number SES-8701108.

7. Saxenian: Origins and Dynamics of Production Networks

Special thanks to Christopher Freeman, David Teece, Chris DeBresson, and two anonymous reviewers for helpful comments and encouragement during earlier drafts of this paper.

1. This paper draws on the findings of more than fifty in-depth interviews with executives and managers in Silicon Valley–based computer systems firms and suppliers during 1988, 1989, and 1990. The sample includes the region's leading computer systems firms, many computer firms started during the 1980s, and a wide range of producers of semiconductors, disk drives, and other components.

2. IBM was forced to rely on outside vendors to an unprecedented extent in the early 1980s in order to bring a personal computer to market rapidly enough to compete with Apple.

3. In 1990, Sun introduced limited printed-circuit board assembly operations, however the firm remains committed to a highly focused strategy.

4. On the trend to customize inputs such as disk drives and power supplies, see Faletra and Elliot (1988).

5. See Richards (1984) for more details.

6. Collaborative supplier relations have been documented in a wide range of industries, including the U.S. and German auto industries (Helper 1990; Sabel 1988), the French machine tool industry (Lorenz 1988), and the Japanese electronics and auto industries (Fruin 1988; Nishiguchi 1989).

7. When HP introduced JIT in the early 1980s, for example, the firm's cost reductions and improvements in manufacturing efficiency were widely publicized in Silicon Valley. JIT has since been widely adopted in the region. See *San Jose Business Journal* (1985).

8. In order to improve its responsiveness, the firm recently moved part of its manufacturing from Hong Kong to Silicon Valley. Sun Microsystems, which is its neighbor, in turn increased its purchases of the firm's power supplies from $500,000 to more than $8 million a year.

9. Flextronics' CEO meets with Sun's senior vice president of operations for breakfast once a month to ensure that trust is maintained at the top and that high-level problems are addressed. Meanwhile, planning, engineering, purchasing, and marketing personnel from the two firms meet still more frequently—often weekly, and in some cases daily—to solve problems and plan

for the future. This involves an immense amount of sharing and typically results in highly personalized relationships between the two firms (Stradford 1988).

10. This expansion was too rapid. In 1989, Flextronics was forced to restructure its worldwide business because of significant excess manufacturing capacity and operating losses that began with a downturn in the disk drive business. To eliminate excess capacity, the production facilities in Massachusetts, South Carolina, Southern California, and Taiwan were sold or closed.

11. The firms are Fujitsu, Ltd. (the first to manufacture the Sparc chip because the leading U.S. semiconductor firms refused to accept external designs), LSI Logic, Bipolar Integrated Technologies, Cypress Semiconductor, and Texas Instruments.

8. Bahrami and Evans: Flexible Recycling

1. There are parallels with Schumpeter's notion (1935) of "creative destruction."

2. Their "ephemeral" nature does not imply the dissolution of all their know-how and intellectual capital. In the disk drive controller industry, for example, the demise of Xebec had a positive impact on the growth of Cirrus Logic, as did the disengagement of Scientific Microsystems, which led to the resurrection of SuperMac Technologies as an independent firm.

3. For additional perspectives on the historical roots of this growth, see the chapters (this volume) by Sturgeon and Leslie.

4. William Hewlett (October 1992) in an address to a meeting of the Churchill Club suggested that the origins of Silicon Valley date back almost to the development of ship-to-shore radio and the early days of television. This is also reflected by Sturgeon and Leslie (this volume).

5. The team comprised, among others, L. D. Stevens and Ken Houghton (later the dean of engineering at Santa Clara University).

6. The first tenant was Varian Associates, a spinoff from the Stanford University Department of Physics. Hewlett Packard followed in 1954. David Packard and William Hewlett, Terman's former students, had founded Hewlett Packard in 1939 to commercialize an electronic device called a "variable frequency oscillator" that Hewlett had developed as part of his graduate work.

7. For example, when the disk drive company, Seagate, was founded by Alan Shugart in 1979, venture capitalists were not initially very interested; private investors—including Norman Dion, the founder of Dyson, and later Texas Instruments' and Compaq's Rod Canion provided the seed money to get the firm off the ground. Similarly, ROLM's founding team initially sought venture capital backing without much success. Each of the four founders invested $15,000 in the business, before Jack Melchor—one of Silicon Valley's early venture capitalists—agreed to become a fifth founder by investing $15,000 and guaranteeing a bank line of credit for $100,000.

8. Departing from the traditional mode of venture funding, a recent trend has been the investment by larger firms in high-technology start-ups. EO Corporation, a new start-up in the multimedia field, was initially funded by the venture capital firm of Kleiner, Perkins, Caufield, and Byers, and subsequently

through a corporate consortium comprising AT&T, Matsushita, Marubeni, and Philips. General Magic and 3DO are two other firms that were initially funded in a similar manner.

9. Venture capitalists seldom invest alone in a deal, but with a group of other venture capital firms. For a historical description of the role of venture capital in Silicon Valley, see Hambrecht 1984.

10. Well-known examples include Italians (Frederico Faggin, cofounder of Synaptics and Zilog, and Giacomo Marini, cofounder of Logitech), Frenchmen (Jean Louis Gassee, formerly of Apple, and Phillipe Kahn of Borland), Britons (Wilf Corrigan of LSI Logic and Dick Moley of Stratacom), Chinese (David Lee of Qume), Hungarians (Andy Grove and Les Vadacz of Intel), Indians (Jugi Tandon of Tandon and Kanwal Rekhi of Excelan), Germans (Michael Spindler of Apple), Iranians (Kamran Elahian of Cirrus Logic and Momenta), Israelis (Arieh Feingold, cofounder of Daisy Systems), and representatives of other nationalities. See also Saxenian (1999).

11. The antecedents of the Silicon Valley culture, however, are the subject of some debate. See, for example, Kenney and von Burg 1999.

12. One example is Trilogy, founded in the early 1980s by Gene Amdahl, who had earlier started Amdahl Corporation in 1970 in order to compete with IBM in the mainframe computer business. Trilogy attracted a lot of interest and venture capital in its formative years but failed to survive because it could not deliver what was initially promised, an advanced microprocessor (Amdahl 1992).

13. SCSI was pioneered by Adaptec, which was founded by three Shugart employees. When an internal business plan was submitted to Shugart's executive team, as part of a new internal venture funding initiative, it was turned down. As a result, the principal developers of this interface, Larry Boucher and two of his colleagues, left Shugart in 1981 to found Adaptec, which would specialize in input-output controllers. By 1992, Adaptec had revenues of $311 million and was ranked among the top two hundred public high-technology companies.

9. Cohen and Fields: Social Capital and Capital Gains

1. In this volume, Kenney and Florida show the origins of this practice with Fairchild Semiconductor.

2. Semiconductor Industry Association. 1998.

3. On how Putnam sets the development trajectory of his regions as fixed by the late Middle Ages, and more generally on the deterministic character of Putnam's concept, see Levy 1998 and Tarrow 1996: 389ff.

4. For a perspective critical of this literature, see Harrison 1994.

5. See also, for the same analysis and omissions, Bernstein 1992.

6. On trust, see Gambetta 1988: 32; Mayntz 1993.

7. Henri Pirenne's celebrated thesis of an eleventh-century trade revival, when placed alongside Putnam's account of social capital's eleventh-century origins, raises several engaging questions about whether prosperity follows or acts as the catalyst for a vibrant civil society. According to Pirenne, the

eleventh-century commercial revolution, occurring in Flanders and Italy, ignited the process of European urbanization, leading to "a new era in the internal history of Western Europe" (Pirenne 1925: 213). From Pirenne's story, supported by numerous other historical accounts, there is a suggestion that the origins of the communes themselves lie in an economic phenomenon as centers of trade and market activity. Presumably, civic life in Italy began to flourish from these economic origins, paving the way for the traditions that are of paramount interest to Putnam. Nevertheless, if the origins of the communes are to be found in the prosperity associated with the rise of commerce, and if, as Putnam suggests, the origins of the civic networks in Italy are to be found in the communes, then it seems difficult to conclude, as Putnam does, that civics is a precondition for prosperity. Instead, the history of the Italian medieval communes suggests that civic engagement is not the cause but the outcome of economic advance.

8. As Leslie shows (this volume), SRI's establishment off-campus was a reaction to the 1960s student protests against military-funded research.

9. Estimates from consulate officials. Census data is (1) out of date (from 1990), and (2) misses dual passport holders. For more information and a visit to these communities, see http://www.tie.org/ (India), or www.dree.org/usa/default.htm (France), http://sf.roc-taiwan.org/ (Taiwan). See also Saxenian 1999, for the best empirical account.

10. Kenney and von Burg: Institutions and Economies

1. Other social actors and institutions may not be rewarded or even thwarted, as is the case with labor unions.

2. See Suchman (this volume) for a discussion of the legal profession in Silicon Valley, and Kenney and Florida (this volume) for a similar discussion of venture capital.

3. Lynn et al. (1996) advances a somewhat similar concept of an "innovation community," however the concept is more general and fits established industries better than it does environments such as Silicon Valley.

4. Of course, the goals of some corporate research laboratories might be only tenuously related to the overall corporate goals of growth and profitability (Rosenberg 1990).

5. For example, in the case of Netscape the basic technology for a graphical browser (Mosaic) was developed at, and the initial technical team came from, the University of Illinois. Marc Andreeson, one of the Mosaic team, had already moved to Silicon Valley. When Andreeson joined Jim Clark, the former Stanford professor and founder of Silicon Graphics, Inc., they recruited most of the remaining Mosaic team and moved them to Silicon Valley.

6. The term "specialist" must be used cautiously. Often a start-up pioneering a new technology must undertake a variety of tasks. For example, Fairchild built its own semiconductor production equipment, grew its own silicon crystals, and designed and manufactured semiconductors. Eventually, equipment and silicon-crystal manufacturing became separate industries. In other words, the definition of a "specialist" changes through time.

7. In high-technology markets the first to the market with a useful product generally has important advantages, ceteris paribus.

8. There is an interesting discussion in legal circles about how the legal system facilitates the ability of entrepreneurs to spin off, and therefore the development of a Silicon Valley–like environment, in which information in the form of employees quickly circulates throughout the region. Hyde (1998) finds that trade secret law is largely unenforceable in Silicon Valley, making it difficult for firms to prevent employees from using knowledge developed at a former employer at a new employer. Gilson (1999), though accepting Hyde's conclusion regarding trade secrets, argues that even more important is California's prohibition of postemployment covenants not to compete. In effect, firms did not have this legal weapon for preventing employees from moving to new firms and using the knowledge developed at their previous employer. Gilson goes further, arguing that California law is quite different from Massachusetts law in this regard, and that this might explain the differential outcomes of the two regions' high-technology growth.

9. Already there were Asian firms that were willing to subcontract semiconductor assembly and testing.

10. Cisco is the premier proponent of this model and is now organized to retain the engineering teams by granting substantial autonomy, even while integrating their efforts. Some would argue that Cisco has generated another new business model. It is worth noting that other firms have been eager to understand how Cisco has been able to do this.

11. Kenney (1986) provides an extended discussion of the role of venture capital, especially KPCB, in providing the initial funding for the biotechnology industry.

References

Abbott, Andrew. 1981. "Status and Status Strain in the Professions." *American Journal of Sociology* 86: 819–35.

Abel, Richard L. 1986. "Lawyers." In *Law and Social Sciences*, edited by L. Lipson and S. Wheeler, 369–444. New York: Russell Sage.

Abernathy, William, and James Utterback. 1978. "Patterns of Industrial Innovation." *Technology Review* (June–July): 40–47.

Aitken, Hugh. 1985. *The Continuous Wave: Technology and American Radio, 1900–1932.* Princeton: Princeton University Press.

Almeida, Paul, and Bruce Kogut. 1997. "The Exploration of Technological Diversity and the Geographic Localization of Innovation." *Small Business Economics* 9, no. 1: 21–31.

Alvarez-Torrez, R. 1986. "More Companies Rent Workers to Fill Gaps." *San Jose Mercury News*, September 28.

Amdahl, Carlton. 1992. "Interview with Carlton Amdahl." *Upside* (February–March): 12–15.

American Heritage. 1982. *American Heritage Dictionary.* 2d college ed. Boston: Houghton-Mifflin.

Amin, Ash. 1989. "Flexible Specialization and Small Firms in Italy: Myths and Realities." *Antipode* 21: 13–34.

Amsden, Alice. 1989. *Asia's Next Giant: South Korea and Late Industrialization.* Oxford: Oxford University Press.

Anderson, Philip, and Michael Tushman. 1990. "Technological Discontinuities and Dominant Designs: A Cyclical Model of Technological Change." *Administrative Science Quarterly* 35: 604–33.

Angel, David. 1991. "High-technology Agglomeration and the Labor Market: The Case of Silicon Valley." *Environment and Planning* A23: 1501–16.

———. 1989. "The Labor Market for Engineers in the U.S. Semiconductor Industry." *Economic Geography* 65, no. 2: 99–112.

Angel, David, and James Engstrom. 1995. "Manufacturing Systems and Technological Change: The U.S. Personal Computer Industry." *Economic Geography* 71, no. 1: 79–102.

Arthur, W. Brian. 1994. *Increasing Returns and Path Dependence in the Economy.* Ann Arbor: University of Michigan Press.

———. 1989. "Competing Technologies, Increasing Returns, and Lock-in by Historical Small Events." *Economic Journal* 99: 116–31.

Astley, W. Graham. 1985. "The Two Ecologies: Population and Community Perspectives on Organizational Evolution." *Administrative Science Quarterly* 30: 224–41.

Aydalot, Philippe, and David Keeble. 1988. *High Technology Industry and Innovative Environments: The European Experience*. New York: Routledge, Chapman and Hall.

Bahrami, Homa. 1992. "The Emerging Flexible Organization: Perspectives from Silicon Valley." *California Management Review* (summer): 33–51.

Bahrami, Homa, and Stuart Evans. 1995. "Flexible Re-Cycling and High-Technology Entrepreneurship." *California Management Review* 37, no. 3: 62–89.

———. 1989a. "Strategy-Making in High Technology Firms: The Empiricist Mode." *California Management Review* (winter): 107–27.

———. 1989b. "Emerging Organizational Regimes in High Technology Firms: The Bi-Modal Form." *Human Resource Management Journal* 28, no. 1 (spring): 25–50.

———. 1987. "Stratocracy in High Technology Firms." *California Management Review* Special Issue (fall): 51–66.

Barkley, David. 1988. "The Decentralization of High Technology Manufacturing to Non-metropolitan Areas." *Growth and Change* 19: 12–30.

Barnett, William P., and Glenn R. Carroll. 1987. "Competition and Mutualism among Early Telephone Companies." *Administrative Science Quarterly* 32: 400–421.

Barron, John, and Otis Gille. 1981. "Job Search and Vacancy Contacts." *American Economic Review* 71: 747–52.

Bartz, Carol. 1993. "Interview with Carol Bartz." *Upside* (April): 44–49.

Baum, Joel, and Christine Oliver. 1992. "Institutional Embeddedness and the Dynamics of Organizational Populations." *American Sociological Review* 57: 540–59.

———. 1991. "Institutional Linkages and Organizational Mortality." *Administrative Science Quarterly* 36: 187–218.

Baum, Joel, and Jitendra Singh. 1994. "Organizational Hierarchies and Evolutionary Processes: Some Reflections on a Theory of Organizational Evolution." In *The Evolutionary Dynamics of Organizations*, edited by J. Baum and J. Singh, 3–20. New York: Oxford University Press.

Benner, Chris. 1998. "Win the Lottery or Organize: Traditional and Non-Traditional Labor Organizing in Silicon Valley." *Berkeley Planning Journal* http://www-dcrp.ced.berkeley.edu/bpj/current.html.

Berger, Peter, and Thomas Luckmann. 1967. *The Social Construction of Reality*. New York: Doubleday.

Bernstein, Lisa. 1992. "Opting Out of the Legal System: Extralegal Contractual Relations in the Diamond Industry." *Journal of Legal Studies* 21, no. 1: 115–57.

Besher, A. 1989. "Asian Investor Feast." *Upside* (November): 43–45.

Best, Michael. 1990. *The New Competition: Institutions of Industrial Restructuring*. Cambridge: Harvard University Press.

Bijker, Wiebe, Thomas Hughes, and Trevor Pinch, eds. 1987. *The Social Construction of Technological Systems: New Directions in the Sociology and History of Technology*. Cambridge: MIT Press.

Birch, David L. 1979. *The Job Generation Process*. Cambridge: MIT Program on Neighborhood and Regional Change.

Blachman, Nelson. 1991. Personal interview, August 21.

Blau, Peter M. 1964. *Exchange and Power in Social Life*. New York: John Wiley.

Bluestein, W. 1988. "How Sun Microsystems Buys Quality." *Electronics Purchasing* (March): 47–51.

Bollinger, Lynn, Katherine Hope, and James Utterback. 1983. "A Review of Literature and Hypotheses on High Technology Firms." *Research Policy* 12: 1–14.

Booz-Allen, Hamilton. 1991. "Foreign Investment in Bay Area Bioscience." A Survey Prepared for the Bay Area Bioscience Center.

Borrus, Michael. 1988. *Competing for Control: America's Stake in Microelectronics*. Cambridge: Ballinger Publishing Co.

Borrus, Michael, James Millstein, and John Zysman. 1983. *U.S.-Japanese Competition in the Semiconductor Industry*. Berkeley: Institute of International Studies.

Bower, J. L., and C. M. Christensen. 1995. "Disruptive Technologies: Catching the Wave." *Harvard Business Review* (January-February): 43–53.

Braun, Ernest, and Stuart Macdonald. 1982. *Revolution in Miniature: The History and Impact of Semiconductor Devices*. Rev. ed. Cambridge: Cambridge University Press.

———. 1978. *Revolution in Miniature: The History and Impact of Semiconductor Electronics*. New York: Cambridge University Press.

Brechin, Gray. 1990. "Imperial San Francisco." *Headlands Journal* 2 (Sausalito, California: Headlands Center for the Arts).

BRIE. 1999. http://brie.berkeley.edu/BRIE.

Brittain, Jack W., and John H. Freeman. 1980. "Organizational Proliferation and Density-Dependent Selection." In *Organizational Life Cycles*, edited by J. Kimberly and R. Miles, 291–338. San Francisco: Jossey-Bass.

Brusco, Sebastian. 1982. "The Emilian Model: Productive Decentralization and Social Integration." *Cambridge Journal of Economics* 6: 167–84.

Bryant, John. 1990. "Microwave Technology and Careers in Transition: The Interests and Activities of Visitors to the Sperry Gyroscope Company's Klystron Plant in 1939–40." *IEEE Transactions in Microwave Theory and Technology MTT-38* (November): 1545–58.

Burt, Ronald S. 1992. *Structural Holes: The Social Structure of Competition*. Cambridge: Harvard University Press.

Business Week. 1992. "Hot Spots." (October 19): 80–87.

Business Week. 1984. "Who's Excellent Now." (November 5): 76–79.

Butcher, Lee. 1989. *Accidental Millionaire: The Rise and Fall of Steve Jobs at Apple Computer*, 108–10. New York: Paragon Books.

Bygrave, William, and Jeffry Timmons. 1992. *Venture Capital at the Crossroads.* Boston: Harvard Business School Press.

Bylinsky, Gene. 1974. "California's Great Breeding Ground for Industry." *Fortune* (June): 129–35, 216–24.

Carlin, Jerome E. 1962. *Lawyers on Their Own: A Study of Individual Practitioners in Chicago.* New Brunswick, N.J.: Rutgers University Press.

Carnoy, Martin, Manuel Castells, and Chris Benner. 1997. *International Labour Review* 136, no. 1: 27–48.

Carroll, G. R., and J. Delacroix. 1982. "Organizational Mortality in the Newspaper Industries of Argentina and Ireland." *Administrative Science Quarterly* 27: 169–98.

Castells, Manuel. 1996. *The Rise of the Network Society.* London: Blackwell Publishers.

———. 1988. "The New Industrial Space: Information Technology, Manufacturing and Spatial Structure in the United States." In *America's New Market Geography,* edited by G. Sternlieb and J. Hughes, 43–100. New Brunswick, N.J.: Center for Urban Policy Research, Rutgers University.

Chambers, Frank. 1986. Personal interview by Richard Florida and Martin Kenney, December 18.

Child, John. 1972. "Organization Structure, Environment and Performance: The Role of Strategic Choice." *Sociology* 6: 1–22.

Christensen, Clayton. 1997. *The Innovator's Dilemma: When New Technologies Cause Great Firms to Fail.* Boston: Harvard Business School Press.

———. 1992. "The Innovator's Challenge: Understanding the Influence of Market Environment on Processes of Technology Development of the Rigid Disk." D.B.A. dissertation, Harvard University.

Clark, Gordon. 1987. "Job Search Theory and Indeterminate Information." In *Regional Labour Markets,* edited by M. Fischer and P. Nijkamp, 169–88. New York: North-Holland.

Clark, Peter, and Neil Staunton. 1989. *Innovation in Technology and Organization.* New York: Routledge, Chapman and Hall.

Clayton, James. 1965. "Defense Spending: Key to California's Growth." *Western Political Science Quarterly* 15: 280–93.

Cohen, Stephen S. 1969. *Modern Capitalist Planning: The French Model.* Berkeley: University of California Press.

Cohen, Steven, and John Zysman. 1987. *Manufacturing Matters: The Myth of the Post-industrial Economy.* New York: Basic Books.

Cohodas, M. 1987. "What Makes JIT Work." *Electronics Purchasing* (January).

———. 1986. "How Apple Buys Electronics." *Electronics Purchasing* (November).

Coleman, Charles. 1952. *PG&E of California, the Centennial Story of Pacific Gas and Electric Company, 1852–1952.* New York: McGraw-Hill.

Coleman, James S. 1988. "Social Capital in the Creation of Human Capital." *American Journal of Sociology* 94, supplement S95–S190: S98–S99.

Cook, Scott, and John Seely Brown. 1999. "Bridging Epistemologies: The Generative Dance between Organizational Knowledge and Organizational

Knowing." In *Path Dependence and Path Creation*, edited by R. Garud and P. Karnoe. New York: Lawrence Earlbaum and Associates.

Cortada, James. 1987. *Historical Dictionary of Data Processing: Organizations.* New York: Greenwood Press.

Cox, Gail D. 1988a. "A Valley of Conflicts." *National Law Journal* (June 20): 1, 46, 48–49.

———. 1988b. "Who's Who: A Silicon Valley Legal Sampler." *National Law Journal* (June 20): 47.

———. 1988c. "The Brave New World of Computer Law." *National Law Journal* (June 20): 46.

Cringely, Robert X. 1992. *Accidental Empires: How the Boys of Silicon Valley Make Their Millions, Battle Foreign Competition, and Still Can't Get a Date.* New York: Harper Business.

Curry, James, and Martin Kenney. 1999. "Beating the Clock: Corporate Responses to Rapid Change in the PC Industry." *California Management Review* 42, no. 2: 8–36.

———. 1999. "E-commerce: Implications for Firm Strategy and Industry Configuration." *Industry and Innovation* 6, no. 2: 131–51.

David, Paul. 1993. "Historical Economics in the Long Run: Some Implications of Path-Dependence." In *Historical Analysis in Economics*, edited by Graeme Donald Snooks, 29–40. London: Routledge.

———. 1986. "Understanding the Economics of QWERTY: The Necessity of History." In *Economic History and the Modern Economist*, edited by W. Parker. New York: Basil Blackwell.

———. 1985. "CLIO and the Economics of QWERTY." *American Economic Review* 75: 332–37.

Davidow, William (partner, Mohr Davidow Ventures). 1988. Personal interview, April 21.

Davidow, William, and Michael Malone. 1992. *The Virtual Corporation.* New York: Harper Collins.

Davis, Dwight. 1989. "Making the Most of Your Vendor Relationships." *Electronic Business* (July 10).

Davis, Thomas. 1986. Personal interview by Richard Florida and Martin Kenney, December 16.

Davis, Wally. 1988. Personal interview by Richard Florida and Martin Kenney, March 31.

Deger, Renee. 1995. "Venture Capital Roundtable." *Venture Capital Journal* (September): 34.

Delbecq, Andre, and Joseph Weiss. 1988. "The Business Culture of Silicon Valley: Is It a Model for the Future?" In *Regional Cultures, Managerial Behavior and Entrepreneurship*, edited by J. Weiss. New York: Quorum Books.

Dennis, Reid. 1986. Personal interview by Richard Florida and Martin Kenney, December 17.

DiMaggio, Paul J. 1983. "State Expansion and Organizational Fields." In *Organizational Theory and Public Policy*, edited by R. Hall and R. Quinn, 147–61. Beverly Hills: Sage.

DiMaggio, Paul J., and Walter W. Powell. 1983. "The Iron Cage Revisited: Institutional Isomorphism and Collective Rationality in Organizational Fields." *American Sociological Review* 48: 147–60.

Dobbs, Gordon B., and Craig E. Wollner. 1990. *The Silicon Forest: High Tech in the Portland Area, 1945–1986.* Portland: Oregon Historical Society Press.

Dorfman, Nancy. 1983. "Route 128: The Development of a Regional High Technology Economy." *Research Policy* 12: 299–316.

Dosi, Giovanni. 1988a. "The Nature of the Innovative Process." In *Technical Change and Economic Theory,* edited by G. Dosi, C. Freeman, R. Nelson, G. Silverberg, and L. Soete, 221–38. New York: Frances Pinter.

———. 1988b. "Sources, Procedures and Microeconomic Effects of Innovation." *Journal of Economic Literature* 26: 1120–71.

Dosi, Giovanni, Franco Malerba, and Luigi Orsenigo. 1994. "Evolutionary Regimes and Industrial Dynamics." In *Evolutionary and Neo-Schumpeterian Approaches to Economics,* edited by Lars Magnusson, 203–29. Boston: Kluwer Academic Publishers.

Dougery, John. 1986. Personal interview by Richard Florida and Martin Kenney, December 15.

Drucker, P. F. 1994. "The Theory of the Business." *Harvard Business Review* (September–October): 95–104.

Durkheim, Emile. 1969. *The Division of Labor in Society.* Translated by G. Simpson. New York: Free Press.

Edmondson, Harold (vice president of corporate manufacturing, Hewlett-Packard Corporation). 1988. Personal interview, February 5.

Edwards, William. 1986. Personal interview by Richard Florida and Martin Kenney, December 16.

Eitel-McCullough, Inc. 1960. *Microwave Journal* (August): 85–90.

Electronic Business. 1987. "For Flexible, Quality Manufacturing, Don't Do It Yourself." (March 15).

Electronics News. 1968. "Signetics." (February 25): 3.

Ellickson, Robert C. 1991. *Order without Law.* Cambridge: Harvard University Press.

Emerson, Richard M. 1962. "Power-Dependence Relations." *American Sociological Review* 27: 31–40.

Emery, Fred E., and E. L. Trist. 1965. "The Causal Texture of Organizational Environments." *Human Relations* 18: 21–32.

Employment Development Department, Labor Market Information Division. 1997. *Occupational Projections* (June) http://www.calmis.cahwnet.gov/htmlfile/msa.htm.

Engstrom, Therese. 1987. "Little Silicon Valleys." *Technology Review* (January): 24–32.

Enochs, Hugh. 1958. "The First Fifty Years of Electronics Research." *Tall Tree* 1 (May): 34.

Ettlie, John. 1980. "Manpower Flows and the Innovation Process." *Management Science* 26: 1086–95.

Evans, S. 1991. "Strategic Flexibility for High Technology Maneuvers: A Conceptual Framework." *Journal of Management Studies* 28, no. 1 (January): 69–89.

Everson, George. 1949. *The Story of Television: The Life of Philo T. Farnsworth*. New York: W. W. Norton and Company.

Faletra, R., and M. Elliot. 1988. "Buying in the Microcomputer Market." *Electronics Purchasing* (October).

Febvre, Lucien, and Henri-Jean Martin. 1976. *The Coming of the Book*. London: Verso Press.

Ferguson, Charles. 1990. "The Coming of the U.S. Keiretsu." *Harvard Business Review* (July–August).

Findlay, John M. 1992. *Magic Lands: Western Cityscapes and American Culture after 1940*. Berkeley: University of California Press.

Fisher, David, and Marshall Fisher. 1996. *Tube: The Invention of the Television*. Washington, D.C.: Counterpoint.

Fisk, James. 1965. "The New Role of Graduate Education in Industrial Innovation." *William Baker Papers*. Murray Hill, N.J.: Bell Laboratories (November 3).

Florida, Richard, and Martin Kenney. 1991. "Organizational Transplants: The Transfer of Japanese Industrial Organization to the U.S." *American Sociological Review* 56, no. 3 (June): 381–98.

———. 1990a. "High-technology Restructuring in the U.S.A. and Japan." *Environment and Planning A* 22: 233–52.

———. 1990b. "Why Silicon Valley and Route 128 Won't Save Us." *California Management Review* 33, no. 1: 68–88.

———. 1990c. *The Breakthrough Illusion: Corporate America's Failure to Move from Innovation to Mass Production*. New York: Basic Books.

———. 1988a. "Venture Capital-Financed Innovation and Technological Change in the USA." *Research Policy* 17: 119–37.

———. 1988b. "Venture Capital and High Technology Entrepreneurship." *Journal of Business Venturing* 3, no. 4: 301–19.

———. 1988c. "Venture Capital, High Technology, and Regional Development." *Regional Studies* 22: 33–48.

Fombrun, Charles J. 1988. "Crafting an Institutionally Informed Ecology of Organizations." In *Ecological Models of Organizations*, edited by G. Carroll, 223–40. Cambridge: Ballinger.

Freeman, Christopher. 1982. *The Economics of Innovation*. London: Frances Pinter.

Freeman, John. 1999. "Venture Capital as an Economy of Time." In *Corporate Social Capital*, edited by R. Leenders and S. Gabbay, 400–19. New York: Addison Wesley.

———. 1990. "Ecological Analysis of Semiconductor Firm Mortality." In *Organizational Evolution: New Directions*, edited by Jitendra Singh, 53–77. Newbury Park, N.J.: Sage.

Freiberger, Paul, and Michael Swaine. 1984. *Fire in the Valley*. Berkeley: Osborne/McGraw Hill.

Friedman, Lawrence M., Robert W. Gordon, Sophie Pirie, and Edwin Whatley.

1989. "Law, Lawyers, and Legal Practice in Silicon Valley: A Preliminary Report." *Indiana Law Journal* 64: 555–67.

Fruin, Mark. 1988. *Cooperation and Competition: Interfirm, Networks and the Nature of Supply in the Japanese Electronics Industry.* Fontainebleau, France: Euro-Asia Center, INSEAD.

Fuller, Leonard (research engineer and professor). 1976. Interviews conducted by A. L. Norberg in 1973, 1974, and 1975 for the History of Science and Technology Project, University of California at Berkeley.

———. 1975. Interview by O. G. Villard, for the History of Science and Technology Project, University of California at Berkeley, June 25.

Galante, Steven. 1996. "An Overview of the Venture Capital Industry and Emerging Changes." Presentation made to the Venture Capital Institute, September 18.

Galanter, Marc. 1983. "Megalaw and Megalawyering in the Contemporary United States." In *The Sociology of the Professions: Lawyers, Doctors and Others,* edited by R. Dingwall and P. Lewis, 152–76. London: Macmillan.

Galanter, Marc, and Thomas A. Palay. 1991. *Tournament of Lawyers: The Transformation of the Big Law Firm.* Chicago: University of Chicago Press.

———. 1990. "Why the Big Get Bigger: The Promotion-to-Partner Tournament and the Growth of Large Law Firms." *Virginia Law Review* 76: 747–814.

Galbraith, Craig. 1985. "High Technology Location and Development: The Case of Orange County." California Management Review 28, no. 1: 99–109.

Galbraith, John Kenneth. 1967. *The New Industrial State.* Boston: Houghton Mifflin Company.

Galison, Peter, Bruce Hevly, and Rebecca Lowen. 1991. "Controlling the Monster: Stanford and the Growth of Physics Research, 1935–1962." In *Big Science: The Growth of Large Scale Research,* edited by P. Galison and B. Hevly, 46–77. Palo Alto: Stanford University Press.

Gambetta, D., ed. 1988. *Trust: Making and Breaking Relationships.* Oxford: Basil Blackwell.

Garud, Raghu, and Peter Karnoe, eds. 1999. *Path Dependence and Path Creation.* New York: Lawrence Earlbaum and Associates.

Gerschenkron, Alexander. 1962. *Economic Backwardness in Historical Perspective.* Cambridge: Harvard University Press.

Gilder, George. 1989. *Microcosm.* New York: Basic Books.

Gilson, Ronald. 1999. "The Legal Infrastructure of High-Technology Industrial Districts: Silicon Valley, Route 128, and Covenants Not to Compete." *New York University Law Review* 74, no. 3: 575–629.

Ginzton, Edward. 1975. "The $100 Idea." *IEEE Spectrum* 10 (February): 30–39.

Glaser, Barney G., and Anselm L. Strauss. 1967. *The Discovery of Grounded Theory: Strategies for Qualitative Research.* Chicago: Aldine.

Glasmeier, Ann, Peter Hall, and Anne Markusen. 1983. "Recent Evidence on High Technology Industries' Spatial Tendencies." Working paper, Department of City and Regional Planning, University of California, Berkeley, CA.

Gordon, R. 1987. "Growth and the Relations of Production in High Technology

Industry." Paper presented at Conference on New Technologies and New Intermediaries, Stanford University.

Gorman, Michael, and William Sahlman. 1989. "What Do Venture Capitalists Do?" *Journal of Business Venturing* 4, no. 4: 231–48.

Granovetter, Mark. 1985. "Economic Action and Social Structure: The Problem of Embeddedness." *American Journal of Sociology* 91: 481–510.

Grass Roots Writing Collective. 1969. *The Promised Land, a Grass Roots Report on Mid-Peninsula Land Use.* Grass Roots Writing Collective in cooperation with Stanford Chaparral, Palo Alto. Pacific Studies Center.

Gray, Mia, Elyse Golob, Ann Markusen, and Sam Ock Park. 1999. "The Four Faces of Silicon Valley." In *Second Tier Cities*, edited by A. Markusen. Minneapolis: University of Minnesota Press.

Gupta, Udayan. 1985. "Stretched to the Limit." *Venture* (June): 38–48.

Hakansson, Hakan. 1987. *Industrial Technological Development: A Network Approach.* Beckenham, England: Croom Helm.

Hall, Peter, M. Breheny, R. McQuaid, and D. Hart. 1987. *Western Sunrise: The Genesis and Growth of Britain's Major High Tech Corridor.* Winchester, Mass.: Allen and Unwin.

Hall, Peter, and Ann Markusen, eds. 1985. *Silicon Landscapes.* Boston: Allen and Unwin.

Hambrecht, W. R. 1984. "Venture Capital and the Growth of Silicon Valley." *California Management Review* 26, no. 2 (winter): 74–82.

Hannan, Michael T., and Glenn R. Carroll. 1992. *Dynamics of Organizational Populations.* New York: Oxford University Press.

Hannan, Michael T., and John H. Freeman. 1989. *Organizational Ecology.* Cambridge, Mass.: Harvard University Press.

———. 1986. "Where Do Organizational Forms Come From?" *Sociological Forum* 1: 50–72.

———. 1984. "Structural Inertia and Organizational Change." *American Sociological Review* 49: 149–64.

———. 1977. "The Population Ecology of Organizations." *American Journal of Sociology* 62: 929–64.

Hanson, Dirk. 1982. *The New Alchemists: Silicon Valley and the Microelectronics Revolution.* Boston: Little, Brown and Company.

Hardy, Quentin. 1998. "Meeting Jerry Weisman, Acting Coach to CEOs." *Wall Street Journal*, April 21.

Harker, J. M., D. W. Brede, R. E. Pattison, G. R. Santana, and L. G. Taft. 1981. "A Quarter Century of Disk File Innovation." *IBM Journal of Research and Development* 25, no. 5 (September): 677–89.

Harrington, J. 1985. "Intraindustry Structural Change and Location Change: U.S. Semiconductor Manufacturing, 1958–80." *Regional Studies* 19: 343–52.

Harris, Donald. 1952. "Countermeasures-guided Missiles Signal Corps Contract." SAFT, series V. Box 17, file 11 (June 2).

Harris, S. E., and J. S. Harris. 1986. "Stanford University Electronics Laboratory and Microwave-Ginzton Laboratory." In *Fortieth Anniversary of the Joint Services Electronics Program*, 104ff. Arlington, Va.: ANSER.

Harris, William B. 1957. "The Electronics Business." *Fortune* (April): 139–41.

Harrison, Bennett. 1994. *Lean and Mean: The Changing Landscape of Corporate Power in the Age of Flexibility*. New York: Basic Books.

Hart, A. G. 1937. "Anticipations, Business Planning, and the Cycle." *Quarterly Journal of Economics* (February): 272–93.

Hauben, Michael, and Ronda Hauben. 1998. *Netizens: On the History and Impact of Usenet and the Internet*. http://www.columbia.edu/~rh120/.

Heintz, Ralph. 1982. "Technical Innovation and Business in the Bay Area," an interview conducted by A. L. Norberg for the History of Science and Technology Project, University of California at Berkeley.

————. 1974. Interview conducted by Thornton Mayes for the History of Science and Technology Project, University of California at Berkeley, June 30.

Heinz, John P., and Edward O. Laumann. 1982. *Chicago Lawyers: The Social Structure of the Bar*. New York: Russell Sage.

Hekman, John. 1980. "The Future of High Technology Industry in New England." *New England Economic Review* (January/February): 5–17.

Helper, Susan. 1990. *Supplier Relations at a Crossroads: Results of Survey Research in the US Auto Industry*. Boston University, Department of Operations Management.

Henderson, John, and Allen J. Scott. 1987. "The Growth and Internationalisation of the American Semiconductor Industry: Labour Processes and the Changing Spatial Organization of Production." In *The Development of High Technology Industries*, edited by M. Breheny and R. McQuaid, 37–79. London: Croom Helm.

Henderson, Rebecca, and Kim Clark. 1990. "Architectural Innovation: The Reconfiguration of Existing Production Technologies and the Failure of Established Firms." *Administrative Science Quarterly* 35, no. 1: 9–30.

Herrigel, Gary. 1996. *Industrial Constructions: The Sources of German Industrial Power*. Cambridge: Cambridge University Press.

Hickson, David J., C. R. Hinings, C. A. Lee, R. E. Schneck, and J. M. Pennings. 1971. "A Strategic Contingencies' Theory of Intraorganizational Power." *Administrative Science Quarterly* 16: 216–29.

Hirsch, Paul M. 1972. "Processing Fads and Fashions: An Organization-Set Analysis of Cultural Industry Systems." *American Journal of Sociology* 77: 639–59.

Hodgson, Geoffrey M. 1994. "Precursors of Modern Evolutionary Economics: Marx, Marshall, Veblen, and Schumpeter." In *Modern Institutional Economics*, edited by Richard W. England, 9–35. Ann Arbor: University of Michigan Press.

Hoefler, Don. 1971. "Semiconductor Family Tree." *Electronics News* (July 8): 1.

Holmes, John. 1986. "The Organization and Locational Structure of Production Subcontracting." In *Production, Work and Territory*, edited by A. Scott and M. Storper. Boston: Allen and Unwin.

Holub, Kathy. 1990. "Larry Sonsini Goes Public." *San Jose Mercury News/West Magazine* (August 26): 16–29.

Hoover, Edgar, and Raymond Vernon. 1959. *Anatomy of a Metropolis.* Cambridge: Harvard University Press.

Howeth, Linwood. 1963. *History of Communications-electronics in the United States Navy.* Introduction by Chester W. Nimitz. Prepared by L. S. Howeth under the auspices of the Bureau of Ships and Office of Naval History. Washington, D.C.: U.S. Government Printing Office.

Hyde, Alan. 1998. "The Wealth of Shared Information: Silicon Valley's High-Velocity Labor Market, Endogenous Growth, and the Law of Trade Secrets." Unpublished manuscript. State University of New Jersey School of Law, Newark, New Jersey.

Imai, Ken-ichi. 1988. "Evolution of Japan's Corporate and Industrial Networks." In *Industrial Dynamics*, edited by B. Carlsson. Dordrecht: Kluwer.

Innovation. 1969. "The Splintering of the Solid-State Electronics Industry." 8: 2–16.

Jardine, Lisa. 1996. *Worldly Goods.* New York: Doubleday.

Jarillo, J. Carlos. 1988. "On Strategic Networks." *Strategic Management Journal* 9: 31–41.

Jarrat, Henri (president and chief operating officer, VLSI Technology). 1988. Personal interview, May 10.

Jensen, Eric, and Jim Fulton. 1996. "The Rich Get Richer." Download from the homepage of Cooley Godward, May 14.

Jessup, A. W. 1957. "Lockheed Attune to USAF Warning, Plans Expansion in Avionics." *Aviation Week* (July 8): 29–30.

Johanson, J., and L. Mattson. 1987. "Interorganizational Relations in Industrial Systems: A Network Approach Compared with the Transactions Cost Approach." *International Studies of Management and Organization* 27, no. 1: 34–48.

Johnson, Chalmers. 1982. *MITI and the Japanese Miracle: The Growth of Industrial Policy, 1925–1975.* Stanford: Stanford University Press.

Johnson, Chalmers, Laura Tyson, and John Zysman. 1989. *Politics and Productivity.* Cambridge: Ballinger.

Johnson, Franklin. 1986. Personal interview by Richard Florida and Martin Kenney, December 7.

Johnston, Moira. 1982. "High Tech, High Risk, and High Life in Silicon Valley." *National Geographic* 162, no. 4 (October): 459–76.

Johnston, Russel, and Paul Lawrence. 1988. "Beyond Vertical Integration—the Rise of the Value-Adding Partnership." *Harvard Business Review* (July–August): 94–101.

Joint Venture: Silicon Valley. 1998. 1998 Index. http://www.jointventure.org/resources/1998index/index.html.

Jones, S. 1987. "Hewlett-Packard Inks Major Chip Deal." *San Jose Business Journal*, May 18.

Jorde, Thomas, and David Teece. 1989. "Innovation, Cooperation and Antitrust." *High Technology Law Journal* 4: 1–112.

Joss, John. 1990. "Ron Johnson, Silicon Alchemist." *Silicon Valley Engineer* 2, no. 1.

Kagan, Robert A., and Robert E. Rosen. 1985. "On the Social Significance of Large Law Firm Practice." *Stanford Law Review* 37: 399–443.

Kenney, Martin. 1986. *Biotechnology: The University-Industrial Complex*. New Haven: Yale University Press.

Kenney, Martin, and James Curry. 1999. "E-Commerce: Implications for Firm Strategy and Industry Configuration." *Industry and Innovation*.

———. 1999. "Knowledge Creation and Temporality in the Information Economy." In *Cognition, Knowledge, and Organizations*, edited by Raghu Garud and Joe Porac. Greenwich: Conn.: JAI Press.

Kenney, Martin, and Urs von Burg. 1999. "Technology and Path Dependence: The Divergence between Silicon Valley and Route 128." *Industrial and Corporate Change* 8, no. 1: 67–103.

Kim, S. 1987. "Diversity in Urban Labor Markets and Agglomeration Economies." *Papers of the Regional Science Association* 62: 57–70.

Kleiner, Eugene. 1988. Personal interview by Richard Florida and Martin Kenney, March 31.

Komag, Inc. 1996. *The First Five Years*. Milpitas, Calif.: Komag, Inc.

Kotkin, J., and P. Grabowicz. 1982. *California, Inc*. New York: Rawson Wade Publishers.

Kramlich, C. Richard. 1995. Personal interview by Urs von Burg and Martin Kenney, July 17.

Kretchmar, L. 1989. "Auspex Serves Notice." *Upside Magazine* (November–December): 17–18.

Ladinsky, Jack. 1963. "Careers of Lawyers, Law Practice and Legal Institutions." *American Sociological Review* 28: 47–54.

Landon, Donald D. 1990. *Country Lawyers: The Impact of Context on Professional Practice*. New York: Praeger.

———. 1988. "Lasalle Street and Main Street: The Role of Context in Structuring Law Practice." *Law & Society Review* 22, no. 2: 213–36.

Langlois, Richard, and Paul Robertson. 1995. *Firms, Markets and Economic Change*. London: Routledge.

———. 1992. "Networks and Innovation in a Modular System: Lessons from the Microcomputer and Stereo Component Industries." *Research Policy* 21: 297–313.

Larson, A. 1988. "Cooperative Alliances: A Study of Entrepreneurship." Ph.D. dissertation, Harvard University, Sociology and Business Administration.

Lasnier, G. 1988. "Solectron to Acquire 10 Advanced Surface Mount Systems." *San Jose Business Journal*, February 8.

Latour, Bruno, and Steve Woolgar. 1986. *Laboratory Life: The Construction of Scientific Facts*. Princeton: Princeton University Press.

Leifer, Meyer, and Walter Sernuik. 1991. Personal interview, May 21.

Leslie, Stuart. 1993. *The Cold War and American Science*. New York: Columbia University Press.

Leslie, Stuart W., and Robert H. Kargon. 1996. "Selling Silicon Valley: Frederick Terman's Model for Regional Advantage." *Business History Review* 70 (winter): 435–72.

Levitt, Barbara, and James G. March. 1988. "Organization Learning." *Annual Review of Sociology* 14: 319–40.

Levy, Jonah. 1998. *Tocqueville's Revenge*. Cambridge: Harvard University Press.

Levy, Ken (president of KLA Instruments). 1988. Personal interview by Richard Florida and Martin Kenney, April 4.

Lewis, Tom. 1991. *Empire of the Air: The Men Who Made Radio*. New York: HarperCollins.

Liles, Patrick. 1977. *Sustaining the Venture Capital Firms*. Cambridge, Mass.: Management Analysis Center.

Lindsey, Robert. 1964. "Philco Division Completes Reorientation." *Missiles and Rockets* (June 15): 28.

Litton Industries. 1957. "Quarterly Fiscal Report, 1956–57." *C. Litton Papers* 75/7C. Special Collections. Bancroft Library, University of California, Berkeley.

Lob, Chester. 1991. Personal interview, August 22.

Lorenz, E. 1988. "Neither Friends nor Strangers: Informal Networks of Subcontracting in French Industry." In *Trust*, edited by D. Gambetta. New York: Basil Blackwell.

Lotchin, Roger. 1992. *Fortress California, 1910–1961*. New York: Oxford University Press.

Lowen, Rebecca. 1992. "Exploiting a Wonderful Opportunity: The Patronage of Scientific Research at Stanford University, 1937–1965." *Minerva* 30, no. 3 (fall): 391–421.

Lowood, Henry. 1988. "From Steeples of Excellence to Silicon Valley." *Stanford Campus Report* (March 9): 11–13.

Luger, Michael, and Harvey Goldstein. 1991. *Technology in the Garden: Research Parks and Regional Economic Development*. Chapel Hill: University of North Carolina Press.

Lynn, Leonard, N. Reddy, and J. Aram. 1996. "Linking Technology and Institutions: The Innovation Community Framework." *Research Policy* 25: 91–106.

Macaulay, Stuart. 1963. "Non-Contractual Relations in Business: A Preliminary Study." *American Sociological Review* 28: 55–67.

Macgregor, B., R. Langridge, J. Adley, and B. Chapman. 1986. "The Development of High Technology Industry in Newbury District." *Regional Studies* 20: 433–48.

Mackay, D., D. Boddy, J. Brack, J. Diack, and N. Jones. 1971. *Labor Markets under Different Employment Conditions*. London: Allen and Unwin.

MacLaurin, W. R. 1949. *Invention and Innovation in the Radio Industry*. MIT Studies in Innovation. New York: Macmillian.

Maidique, M. A., and B. J. Zirger. 1985. "The New Product Learning Cycle." In *Strategic Management of Technology and Innovation*, edited by R. A. Burgelman and M. A. Maidique, 320–37. Homewood, Ill.: Irwin.

Malecki, Edward J. 1989. "What About People in High Technology?: Some Research and Policy Considerations." *Growth and Change* 20: 67–79.

————. 1987. "The R&D Location Decision of the Firm and 'Creative' Regions: A Survey." *Technovation* 6: 205–22.

————. 1984. "High Technology and Local Economic Development." *Journal of the American Planning Association* 50: 262–69.

————. 1981. "Science, Technology and Regional Economic Development: Review and Prospects." *Research Policy* 10, no. 1: 312–34.

Malecki, Edward J., and P. Nijkamp. 1988. "Technology and Regional Development: Some Thoughts on Policy." *Environment and Planning C.* 6: 383–99.

Malone, Michael. 1985. *The Big Score: The Billion Dollar Story of Silicon Valley.* New York: Doubleday Books.

Markusen, Anne, and R. Bloch. 1985. "Defensive Cities: Military Spending, High Technology and Human Settlements." In *High Technology, Space and Society,* edited by M. Castells. Beverly Hills: Sage.

Markusen, Anne, Peter Hall, Scott Campbell, and Sabina Deitrick. 1991. *The Rise of the Gunbelt: The Military Remapping of Industrial America.* New York: Oxford University Press.

Marsden, Peter V. 1982. "Brokerage Behavior in Restricted Exchange Networks." In *Social Structure and Network Analysis,* edited by P. Marsden and N. Lin, 201–19. Beverly Hills: Sage.

Marshall, Alfred. 1919. *Industry and Trade.* London: Macmillan and Company.

————. 1890. *Principles of Economics.* London: Macmillan and Company.

Mayadas, Frank (former director of research, IBM San Jose Laboratory). 1998. Personal interview by Martin Kenney, March 17.

Mayntz, R. 1993. "Modernisation and the Logic of Interorganizational Networks." *Knowledge and Policy* (spring): 3–16.

McCall, John Joseph, and Anthony H. Pascal. 1979. *Agglomeration Economies, Search Costs, and Industrial Location.* Santa Monica, Calif.: Rand.

McKelvey, William. 1982. *Organizational Systematics: Taxonomy, Evolution, Classification.* Berkeley: University of California Press.

McKelvey, William, and Howard Aldrich. 1983. "Population, Natural Selection and Applied Organizational Science." *Administrative Science Quarterly* 28: 101–28.

McKenna, Regis. 1998. Interview by Rob Walker. http: //www-sul.stanford. edu/depts/hasrg/histsci/silicon%20genesis/regis-ntb.html.

————. 1989. *Who's Afraid of Big Blue?* New York: Addison Wesley.

McMahon, A. Michael. 1984. *The Making of a Profession: A Century of Electrical Engineering in America.* New York: IEEE Press.

McMurtry, Burton. 1986. Personal interview by Richard Florida and Martin Kenney, December 15.

McWilliams, Carey. 1949. *California: The Great Exception.* New York: Current Books.

Merrill, Steve. 1986. Personal interview by Richard Florida and Martin Kenney, December 16.

Merwin, John. 1981. "Have You Got What It Takes?" *Forbes* (August 3): 60–64.

Metcalf, Scott (director of materials, Sun Microsystems). 1988. Personal interview, March 30.

Meyer, John W., and Brian Rowan. 1977. "Institutionalized Organizations: Formal Structure as Myth and Ceremony." *American Journal of Sociology* 83: 340–63.

Meyer, John W., and W. Richard Scott. 1983. *Organizational Environments: Ritual and Rationality.* Beverly Hills: Sage.

Microwave Journal. 1963. "MEC." (August): 120–27.

Microwave Journal. 1961a. "Huggins Laboratories, Inc." (February): 109–12.

Microwave Journal. 1961b. "Applied Technology, Inc." (June): 122–24.

Microwave Journal. 1960. "Eitel-McCullough, Inc." (August): 85–86.

Microwave Journal. 1959a. "MELabs, Inc." (July): 44–47.

Microwave Journal. 1959b. "Hewlett-Packard Company." (October): 56–57.

Miles, Raymond, and Charles Snow. 1986. "Organizations: New Concepts for New Forms." *California Management Review* 28, no. 3: 62–73.

Miles, Raymond, Charles Snow, Alan Meyer, and H. Coleman. 1978. "Organizational Strategy, Structure and Process." *Academy of Management Review* 3: 546–62.

Miller, Jeffrey (vice president of marketing, Adaptec Corporation). 1988. Personal interview, May 10.

Miller, Roger-Emile. 1987. *Growing the Next Silicon Valley: A Guide for Successful Regional Planning.* Lexington: Lexington Books.

Miller, Roger, and Marcel Côté. 1985. "Growing the Next Silicon Valley." *Harvard Business Review* (July–August): 114–23.

Millikan, Robert. 1931. "Radio's Past and Future." Lecture series sponsored by the National Council on Radio in Education, University of Chicago Press.

Mitchell, James J. 1991. "Silicon Valley Wannabes." *San Jose Mercury News,* August 25.

Mokyr, Joel. 1990. *The Lever of Riches: Technological Creativity and Economic Progress.* Oxford: Oxford University Press.

Morgan, Jane. 1967. *Electronics in the West: The First Fifty Years.* Palo Alto, Calif.: National Press Books.

Morgan, Kevin, and Andrew Sayer. 1988. *Microcircuits of Capital: Sunrise Industry and Uneven Development.* Boulder: Westview Press.

Moritz, Michael. 1984. *The Little Kingdom: The Private Story of Apple Computer.* New York: William Morrow and Company.

Morris, J. 1988. "New Technologies, Flexible Work Practices, and Regional Sociospatial Differentiation: Some Observations from the United Kingdom." *Environment and Planning D: Society and Space* 6: 301–19.

Mulvany, R. B., L. H. Thompson, and K. E. Haughton. 1975. "Innovations in Disk File Manufacturing: An Overview of Disk Storage Systems." *Proceedings of the IEEE* 63: 1148–52.

Nalos, Erwin. 1991. Personal interview, August 21.

———. 1955. "General Electric Microwave Laboratory at Stanford, Proposed 1956 Project Budget." *Erwin Nalos Papers.*

Nelson, Richard, and Sidney Winter. 1982. *An Evolutionary Theory of Economic Change.* Cambridge: Harvard University Press.

Nelson, Robert. 1989. *Partners with Power: Social Transformation of the Large Law Firm*. Berkeley: University of California Press.

Nishiguchi, Toshihiro. 1989. "Strategic Dualism: An Alternative in Industrial Societies." Ph.D. dissertation, Oxford University, Nuffield College.

Nohria, Nitin. 1992. "Information and Search in the Creation of New Business Ventures: The Case of the 128 Group." In *Networks and Organizations: Structure, Form, and Action*, edited by N. Nohria and R. J. Eccles, 240–61. Boston: Harvard University Press.

Norberg, Arthur L. 1976. "The Origins of the Electronics Industry on the Pacific Coast." *Proceedings of the Institute of Electrical and Electronics Engineers* 64, no. 9 (September): 1314–19.

North, Douglass C. 1990. *Institutions, Institutional Change and Economic Performance*. Cambridge: Cambridge University Press.

Oakey, Ray. 1985. "High Technology Industry and Agglomeration Economies." In *Silicon Landscapes*, edited by P. Hall and A. Markusen, 94–117. Winchester, Mass.: Allen and Unwin.

———. 1984. *High Technology Small Firms*. New York: St. Martin's Press.

Oakey, Ray, and S. Cooper. 1989. "High Technology Industry, Agglomeration, and the Potential for Peripherally Sited Small Firms." *Regional Studies* 23: 347–60.

O'Brien, Tia. 1998. "Feasting on Failure." *Upside* (August): 70–74, 120–26.

OECD. 1986. *Labour Market Flexibility Report by a High Level Group of Experts to the Secretary General*. Paris: OECD.

O'Green, Fred. 1989. *Putting Technology to Work: The Story of Litton Industries*. New York: Newcomen Society of the United States.

O'Reilly, C. 1989. "Corporations, Culture, and Commitment." *California Management Review* (summer): 9–25.

Osborne, David. 1988. *Laboratories of Democracy*. Cambridge: Harvard University Press.

Packard, David. 1995. *The HP Way: How Bill Hewlett and I Built Our Company*. New York: Harper Business.

Paine, Adelaide. 1963. "Microwave People—Dr. Wesley P. Ayers." *Microwave Journal* (July): 30–34.

———. 1962a. "Ray Stewart." *Microwave Journal* (November): 35–39.

———. 1962b. "Dr. Romayne Whitmet." *Microwave Journal* (June): 37–42.

———. 1962c. "Stanley F. Kaisel." *Microwave Journal* (December): 19–26.

Parden, Robert. 1981. "The Manager's Role and the High Mobility of Technical Specialists in the Santa Clara Valley." *IEEE Transactions on Engineering Management* EM-28, no. 1: 2–8.

Perkins, Thomas. 1994. Personal interview. *Red Herring* (March).

Perry, William. 1991. Personal interview, August 21.

Peters, T., and R. Waterman. 1982. *In Search of Excellence*. New York: Harper & Row.

Pfeffer, Jeffrey, and Gerald R. Salancik. 1978. *The External Control of Organizations: A Resource Dependence Perspective*. New York: Harper & Row.

Piore, Michael. 1986. "Perspectives on Labor Market Flexibility." *Industrial Relations* 25: 147–66.

Piore, Michael, and Charles Sabel. 1984. *The Second Industrial Divide*. New York: Basic Books.

Pirenne, Henri. 1925. *Medieval Cities: Their Origins and the Revival of Trade*. Princeton: Princeton University Press.

Polanyi, Karl. 1944. *The Great Transformation*. Boston: Beacon Press.

Pollard, Sidney. 1981. *Peaceful Conquest: The Industrialization of Europe 1760–1870*. Oxford: Oxford University Press.

———. 1973. "Industrialization and the European Economy." *Economic History Review* 26: 636–48.

Pollert, Anne. 1988. "Dismantling Flexibility." *Capital and Class* 34: 42–75.

Poniatoff, Alexander. 1974. Interview Conducted by A. L. Norberg, History of Science and Technology Project, Bancroft Library, University of California at Berkeley.

Popper, K. R. 1972. *Conjectures & Refutations: The Growth of Scientific Knowledge*. 4th ed. London: Routledge & Kegan Paul.

Porter, Michael. 1998. "Clusters and the New Economics of Competition." *Harvard Business Review* (November–December): 77–90.

———. 1990. *The Competitive Advantage of Nations*. New York: Free Press.

Powell, Walter. 1990. "Neither Market nor Hierarchy: Network Forms of Organization." *Research in Organizational Behavior* 12: 295–336.

Powell, Walter, and Paul DiMaggio, eds. 1991. *The New Institutionalism in Organizational Analysis*. Chicago: University of Chicago Press.

Prahalad, C. K., and Gary Hamel. 1990. "The Core Competence of the Corporation." *Harvard Business Review* (May–June).

Premus, Robert. 1982. *Location of High Technology Firms and Regional Economic Development*. Washington, D.C.: U.S. Government Printing Office.

President's Commission. 1984. *Report on the President's Commission on Competitiveness III*. Washington, D.C.: U.S. General Printing Office.

Pricewaterhouse, Coopers. 1998. "Venture Capital Investments by Region." http://209.67.194.61/region.asp?year=1998&qtr=2.

———. 1998. *Venture Capital Survey*. http://204.198.129.80/region.asp?year=1999&qtr=1.

Priest, George L., and Benjamin Klein. 1984. "The Selection of Disputes for Litigation." *Journal of Legal Studies* 13: 1–55.

Pursell, Carroll. 1976. "The Technical Society of the Pacific Coast 1884–1914." *Technology and Culture* 17, no. 4: 702–17.

Putnam, Robert D. 1993a. *Making Democracy Work: Civic Traditions in Modern Italy*. Princeton: Princeton University Press.

Putnam, Robert D. 1993b. "The Prosperous Community: Social Capital and Public Life." *American Prospect* (spring): 35–42.

Quinn, J., T. Doorley, and P. Paquette. 1990. "Technology in Services: Rethinking Strategic Focus." *Sloan Management Review* (winter): 79–87.

Red Herring. 1994. Personal interview with Thomas Perkins, March.

Reiner, Martha Louise. 1989. "The Transformation of Venture Capital: A History of the Venture Capital Organizations in the Untied States." Ph.D. dissertation, University of California, Berkeley, Business Administration.

Richards, E. 1984. "IBM Pulls the Strings." *San Jose Mercury News*, December 31.

Richardson, G. 1972. "The Organisation of Industry." *Economic Journal* (September): 3883–96.

Richie, R., D. Hecker, and J. Burgan. 1983. "High Technology Today and Tomorrow: A Small Slice of the Employment Pie." *Monthly Labor Review* 11: 50–58.

Riordan, Michael, and Lillian Hoddeson. 1997. *Crystal Fire*. New York: Norton and Company.

Robertson, Paul, and Richard Langlois. 1995. "Innovation, Networks and Vertical Integration." *Research Policy* 24, no. 4: 543–62.

Rock, Arthur. 1989. "Arthur Rock on Faith and Luck." *Upside* (summer): 15.

———. 1988. Personal interview by Richard Florida and Martin Kenney, April 15.

Rogers, Everett. 1982. "Information Exchange and Technological Innovation." In *The Transfer and Utilization of Technical Knowledge*, edited by D. Sahal. Lexington, Mass.: Lexington Books.

Rogers, Everett, and Annie Chen Ying-Chung. 1990. "Technology Transfer and the Technopolis." In *Managing Complexity in High Technology Organizations*, edited by M. A. Von Glinow and S. A. Mohrman. New York: Oxford University Press.

Rogers, Everett, and Judith Larsen. 1984. *Silicon Valley Fever*. New York: Basic Books.

Romer, Paul M. 1993. "Two Strategies for Economic Development: Using Ideas and Producing Ideas." *Proceedings of the World Bank Annual Conference on Development Economics 1992*. Washington, D.C.: International Bank for Reconstruction of Development/The World Bank: 63–91.

Rosa, Felix. 1960. "Radio Telegraph and Telephone Pioneer 1909–1959, Inception of the Electronics Era: A Biography of C. F. Elwell." Unpublished manuscript. History of Science and Technology Project, Bancroft Library, University of California, Berkeley.

Rosenberg, Nathan. 1990. "Why Do Firms Do Basic Research (with Their Own Money)." *Research Policy* 18: 165–74.

———. 1982. *Inside the Black Box: Technology and Economics*. Cambridge: Cambridge University Press.

Rosenkopf, Lori, and Michael L. Tushman. 1994. "The Coevolution of Technology and Organization." In *The Evolutionary Dynamics of Organizations*, edited by J. Baum and J. Singh, 403–24. New York: Oxford University Press.

Sabel, Charles. 1993. "Studied Trust: Building New Forms of Cooperation in a Volatile Economy." In *Explorations in Economic Sociology*, edited by Richard Swedberg, 104–44. New York: Russell Sage Foundation.

———. 1988. "Flexible Specialization and the Re-emergence of Regional Economies." In *Reversing Industrial Decline*, edited by Paul Hirst and Jonathan Zeitlin, 17–70. Oxford: Berg.

Sabel, Charles, Horst Kern, and Gary Herrigel. 1989. *Collaborative Manufacturing: New Supplier Relations in the Automobile Industry and the Redefinition of the Industrial Corporation.* Working Paper No. 1. International Motor Vehicle Program. Massachusetts Institute of Technology.

Sanger, David. 1987. "A Peek at IBM's Trump Card." *New York Times*, March 8.

San Jose Business Journal. 1985. "Hewlett Packard swears by 'Just-in-Time' System." (June).

San Jose Mercury News. 1993. "Venture Tree Quarterly Survey." (November 29): 27–33.

San Francisco Chronicle. 1984. "IBM Talks Merger with Santa Clara's ROLM." (September 26): 25–30.

Saxenian, AnnaLee. 1999. *Silicon Valley's New Immigrant Entrepreneurs.* San Francisco: Public Policy Institute of California.

———. 1994. *Regional Advantage: Culture and Competition in Silicon Valley and Route 128.* Cambridge: Harvard University Press.

———. 1991. "A Response to Richard Florida and Martin Kenney." *California Management Review* 33 (spring): 136–42.

———. 1990. "Regional Networks and the Resurgence of Silicon Valley." *California Management Review* 33, no. 1: 89–112.

———. 1989a. "In Search of Power: The Organization of Business Interests in Silicon Valley and Route 128." *Economy and Society* 18: 25–50.

———. 1989b. "Regional Networks and the Resurgence of Silicon Valley." WP-508, Institute of Urban and Regional Development, University of California, Berkeley.

———. 1988a. "The Political Economy of Industrial Adaptation in Silicon Valley." Ph.D. dissertation, Department of Political Science, MIT.

———. 1988b. "The Cheshire Cat's Grin: Innovation and Regional Development in England." *Technology Review* 71 (February/March): 67–75.

———. 1986. "In Search of Power: The Organization of Business Interests in Silicon Valley and Route 128." Working paper, E53-470, Department of Political Science, MIT, Cambridge.

———. 1985. "Silicon Valley and Route 128: Regional Prototypes or Historic Exceptions?" In *Technology, Space, and Society, Urban Affairs Annual Review* 28, edited by M. Castells. Los Angeles: Sage.

———. 1983a. "The Urban Contradictions of Silicon Valley." *International Journal of Urban and Regional Research* 17: 237–61.

———. 1983b. "The Genesis of Silicon Valley." *Built Environment* 9, no. 1: 7–17.

Schaller, Bob. 1996. "The Origin, Nature, and Implications of Moore's Law." http://www.research.microsoft.com/~Gray/Moore_Law.html (September 26).

Schlender, Brenton. 1988. "Computer Maker Aims to Transform Industry and Become a Giant." *Wall Street Journal*, March 18.

Schoenberger, Erica. 1996. *The Culture of the Firm.* Oxford: Blackwell.

Scholtz, Robert A. 1982. "The Origins of Spread-Spectrum Communications." *IEEE Transactions on Communications* 30 (May): 822–54.

Schoonhoven, Claudia Bird, and Kathleen Eisenhardt. 1989. "The Impact of Incubator Region on the Creation and Survival of New Semiconductor Ventures in the U.S. 1978–1986." Report to the Economic Development Administration, U.S. Department of Commerce (August).

Schulman, S. J. 1964. "EDL-Yesterday and Today." U.S. Army Communications-Electronics Command Archives, Fort Monmouth, N.J. (September 14).

Schultz, James. 1983. "Inside the Blue Cube." *Defense Electronics* (April): 52–58.

Schumpeter, Joseph. 1969. *Business Cycles.* Abridged by Reindig Fels. New York: McGraw Hill.

———. 1947. "The Creative Response in Economic History." *Journal of Economic History* 7 (November): 149–59.

———. 1935. "An Analysis of Economic Change." *Review of Economic Statistics* 27 (May): 2–10.

Scott, Allen J. 1988a. *Metropolis.* Berkeley: University of California Press.

———. 1988b. "Flexible Production Systems and Regional Development: The Rise of New Industrial Spaces in North America and Western Europe." *International Journal of Urban and Regional Research* 23: 171–85.

———. 1986. "High Technology Industry and Territorial Development: The Rise of the Orange County Complex, 1955–84." *Urban Geography* 7: 3–45.

Scott, Allen J., and David P. Angel. 1988. "The Global Assembly-operations of U.S. Semiconductor Firms: A Geographical Analysis." *Environment and Planning A* 20: 1047–67.

———. 1987. "The U.S. Semiconductor Industry: A Locational Analysis." *Environment and Planning A* 19: 875–912.

Scott, Allen J., and A. S. Paul. 1990. "Collective Order and Economic Coordination in Industrial Agglomerations: The Technopoles of Southern California." *Environment and Planning C* 8: 179–93.

Scott, Allen, and Michael Storper. 1987. "High Technology Industry and Regional Development: A Theoretical Critique and Reconstruction." *International Social Science Journal* 34: 215–32.

Scott, Mel. 1985. *The San Francisco Bay Area: A Metropolis in Perspective.* Berkeley: University of California Press.

Scott, Otto. 1974. *The Creative Ordeal: The Story of Raytheon.* New York: Atheneum.

Scott, W. Richard. 1992. *Organizations: Rational, Natural and Open Systems.* 3d ed. Englewood Cliffs, N.J.: Prentice Hall.

Scranton, Philip. 1997. *Endless Novelty: Specialty Production and American Industrialization, 1865–1925.* Princeton: Princeton University Press.

Segal, Martin. 1960. *Wages in the Metropolis.* Cambridge: Harvard University Press.

Sengenberger, W., G. Loveman, and M. J. Piore, eds. 1990. *The Reemergence of Small Enterprises.* Geneva: International Labor Institute.

Shaiken, Harley, S. Hershenberg, and Sarah Kuhn. 1986. "The Work Process under More Flexible Production." *Industrial Relations* 25: 167–83.

Siegel, Lenny, and Herb Borock. 1982. "Background Report on Silicon Valley." Report prepared for the U.S. Commission on Civil Rights (September). Mountain View, Calif.: Pacific Studies Center.

Siekman, Philip. 1966. "Henry Ford and His Electronic Can of Worms." *Fortune* (February): 119.

Simon, David. 1960. "Dr. John Van Nuys Granger." *Microwave Journal* (June): 25–29.

Sims, John (director of materials, Tandem Computers). 1988. Personal interview, April 13.

Singh, Jitendra V., David J. Tucker, and Agnes G. Meinhard. 1991. "Institutional Change and Ecological Dynamics." In *The New Institutionalism and Organizational Analysis*, edited by W. W. Powell and P. J. DiMaggio, 390–422. Chicago: University of Chicago Press.

Smigel, Erwin O. 1969. *The Wall Street Lawyer*. Bloomington: Indiana University Press.

Smith, Douglas, and Robert Alexander. 1988. *Fumbling the Future*. New York: William Morrow and Company.

Smith, Merritt Roe, ed. 1985. *Military Enterprise and Technological Change: Perspectives on the American Experience*. Cambridge: MIT Press.

———. 1977. *Harper's Ferry Armory and the New Technology: The Challenge of Change*. Ithaca, N.Y.: Cornell University Press.

Smith, Robert (president, Computer Products/Boschert). 1988. Personal interview, September 1.

Snow, R. 1983. "The New International Division of Labor and the U.S. Work Force: The Case of the Electronics Industry." In *Women, Men, and the International Division of Labor*, edited by M. Fernandez-Kelly and J. Nash, 39–69. Albany: State University of New York Press.

Sobel, Robert. 1982. *ITT: The Management of Opportunity*. New York: Times Books.

Soussou, Helen. 1985. "Note on the Venture Capital Industry, 1981." Harvard Business School Case Study No. 9-285-096.

Stanford Engineering News. 1950. "Stanford Engineering Attracts National Attention: The Traveling Wave Tube." (May 6).

Stanford University. 1985. "Shugart Corporation: Planning Manufacturing Capabilities and Its Accompanying Industry Note." Stanford University, Graduate School of Business #S-MM-6N.

———. 1983. "Disk Drives for Small and Microcomputer Systems, 1983." Stanford University, Graduate School of Business, Case Study #S-MM-8.

Stevens, L. D. 1981. "The Evolution of Magnetic Storage." *IBM Journal of Research and Development* 25, no. 5 (September): 663–75.

Stigler, G. J. 1939. "Production and Distribution in the Short Run." *Journal of Political Economy* 47: 305–27.

Stinchcombe, Arthur. 1965. "Organization-Creating Organizations." *Trans-Actions* 2: 34–35.

Storper, Michael. 1995. "The Resurgence of Regional Economies, Ten Years Later: The Region as a Nexus of Untraded Interdependencies." *European Urban and Regional Studies* 2, no. 3: 191–221.

———. 1993. "Regional 'Worlds' of Production: Learning and Innovation in the Technology Districts of France, Italy and the USA." *Regional Studies* 27, no. 5: 433–55.

Storper, Michael, and Susan Christopherson. 1987. "Flexible Specialization and Regional Industrial Agglomeration: The Case of the U.S. Motion Picture Industry." *Annals of the Association of American Geographers* 77: 104–17.

Storper, Michael, and Robert Salais. 1997. *Worlds of Production.* Cambridge: Harvard University Press.

Storper, Michael, and Allen Scott. 1988. "The Geographical Foundations and Social Regulation of Flexible Production Complexes." In *Territory and Social Reproduction*, edited by J. Wolcher and M. Dear. London: Allen & Unwin.

Storper, Michael, and Richard Walker. 1989. *The Capitalist Imperative: Territory, Technology, and Industrial Growth.* London: Basil Blackwell.

Stowsky, Jay. 1988. "The Weakest Link: Semiconductor Equipment, Linkages, and the Limits to International Trade." Working Paper No. 27, Berkeley Roundtable on the International Economy, University of California, Berkeley.

Stradford, Dennis (vice president of marketing, Flextronics). 1988. Personal interview, March 3.

Stuart, C. 1979. "Search and the Spatial Organization of Trading." In *Studies in the Economics of Search*, edited by S. Lippman and J. McCall, 17–33. Amsterdam: North-Holland.

Sturgeon, Timothy. 1999. "Turn-key Production Networks: The Organizational Delinking of Production from Innovation." In *New Product Development and Production Networks: Global Industrial Experience*, edited by U. Juergens. New York: Springer Verlag.

———. 1992. "The Origins of Silicon Valley: The Development of the Electronics Industry in the San Francisco Bay Area." Masters thesis, University of California at Berkeley, Department of Geography.

Suchman, Mark C. 1996. "Constructed Ecologies: Reproduction and Structuration in Emerging Organizational Communities." Paper presented to the Workshop in Institutional Analysis in Tucson, Arizona.

———. 1994. "On Advice of Counsel: Law Firms and Venture Capital Funds as Information Intermediaries in the Structuration of Silicon Valley." Unpublished Ph.D. dissertation, Department of Sociology, Stanford University.

———. 1988. "Constructing an Institutional Ecology: Notes on the Structural Dynamics of Organizational Communities." Paper presented to the annual meeting of the American Sociological Association in Atlanta, Georgia.

Suchman, Mark C., and Mia L. Cahill. 1996. "The Hired-Gun as Facilitator: Lawyers and the Suppression of Business Disputes in Silicon Valley." *Law and Social Inquiry* 21, no. 3: 679–712.

Swanger, C. C. 1985. "Apple Computer: The First Ten Years." Case Study # S-BP-245, Graduate School of Business, Stanford University.

Swartz, James. 1995. Personal interview by Urs von Burg and Martin Kenney, June 22.

Tarrow, Sidney. 1996. "Making Social Science Work across Space and Time: A Critical Reflection on Robert Putnam Making Democracy Work." *American Political Science Review* 90, no. 2: 389–97.

Taylor, Tony. 1983. "High-technology Industry and the Development of Science Parks." *Built Environment* 9, no. 1: 72–78.

Teece, D. J. 1992. "Foreign Investment in Silicon Valley." *California Management Review* (winter): 88–106.

Teitz, Michael B., Amy Glasmeier, and Douglas Svensson. 1981. "Small Business and Employment Growth in California." Working Paper No. 348. Berkeley: Institute of Urban and Regional Development.

Terman, Frederick. 1978. Interviews conducted by A. L. Norberg, Charles Susskind, and Rodger Hahn, History of Science and Technology Project, Bancroft Library, University of California at Berkeley.

———. 1947. "Dean's Report, School of Engineering, 1946–47." *S. E. Wallace-Sterling Papers*. Stanford University Special Collections 39/School of Engineering.

Terman, F., to W. Cooley. 1958. *Terman Papers* SC 160 V/7/7 (April 9).

Terman, F., to W. Cooley. 1957. *Terman Papers* SC 160 V/5/6 (December 11).

Terman, F., to W. Cooley. 1955. *Terman Papers* SC 160 V/7/7 (May 2).

Terman, F., to J. Hawkinson. 1966. *Terman Papers* SC 160 V/7/12 (February 1).

Terman, F., to J. Hawkinson. 1964. *Terman Papers* SC 160 V/7/9 (February 3).

Terman, F., to J. Hawkinson. 1963. *Terman Papers* SC160 V/7/9 (November 1).

Terman, F., to J. Hawkinson. 1962. *Terman Papers* SC 160 V/7/9 (November 30).

Terman, F., to H. Laun. 1953a. *Terman Papers* SC 160 V/6/13 (November 5).

Terman, F., to H. Laun. 1953b. *Terman Papers* SC 160 V/6/13 (December 17).

Terman, F., to H. Skilling. 1944a. *Terman Papers* SC I/1/11 (June 20).

Terman, F., to D. Tresidder. 1944b. *Sterling Papers* SC 216 39/School of Engineering (April 25).

Thibaut, John W., and Harold H. Kelley. 1959. *The Social Psychology of Groups.* New York: John Wiley.

Thompson, C. 1989. "High-technology Theories and Public Policy." *Environment and Planning C: Government and Policy* 7: 121–52.

Thompson, James D. 1967. *Organizations in Action.* New York: McGraw-Hill.

Tierston, S. 1989. "The Changing Face of Purchasing." *Electronic Business* (March 20).

Tilton, John. 1971. *International Diffusion of Technology: The Case of Semiconductors.* Washington, D.C.: Brookings Institution.

Time. 1961. "Marriage of the Giants." (September 22): 112.

Timmons, Jeffry A., and Harry J. Sapienza. 1991. "Venture Capital: More than Money?" In *Pratt's Guide to Venture Capital Sources,* 15th ed., edited by S. M. Pratt and J. Morris, 35–41. Needham, Mass.: Venture Economics.

Todd, Robert (CEO, Flextronics). 1988. Personal interview, February 2.

Todtling, Franz. 1994. "Regional Networks of High-technology Firms—The Case of the Greater Boston Region." *Technovation* 14, no. 5: 323–43.

Torres, David L. 1988. "Professionalism, Variation, and Organizational Survival." *American Sociological Review* 53: 380–94.

Turriff, Lowell (vice president of marketing, Cypress Semiconductor). 1988. Personal interview, March 7.

Tushman, Michael, and Philip Anderson. 1986. "Technological Discontinuities and Organizational Environments." *Administrative Science Quarterly* 31: 439–65.

University of California. 1998. *The BioSTAR Project: Critical Linkages Project.* President's Industry-University Cooperative Research Initiative.

University of California, Berkeley, Graduate Division. 1997. *Department of Electrical Engineering and Computer Science Statistics.* Berkeley: University of California, Berkeley, Graduate Division.

Urhande, F. F., to Chief, Engineering and Technical Division, Office of the Chief Signal Officer. 1953. Fort Monmouth, N.J.: U.S. Army Communications—Electronics Command Archives. (September 17).

U.S. Army. 1952. "Briefing on Department of Army Quick Reaction Capability in Electronic Warfare." Fort Monmouth, N.J.: U.S. Army Communications—Electronics Command Archives.

U.S. Congress, Joint Economic Committee. 1984. *Climate for Entrepreneurship and Innovation in the United States.* Hearings before the Joint Economic Committee, Congress of the United States, Ninety-eighth Congress, 2d session (August 27–28): 34–45.

Uzzi, Brian. 1996. "The Sources and Consequences of Embeddedness for the Economic Performance of Organizations: The Network Effect." *American Sociological Review* 61, no. N4: 674–98.

Valentine, Donald. 1988. Personal interview by Richard Florida and Martin Kenney, March 29.

Van de Ven, Andrew H., and Raghu Garud. 1989. "A Framework for Understanding the Emergence of New Industries." *Research on Technological Innovation, Management and Policy* 4: 195–225.

Varian, Dorothy. 1983. *The Pilot and the Inventor.* Palo Alto, Calif.: Pacific Press.

Varian. 1973. *Varian: 25 Years, 1948–1973.* Palo Alto, Calif.: Varian.

Varian. 1952. *Varian Associates Minute Books.* (October 7). Palo Alto, Calif.: Varian.

Varian. 1951. *Varian Associates Minute Books.* (June 3). Palo Alto, Calif.: Varian.

Veblen, Thorstein. 1915. *Imperial Germany and the Industrial Revolution.* New York: Macmillan.

———. 1899. *The Theory of the Leisure Class: An Economic Study of Institutions.* New York: B. W. Huebsch.

———. 1898. "Why Is Economics Not an Evolutionary Science?" *Quarterly Journal of Economics* 12: 373–97.

Venture Capital Journal. 1982. (February, March, May).

Venture Capital Journal. 1981. (January, March, November, December).

Venture Capital Journal. 1980. (February, March).

Venture Capital Yearbook. 1983. Wellesley Hills, Mass.: Venture Economics.

Voakes, Paul. 1978. "Sylvania One of the First in the Valley—25 Years Ago." *Palo Alto Times,* July 18.

von Burg, Urs, and Martin Kenney. 2000. "Venture Capital and the Creation of the Local Area Networking Industry." *Research Policy.*

von Hippel, Eric. 1988. *The Sources of Innovation.* New York: Oxford University Press.

———. 1986. "Cooperation between Rivals: Information Know-How Trading." Working Paper #1759–86. Cambridge, Mass.: MIT Sloan School.

Walker, Richard. 1996. "Another Round of Globalization in San Francisco." *Urban Geography* 17, no. 1: 60–94.

———. 1988. "The Geographical Organization of Production-Systems." *Environment and Planning D: Society and Space* 6: 377–408.

———. 1985. "Technological Determination and Determinism: Industrial Growth and Location." In *High Technology, Space and Society*, edited by M. Castells, 226–64. Beverly Hills, Calif.: Sage.

WASBIC. 1969. "Minutes of a Special Meeting of the Members of Western Association of Small Business Investment Companies, A California Corporation." (October 29).

Watkins-Johnson Company. 1964. *Prospectus*. (June 18).

Weber, Max. 1947. "Bureaucracy." In *From Max Weber: Essays in Sociology*, edited by H. H. Gerth and C. W. Mills, 196–244. New York: Oxford University Press.

Wegmann, David. 1986. Personal interview by Richard Florida and Martin Kenney, December 19.

Weick, Karl E. 1979. *The Social Psychology of Organizing*. Reading, Mass.: Addison-Wesley.

Weiss, Joseph, and Andre Delbecq. 1990. "A Regional Culture Perspective of High Technology Management." In *Strategic Management in High Technology Firms*, edited by M. Lawless and L. Gomez-Meija, 83–94. Greenwich, Conn.: JAI Press.

Weiss, Linda. 1988. *Creating Capitalism: The State and Small Business since 1945.* Oxford: Blackwell Publishers.

Wendt, Paul. 1947. "The Availability of Capital to Small Business in California." Unpublished mimeo. Berkeley: University of California: 145–47.

Western Association of Venture Capitalists (WAVC). 1971. "Membership List 1970/1971."

Williams, James C. 1990. "The Rise of Silicon Valley." *Invention and Technology* (spring/summer).

———. 1987. "Regional Development in the Technical Sciences in California's Electric Power Industry, 1890–1920." In *Technology and Technical Sciences in History, Proceedings of the ICOHTEC-Symposium, Dresden, 25–29 August, 1986*, edited by Rolf Sonnemann and Klaus Krug. Berlin: VEB Deutscher Verlag der Wissenschaften.

Williams, Jeffrey R. 1992. "How Sustainable Is Your Competitive Advantage?" *California Management Review* (spring): 29–51.

Wilson, John. 1988. Personal interview by Richard Florida and Martin Kenney, March 29.

———. 1985. *The New Venturers*. Reading, Mass.: Addison-Wesley.

Wilson, Mike. 1997. *The Difference between God and Larry Ellison*. New York: William Morrow and Company.

Wythes, Paul. 1986. Personal interview by Richard Florida and Martin Kenney, December 15.

York, Herbert, and G. Allen Greb. 1977. "Strategic Reconnaissance." *Bulletin of the Atomic Scientists* (April): 33–42.

Young, Jeffrey. 1988. *Steve Jobs: The Journey is the Reward*. Glenview, Ill.: Scott, Foreman and Company.

Zider, Bob. 1998. "How Venture Capital Works." *Harvard Business Review* (November–December): 131–39.

Zucker, Lynne G. 1988. *Institutional Patterns and Organizations: Culture and Environment*. Cambridge, Mass.: Ballinger.

————. 1983. "Organizations as Institutions." *Research in the Sociology of Organizations* 2: 1–47.

————. 1977. "The Role of Institutionalization in Cultural Persistence." *American Sociological Review* 42: 726–43.

Zysman, John. 1994. "How Institutions Create Historically Rooted Trajectories of Growth." *Industrial and Corporate Change* 3, no. 1: 243–83.

————. 1983. *Government, Markets, and Growth*. Ithaca, N.Y.: Cornell University Press.

Index

In this index an "f" after a number indicates a separate reference on the next page, and an "ff" indicates separate references on the next two pages. A continuous discussion over two or more pages is indicated by a span of page numbers, e.g., "57–59." *Passim* is used for a cluster of references in close but not consecutive sequence.